The Patience Payoff

The Patience Payoff

Emotional resilience as the most underrated wealth builder

Leandro Vos

Mindful Pages

Published in 2025

ISBN: 9789371340557 (PB)
ISBN: 9789371348065 (eBook)

Published by

Mindful Pages
Imprint of Alpha Editions LLC
312 W. 2nd St #1834
Casper, WY 82601, USA

This book was developed using advanced writing tools to support the drafting and ideation process. All content has been thoughtfully curated, refined, and reviewed to ensure quality and relevance.

Content

Introduction
The Wealth No One Talks About

For much of human history, wealth was something you could hold in your hands or see with your eyes. Land, coins, titles, homes—tangible signs of prosperity and standing. Today, the symbols have evolved, or perhaps just multiplied: portfolios, equity holdings, passive income charts, net worth trackers updated in real time. We quantify obsessively, pursue relentlessly, and display conspicuously. Yet, beneath all this noise, one form of wealth has quietly slipped through the cracks of our cultural awareness—overlooked, underappreciated, and often misunderstood. It's the ability to endure. Not merely to survive hardship, but to remain composed in its presence; to make decisions not from fear or urgency, but from foresight. To persist—not recklessly, but deliberately—through confusion, change, and delay. This is emotional resilience, and it may well be the most undervalued asset in our entire economy.

The core thesis of this book is disarmingly simple, though it cuts against the grain: emotional resilience isn't a soft trait, a psychological footnote, or a pleasant bonus in times of stress. It's foundational. It is the multiplier that strengthens every other form of capital—be it financial, relational, intellectual, or reputational. Those who possess it do not succeed by outpacing the rest, but by outlasting the chaos. They weather volatility without veering off course. They stay measured when others spiral. And they make decisions with consequences in mind, not just optics. Emotional resilience, in this telling, is the hidden scaffolding behind the grand structures we admire—structures that look effortless, but are anything but.

Still, this truth rarely gets airtime. We are, after all, living in an era intoxicated by speed. The prevailing narrative idolises urgency, celebrates rapid wins, and applauds visibility over substance. Attention is the currency, and the platforms reward performance—sometimes even performance of the hollowest kind. A start-up raises millions without a working product and is instantly hailed as visionary. A teenager with a viral post becomes a business sage overnight. Investors showcase their latest windfall, while conveniently omitting the years they bled in obscurity. Patience—once the cornerstone of wisdom—has begun to resemble foolishness in the eyes of a culture that equates delay with failure.

But speed, when not anchored by depth, often leads to disaster. Decisions made in emotional turbulence don't just chip away at our financial standing—they corrode our judgement. The inability to wait, to sit with discomfort, to resist the lure of the immediate—it generates its own kind of poverty. One marked by poor choices, burnout, and a persistent sense of being unmoored. We celebrate the meteoric rise, yes—but we rarely study the implosion. And so the myth persists: that success must be fast, and that resilience is optional.

The Patience Payoff is a conscious rejection of that myth. It offers a reframing—one that defines wealth not by what can be accumulated, but by what can be sustained without compromising one's core. It's not about the speed of achievement, but the steadiness with which one carries on. This isn't sentimentality dressed up as strategy. It's a hard-nosed argument about infrastructure: that if you cannot keep your nerve when faced with uncertainty, delay, or unpredictability, you will, sooner or later, sabotage your own progress. Whether in business, family life, investment, or creative work—inner steadiness determines external success.

In this light, emotional resilience ceases to be a coping mechanism and emerges as a form of intelligence. Not a trait you're born with, but a skill that can be built, honed, and deployed. The emotionally resilient person isn't simply calm—they are strategic. They know when to pause, when to speak, and when to step back. They conserve energy rather than reacting reflexively. They understand the long game, and more importantly, they're willing to play it. And as with any investment, the returns of such emotional discipline compound dramatically over time.

This book views emotional resilience through an economic lens. It dissects the cultural conditions that reward haste and examines the true cost of impatience. It delves into the neurobiology of reactivity—how our brains, wired for immediacy, can betray our long-term interests. By understanding dopamine loops, cognitive fatigue, and the nature of fear, we not only gain insight—we gain leverage. The illusion of the "overnight success" is gently unravelled here, revealing that visibility often lags far behind value. In fact, some of the most impactful efforts happen out of view. Strategic invisibility, as paradoxical as it may sound, can be a position of immense strength.

You'll encounter the concept of emotional capital—an internal reservoir that governs not just how we feel, but what we're able to carry, create, and protect. Like financial capital, it must be stewarded wisely. Those who let it drain, unchecked, find themselves reactive, exhausted, and far more susceptible to distraction and defeat. And unlike money, emotional capital can't be borrowed or outsourced—it's self-generated, and self-sustaining only through care and consciousness.

Don't expect tips, tricks, or silver-bullet tactics here. You won't find financial modelling or quick-fix routines. What you will find are frameworks for clarity. Real stories from entrepreneurs, thinkers, parents, and investors who built their success not by racing ahead, but by standing firm—by choosing substance over noise. The pages ahead explore how emotion skews logic, why some people quit just before a breakthrough, and how to fortify yourself against the storm, not by denying it, but by becoming less movable in its midst.

There will be friction. You'll be invited—perhaps even dared—to slow down. Not in defeat, but in defiance. To interpret silence as composure, not absence. To treat waiting not as idleness, but as discipline in action. To realise that discipline itself is not an act of suppression, but of inner alignment. The truly resilient are not numb or detached—they feel everything, but aren't ruled by any of it.

At its heart, *The Patience Payoff* is about constructing a self that doesn't fracture at the first sign of disruption. It's a guide to building a kind of quiet toughness—one that holds steady across economic downturns, creative droughts, relational uncertainties, and inner storms. If you've grown weary of volatility—emotional, financial, or otherwise—this book offers a path back to steadiness. Not by eliminating chaos, but by learning to anchor yourself within it.

Why this, and why now? Because the cultural tempo is only accelerating. Because we are losing the distinction between attention and value. Because we are deciding more, regretting faster, and rarely pausing to ask why. In a world where everyone seems to be shouting over one another, the ability to wait, to listen, to think slowly—has become not just a strength, but a form of radical intelligence. Quiet doesn't mean absent. Patience doesn't mean inert.

This book is not a manual for getting rich. It is, rather, a blueprint for becoming unshakeable. And in a world obsessed with spectacle but sustained by endurance, that may prove to be the most enduring form of wealth there is.

Chapter 1
The Illusion of Fast Wins

The contemporary tale of success has, quite plainly, lost its grip on time. It's not just that the structure has dissolved—though it often has—but that the tempo has been pushed into a frenzy. Everything is fast, flash-lit, and increasingly fragile. We are surrounded by accounts of meteoric rise: the twentysomething tech founder pulling in millions with a pitch deck and a grin; the influencer cashing in on a curated morning routine; the investor who makes a fortune catching a market wave at just the right moment. These narratives catch fire not because they reflect the norm—they don't—but because they're easy to digest. Speed flattens nuance. It lets us skip over the slow, awkward, and frequently unrewarded work from which most meaningful achievement actually emerges. The irony, of course, is painful: in trying to find inspiration, we often end up absorbing stylised fiction dressed up as fact—and, worse, we begin to believe our own lives should perform similarly.

There's something deeper at play here—something not incidental but built into the very systems that shape our behaviour. This chapter is not simply an attempt to correct a popular myth. It's an effort to reveal a more dangerous misalignment: the growing dissonance between how fast we think results should come and how real progress actually unfolds. We're inhabiting a cultural environment in which delayed gratification isn't just rare—it's viewed with suspicion. The kind of long-term thinking that once underpinned wisdom now feels like a luxury, or worse, a liability.

To make sense of how we landed here, we have to begin with the brain—not because biology holds all the answers, but because it gives us our first orientation. The human brain, contrary to the way we often treat it, wasn't built to secure long-term prosperity. It evolved to keep us alive. It rewards whatever delivers immediate feedback—whether that's food, sex, or social validation. And the currency it uses to reinforce this behaviour is dopamine. Contrary to popular belief, dopamine doesn't signal pleasure itself—it signals anticipation. The itch to check your phone one more time, to refresh that page again, to scroll just a bit further—it's not discipline steering you. It's dopamine. And no, this doesn't make you weak. It makes you human, caught in a modern architecture designed to capitalise on your brain's most ancient instincts.

Social media platforms aren't inert tools; they are meticulously engineered ecosystems built to monetise your attention by exploiting precisely these neurological triggers. The endless scroll, the sporadic buzz of a notification, the public scoring of your popularity—they all feed into a closed loop of stimulus and response. What's rewarded is not depth, but frequency. Not mastery, but motion. And as this pattern settles into our neural wiring, we begin to confuse the signs of progress with progress itself. The signs, of course, are quicker. They're cleaner. They give us a fix. But they don't build anything.

For anyone attempting to build something of substance—whether a company, a creative practice, a family, or a life rooted in integrity—this is more than just a distraction. It's a distortion. These dopamine-driven patterns reduce our capacity to handle complexity, blunt our tolerance for uncertainty, and leave us almost allergic to anything that doesn't yield immediate reward. But the truth is unavoidable: enduring success doesn't sprint. It lumbers, stumbles, regroups. It requires a quiet, often invisible kind of endurance—the psychological capacity to keep going when nothing seems to be paying off.

In this sense, discipline isn't about gritting your teeth and charging forward. It's about learning to override your brain's default settings with structures and habits that reinforce the long view. It's the quiet act of saying, "Yes, this feels good now—but I'm choosing what will matter more later." And that kind of discipline is getting harder to sustain in a culture where immediate reward is visible, amplified, and endlessly celebrated—while patience is unglamorous, and often ignored altogether.

Which brings us to one of the most corrosive tropes of our time: the myth of the overnight success. Despite its obvious implausibility, it persists—bolstered by our own biases and our fondness for shortcuts. The narrative is seductive: struggle, if it appears at all, is brushed aside or stylised into a noble montage. Success arrives as a kind of destiny, conferred upon those with extraordinary talent or uncanny timing. But speak privately to anyone who's actually built something real, and the tone changes. They'll speak of years in the wilderness—of plans that didn't pan out, of feedback loops that offered nothing but silence, of the work continuing long after the audience had wandered off. What looks like sudden ascent is so often just long effort finally reaching the surface. The work was there all along. The spotlight simply hadn't landed on it yet.

The real damage this myth inflicts is not envy—it's distortion. It warps our perception of time. It makes steadiness feel like falling behind. It tricks us into walking away from what's working simply because it isn't working quickly. We abandon projects, shift direction too soon, drain our energy chasing novelty, and ultimately burn out not because we failed—but because we misread the tempo of the game.

At the root of this misreading is a resource that almost never makes it onto the balance sheet, yet governs nearly every long-term outcome: emotional capital. Financial capital is tracked down to the last decimal. Emotional capital, on the other hand, is barely acknowledged—though it is, arguably, the more crucial of the two. It is the internal reservoir from which you draw when outcomes delay, when feedback is scarce, when uncertainty bites. It is your capacity to hold tension, to maintain perspective, to act without applause. And, like any resource, it can be exhausted.

Every time you face ambiguity, every time you push forward without validation, every time you absorb a setback without flinching, you're drawing on that emotional reserve. People don't abandon promising paths because they've run out of money—they walk away because they've run out of nerve. The pressure, the waiting, the noise—when it outlasts our emotional stamina, we flinch. And when that happens, decisions become short-sighted. We rush into poor partnerships, exit prematurely, second-guess our own strategy. Emotional insolvency is real. And like financial insolvency, it leaves us in survival mode—seeking relief over wisdom.

Think of the entrepreneur staring down another quarter of flat growth. Or the artist producing work in silence. The investor in the middle of a prolonged drawdown. Or the parent navigating a long, unpredictable developmental journey. Success in these cases isn't determined by cleverness or charisma. It's governed by the ability to stay centred over time—to weather uncertainty without folding, to act thoughtfully without external validation. That's emotional capital in motion. And most people have no idea they're spending it—until it's gone.

So the question isn't merely whether we desire success. The deeper question is whether we're building the interior capacity to receive and sustain it. Beyond skillsets and contacts, are we developing the mental scaffolding to withstand the long, quiet stretches? Can we stay anchored while others chase the next shiny thing? Because sometimes the difference between breakthrough and burnout comes down to little more than who blinked first.

This chapter makes the case for long games—not as acts of idealism, but as tactical necessity. This is not a romantic call to slowness for its own sake. It is a rigorous, evidence-based exploration of why deliberate, emotionally-resilient progress outperforms speed that's reactive, erratic, and thin. We'll look at how the brain responds to short-term stimulus, why willpower is less about grit than about design, and how the myth of rapid success hides the true costs of achievement. And we'll introduce a working model of emotional capital—how it functions, how it frays, and how it can be replenished like any other resource.

Because the illusion of rapid wins doesn't just waste time—it drains us. It leads us to confuse motion with meaning, to act when observation is needed, to pivot when we should persist. What's needed is a recalibration—not just of strategy, but of instinct. A shift away from frantic pursuit, and towards purposeful positioning. The outcomes that last, the ones that alter trajectories—they tend to grow in silence. Until, suddenly, they don't. And those who reach them are usually the ones who could sit in the quiet the longest.

So let's start where so many falter: with the brain's appetite for immediacy. It's not your fault that it craves the quick hit. But it is your responsibility to learn what that craving costs—and how to reclaim your choices from it.

The Culture of Urgency

If there is one value modern society seems to hold above all others, it is speed. Faster responses. Immediate results. Real-time updates. Productivity tools promise minutes saved. Trading platforms reward microsecond advantage. Communication has become instantaneous, feedback loops have shrunk to hours, and expectations have followed suit. In this climate, slowness is not merely inefficient—it is suspect. Waiting, once an unavoidable rhythm of life, is now treated as a system flaw. We no longer tolerate slow progress; we pathologise it.

The culture of urgency is not just a byproduct of technology. It is a worldview—a collectively reinforced operating system that equates speed with competence, visibility with value, and busyness with importance. It permeates corporate structures, academic institutions, social networks, and even our private self-assessments. Its most seductive promise is that moving fast means getting ahead. But the unspoken cost is cumulative: eroded patience, impaired judgment, shallow work, and, perhaps most insidiously, the loss of any meaningful connection to duration itself.

At the heart of this accelerationist mindset is a psychological vulnerability. Human beings are neurologically drawn to closure. Uncertainty creates cognitive load; ambiguity taxes our emotional energy. The promise of quick results alleviates this tension—temporarily. When speed is mistaken for progress, we experience a kind of emotional relief that feels like clarity. But it is often a shortcut around complexity, not through it. The result is decision-making skewed by immediacy rather than guided by strategic timing. What masquerades as efficiency is often just premature resolution.

The rise of hustle culture in the past two decades exemplifies this shift. Originally framed as a form of empowerment—own your time, build your brand, monetise your passion—it has evolved into a near-religious work ethic that moralises busyness. It valorises those who sacrifice sleep, skip weekends, and optimise every second. The messaging is clear: to pause is to fall behind. But behind this façade of ambition lies an unsustainable emotional economy. Hustle culture externalises value and internalises pressure. It does not teach endurance; it incentivises depletion.

The physiological consequences are well-documented. Chronic stress, driven by relentless urgency, leads to elevated cortisol levels, impaired immune function, and cognitive fatigue. More importantly, it distorts the very faculties we rely on for thoughtful work: attention, memory, patience, and emotional regulation. What begins as a motivational framework often ends in burnout. The body cannot distinguish between a real emergency and a calendar saturated with artificial urgency. It simply responds in kind—with exhaustion, anxiety, and eventually withdrawal.

This is not to say that speed is inherently harmful. Speed in the right context—emergency response, innovation sprints, adaptive iteration—can be vital. The problem arises when speed becomes default. When the logic of urgency is applied indiscriminately, it displaces deeper forms of value creation: contemplation, craftsmanship, and strategic restraint. These are slow processes by design. They require time not as a luxury, but as a condition for quality.

The education system offers a telling microcosm. Students are encouraged to produce more, sooner: submit essays in tighter windows, respond to assessments in real-time, master complex skills on compressed schedules. Rarely are they taught how to dwell with ideas, to explore nuance, or to tolerate the discomfort of not knowing. The result is not just academic fatigue, but a generation of thinkers for whom ambiguity feels like failure. And when that mindset transfers into professional life, it results in decision-makers who value speed over insight, reactivity over reflection.

Corporate structures mirror this impatience. Quarterly targets, performance dashboards, and instant KPIs dominate how organisations evaluate success. Long-term planning is often subordinated to optics—what can be presented, posted, or pitched. Leaders are under constant pressure to demonstrate visible momentum, even if that momentum is strategically incoherent. The tyranny of the quarterly report leaves little room for the kind of slow, sometimes invisible groundwork that actually creates sustainable value. Productive patience is hard to justify in a metrics-first economy.

Technology has certainly amplified the velocity of life, but the culture of urgency predates Silicon Valley. Its philosophical roots can be traced to the industrial revolution, when time became money and labour was broken into units of measurable productivity. But unlike in previous eras—where rest and contemplation still had some recognised place in the rhythm of the day—the digital environment has eliminated natural boundaries. The workday has no edge. We carry our inbox in our pocket, our analytics dashboard in our palm, and our anxiety like a background app never quite closed. The default mode is not presence, but perpetual response.

Ironically, the more we try to speed up, the more fragile we become. Systems that move too fast become brittle. They rely on uninterrupted flow and constant feedback, which makes them vulnerable to any disruption. This applies not only to institutions, but to individuals. A mind trained to operate in constant urgency loses the ability to *hold* complexity. It becomes reactive. And reactivity, while sometimes necessary, is a poor long-term strategy.

Contrast this with the slow disciplines: architecture, science, philosophy, deep research. These domains demand something the urgent mind cannot easily access—patience without paralysis. A tolerance for partial understanding. A comfort with questions that may not resolve quickly, or ever. In these disciplines, value is not produced in bursts but cultivated over time. Mistakes are part of the process, not public failures to be optimised away. In short, they operate on human time, not algorithmic time.

There is a growing countercurrent—what some call the "slow movement"—but it remains niche, often dismissed as nostalgic or impractical. The truth is, slowness has a branding problem. It lacks the visual drama of the hustle. It doesn't produce immediate metrics or viral content. But that is precisely the point. Its value is revealed over longer arcs. Those who practise it may not always be visible, but they are more likely to be durable.

So what does it mean to opt out of the culture of urgency—not as a retreat into passivity, but as a recalibration of attention and energy? It begins with redefining success in terms of *sufficiency* rather than velocity. It means choosing depth over breadth, clarity over volume, timing over frequency. It involves designing systems—personal and organisational—that reward strategic patience and create buffers against reactive pressure.

On a practical level, this could mean protecting unstructured time for reflection, enforcing communication boundaries, or building feedback cycles that prioritise learning over speed. At a cognitive level, it requires retraining attention—to focus not on the most stimulating inputs, but the most significant ones. And emotionally, it demands a kind of quiet courage: the willingness to delay action until it aligns with deeper values, not just with shorter timelines.

The real challenge is cultural. It is harder to celebrate what is not immediately seen. Progress without spectacle is rarely rewarded. But this is precisely why emotional resilience matters. Because enduring success—the kind built on clarity, consistency, and character—requires withstanding invisibility. It requires saying no to distractions that look like opportunities and resisting the compulsion to respond just because someone is watching.

Urgency, when habitual, narrows our vision. It pulls us into the immediate and away from the meaningful. To live entirely by its rules is to forfeit the long view—the only view that sees beyond performance into purpose.

The culture of urgency is loud, but not wise. It demands your attention, but rarely your understanding. Reclaiming the patience to move deliberately is not just a personal rebellion; it is a strategic imperative. And it begins by recognising that time is not merely something to be managed. It is something to be respected.

Dopamine vs Discipline

The modern brain is not malfunctioning. It's responding—perfectly, predictably, and often destructively—to the incentives and stimuli it's been fed. What we interpret as a lack of willpower, laziness, or distraction is, in most cases, the by-product of a highly efficient neurological system doing exactly what it's designed to do: pursue pleasure, avoid discomfort, and conserve energy. The tension between short-term impulse and long-term strategy—the battle between dopamine and discipline—is not simply a moral struggle. It is a neurochemical negotiation, shaped as much by environment as by intention. Understanding this tension is foundational to reclaiming our capacity for patience, focus, and delayed gratification—the real building blocks of sustainable success.

At the centre of this conflict is dopamine. Often misunderstood as the brain's "pleasure chemical," dopamine is more accurately described as the molecule of *anticipation*. It drives motivation and desire, not satisfaction itself. Dopamine spikes when we expect a reward—whether it's the buzz of a message notification, the thrill of a new investment, or the fleeting high of social validation. It is the anticipation, not the attainment, that hooks us. This mechanism was once vital for survival. It helped early humans seek out food, social connection, and shelter. But in a digital context saturated with hyper-stimuli, this once adaptive system has become chronically overstimulated.

Consider the average person's daily routine. Before the first coffee, they've likely scrolled through headlines, skimmed social media, and processed dozens of digital prompts—all of which trigger dopamine surges. These micro-hits are not neutral. They condition the brain to seek novelty, reward, and stimulation with ever-increasing frequency. Over time, this erodes our capacity to tolerate boredom or engage with sustained, effortful tasks. What was once a healthy anticipation system becomes a feedback loop of craving and reward—a neurological treadmill that exhausts without progressing.

This has profound implications for how we pursue goals. Delayed gratification—the cornerstone of meaningful achievement—requires the ability to sit with discomfort, to postpone reward, and to operate without immediate reinforcement. But this ability is diminished when dopamine's signalling system is hijacked. The more often we satisfy our impulses instantly, the less tolerance we have for the slow burn of progress. This is not a motivational defect; it is a conditioned response. And unless disrupted deliberately, it becomes the default operating mode.

The problem is compounded by decision fatigue—a phenomenon first studied in judicial systems but now observable across domains. The brain has a finite capacity for conscious decision-making in any given day. Each choice, no matter how trivial, depletes this cognitive resource. In environments where we are bombarded by choice architecture—endless tabs, apps, options, prompts—the drain is rapid and relentless. By the time we reach our most important work, we are often mentally bankrupt. And the depleted brain defaults not to discipline, but to convenience.

It is no coincidence that many of the world's most disciplined thinkers—from Steve Jobs to Barack Obama—minimised their daily choices in trivial domains (such as clothing or breakfast) in order to preserve cognitive bandwidth for higher-order tasks. What they understood, whether intuitively or deliberately, is that discipline is not an inexhaustible trait. It is a limited resource, subject to depletion. And in an environment designed to seduce attention, *structure* becomes a better strategy than willpower.

This is where the traditional self-help narrative breaks down. The common prescription—to "try harder," "stay focused," or "resist temptation"—fails because it ignores the systemic forces at play. We are not facing a personal failing, but an environmental one. The platforms we use, the content we consume, the notifications we allow, and the pace we tolerate are all shaping our neurological defaults. Discipline, then, must be reframed—not as a character trait to be summoned in moments of weakness, but as a *design principle* embedded into the architecture of our days.

Let's take a practical example. A person trying to build a long-term financial portfolio must resist the temptation of reactive trading based on short-term market fluctuations. But every time they check a trading app, see a headline, or compare their performance to someone on social media, their dopamine circuits are triggered. The anticipation of gain or the fear of loss activates emotional pathways that impair rational decision-making. Without a pre-committed framework—a structure of rules, limits, and self-imposed constraints—the likelihood of succumbing to short-term reactivity rises dramatically. It's not just that the person lacks discipline; it's that their dopamine system is being pinged faster than their prefrontal cortex can respond.

The same applies to knowledge workers attempting deep work in shallow environments. The constant availability of novelty—emails, messages, metrics—disrupts the continuity required for creative or strategic thinking. And because each disruption delivers a small, measurable reward, it becomes self-reinforcing. Over time, the brain begins to *prefer* the distraction. It mistakes activity for productivity. Urgency eclipses importance. And the long-term vision—the book, the research, the strategy—is sidelined not because it isn't valued, but because it doesn't *feel* immediately rewarding.

This is the silent hijacking of ambition. The long-term becomes emotionally inaccessible, not intellectually unattractive.

There is, however, a path to correction. And it begins with *recognising the biological mechanics* of impulse, rather than moralising them. Discipline is not about white-knuckling your way through discomfort. It is about creating systems that reduce the frequency of impulse triggers, protect decision-making bandwidth, and realign your attention with what matters most.

Neuroscientist Dr Anna Lembke, in her study of addiction and dopamine regulation, describes the process of "dopamine fasting"—a deliberate reduction in compulsive reward-seeking behaviours to reset the brain's reward threshold. While not all readers need to undergo such protocols, the principle is powerful: less stimulation creates more sensitivity. When we reduce our exposure to fast-rewarding stimuli, we re-sensitise ourselves to slower, deeper forms of satisfaction. The discipline to endure the initial discomfort pays dividends in emotional resilience.

Philosophically, this aligns with the concept of *eudaimonia*—the ancient Greek idea of flourishing through alignment with one's deeper purpose, rather than through momentary pleasures. Aristotle distinguished between *hedonia* (pleasure) and *eudaimonia* (meaning), arguing that the latter required restraint, intention, and cultivation. Modern neuroscience now confirms what ancient philosophy intuited: that meaning is rarely dopamine-rich, but always discipline-dependent.

Crucially, this doesn't mean that pleasure is to be demonised. The goal is not to eliminate dopamine, but to *rebalance* it—to make space for slower rewards that compound over time: mastery, integrity, contribution, clarity. These are not dopamine spikes. They are emotional investments that accrue interest. But only when we have the discipline to defer.

In practical terms, this may involve creating digital guardrails: turning off notifications, scheduling deep work blocks, or maintaining time away from screens entirely. It might mean rethinking consumption habits—not just what we consume, but *how* and *why*. It also means creating rituals that honour slowness: reading physical books, writing by hand, walking without purpose. These practices are not nostalgic—they are neurological counterweights. They remind the brain how to be present with process, not just outcomes.

Ultimately, the goal is not to vanquish dopamine, but to train attention. Because where attention goes, behaviour follows. And where behaviour is repeated, identity is formed. Discipline, in this light, is not the suppression of desire—it is the intelligent redirection of it. It is a refusal to outsource your mind to systems designed to monetise your instincts.

The long-term vision you carry—whether financial, creative, relational, or personal—depends not on your ambition, but on your ability to *hold your attention steady*. That is the discipline the modern world quietly erodes. And that is the discipline this book seeks to help you recover.

The Myth of the Overnight Success

Success has always been more attractive than effort. But never has the appeal of rapid success been so dangerously oversimplified, amplified, and exported as it is today. In a culture saturated by curated stories and compressed timelines, we have inherited a dangerously distorted narrative: that real achievement happens suddenly, dramatically, and in public view. The "overnight success" has become a shorthand for brilliance, a justification for luck, and a myth that rewrites history in favour of virality. Yet behind nearly every such headline lies a longer, far less glamorous reality—one of painstaking consistency, invisible setbacks, and strategic patience. *What looks like magic is almost always just timing meeting tenacity.*

The allure of the overnight success story is not hard to understand. It simplifies complexity. It offers a digestible narrative in an attention-starved world: a founder pitches once, a creator goes viral, a product launches and the world suddenly notices. But what these stories conceal—or often omit entirely—is the *timeline.* The years spent refining, the rejections endured, the work done in silence. The result is a cultural paradox: we celebrate outcomes that only patience can produce, but elevate models that suggest patience is optional.

This distortion is reinforced by modern platforms and algorithms that reward spectacle over substance. Success stories now travel at the speed of shareability. But what becomes viral is not what is most instructive—it is what is most clickable. A social media post about quitting a job to build a million-dollar business attracts attention; a decade of bootstrapping rarely does. The medium flattens the message, collapsing a complex process into a singular, digestible event. In doing so, it breeds a dangerous inference: *if your success isn't visible yet, perhaps you're failing.*

To believe in overnight success is not merely to misread the external world—it is to erode internal resilience. It fosters impatience, comparison, and self-doubt. People begin to question their path not because it's wrong, but because it's quiet. They interpret slowness as inadequacy. And this can be fatal to endeavours that require long arcs—whether in business, academia, creative work, or personal mastery.

Consider the case of J.K. Rowling. The global phenomenon that is *Harry Potter* began not with instant acclaim, but with rejection—twelve of them from major publishers. Rowling wrote the first manuscript as a single mother on government assistance, scribbling notes in cafés while her daughter slept. The world eventually saw a billion-dollar franchise; what it did not see were the seven years of development, the loneliness, the edits, the perseverance through near-total invisibility.

Or take the story of Airbnb, now a household name. Most people know the platform as one of Silicon Valley's major unicorns. What they often don't know is that for years, the company teetered on collapse. The founders were unable to secure venture funding, resorted to maxing out credit cards, and even sold novelty cereal boxes to stay afloat. Their platform was dismissed by most investors as implausible. It was only after relentless iteration and slow traction that their breakthrough came—and even then, only gradually.

These are not isolated exceptions. Almost every lasting success story contains an invisible phase—a long, often discouraging period of foundational work that produces no applause. In organisational theory, this phase is sometimes referred to as the *latency period*: the time between an action and its visible consequence. But the latency period is also where emotional capital is built. It's where conviction is tested and frameworks are refined. Those who can endure this phase without external validation are not lucky; they are structurally advantaged. Because once momentum arrives, they are already ready.

Psychology provides further context. In his research on mastery and motivation, psychologist Anders Ericsson emphasised the importance of *deliberate practice*—long-term, effortful engagement in a specific skill, guided by feedback and refinement. This process is slow by design. It requires boredom tolerance, high error rates, and long periods with no external rewards. Ericsson's work was often misrepresented by the popularised "10,000-hour rule," but the core insight remains untouched: *competence is cumulative*. You cannot hack your way to deep expertise.

The myth of overnight success also creates structural blind spots. It favours visibility over viability, charisma over consistency. When society elevates stories of sudden triumph, it inadvertently dismisses the infrastructure that makes success sustainable. Systems thinking teaches us that outcomes are not singular events; they are the end-points of repeated inputs. What matters is not the spike, but the stability that follows it. A product that explodes in popularity without operational readiness often collapses under its own growth. A personal brand that scales too fast without substance becomes a hollow projection.

There is an ethical cost, too. When we elevate "overnight" narratives without context, we feed into a broader culture of performance anxiety. Young professionals feel behind before they've even begun. Creators abandon promising work after short testing cycles. Entrepreneurs make risky pivots based on attention metrics instead of durable strategy. The myth not only misleads—it depletes. It shortens time horizons and devalues persistence.

So, how do we reclaim a more truthful understanding of success—one that preserves aspiration but restores realism?

First, we must learn to honour what is *invisible.* True progress often happens underground, like roots before a bloom. The absence of recognition is not always a signal of inadequacy; often, it's a sign that the foundation is still forming. Patience is not inaction—it is preparation.

Second, we must learn to distinguish *momentum* from *maturity*. Early success, if not grounded in emotional and operational resilience, can collapse under scrutiny. What matters is not how fast something scales, but how well it sustains. Mature success is often unflashy. It's built in iterations, not explosions.

Third, we must challenge the metrics we use to judge progress. Visibility is not proof of value. Followers are not the same as fans. Revenue is not the same as resilience. Learning to differentiate these allows us to design our work around endurance rather than optics.

Finally, we must invest in *emotional patience*—the capacity to withstand delayed returns, silent effort, and internal doubt. This isn't a feel-good virtue. It is a competitive edge. Because in a world optimised for speed, the willingness to go slow—strategically, deliberately, repeatedly—is what separates signal from noise.

The myth of the overnight success is, in the end, a cultural fantasy: seductive, profitable, and incomplete. It feeds our hunger for inspiration while starving us of truth. But when we peel back the surface, we see a different story. One in which the most enduring success is not immediate, but *inevitable*—because it was built quietly, patiently, and with structural integrity. And that is the kind of success worth aspiring to.

Emotional Capital: The Wealth You're Ignoring

If you were asked to list your assets, you would likely name your savings, your property, your investments, perhaps your professional qualifications. But what would happen if we asked you to account for something less tangible—your emotional capital? Not your mood, not your personality, but a deeper reservoir: your capacity to endure stress without breaking, to make decisions without reactivity, to hold your ground when circumstances shift. Most people have never been taught to quantify or even recognise this form of wealth. And yet, *emotional capital is the single most underutilised, yet essential, asset in determining the longevity and quality of success.*

Unlike financial capital, emotional capital doesn't show up on a balance sheet. It doesn't announce itself in metrics or yield quarterly returns. But its effects are everywhere—subtle yet decisive. It determines how you respond under pressure, how you interact in conflict, how long you stay in the game when the outcomes are not immediate. It's the fuel behind composure, the architecture behind resilience, and the bedrock of long-term decision-making. Without it, talent becomes erratic, and potential remains unbanked.

To understand emotional capital as a resource, we must begin by making an uncomfortable admission: we are collectively overdrawn. The modern landscape—fast-paced, hyperstimulating, constantly interrupting—is emotionally expensive. Every notification, every demand for attention, every pressured decision depletes our reserves. What's worse, most of us are operating without any understanding of how to replenish them. We monitor our physical health with step counters and wearables. We track our money through apps and dashboards. But we rarely ask the most fundamental questions: *How much emotional capital do I actually have today? What am I spending it on? What is giving me a return—and what is eroding it?*

This framing matters. It changes the conversation from abstract self-care to strategic resource management. Emotional capital, once properly understood, becomes something you can *invest*, *protect*, and *grow.* Just as a financially intelligent person knows not to overspend during a downturn, an emotionally intelligent person recognises that certain people, situations, or choices cost more than they return—and adjusts accordingly.

Let's clarify what emotional capital is not. It's not about being emotionally expressive, or even emotionally intelligent in the conventional sense. Those can be components, but emotional capital goes further. It encompasses your *total usable reserve* of inner stability, presence, and self-regulation. It is what allows you to sit with discomfort without defaulting to escape behaviours. It is what steadies you when your plans unravel. It is what keeps you from making impulsive decisions when the stakes are high. It is, quite literally, the currency of your composure.

Take decision-making under pressure. Research from behavioural economics and neuroscience shows that human choices are far more emotionally driven than we'd like to admit. Stress narrows cognitive bandwidth. Uncertainty triggers loss aversion. Emotional fatigue leads to a reliance on heuristics and default patterns. In other words, when your emotional capital is low, your decisions become reactive rather than reflective. This is not just a personal problem—it's an economic one. Entrepreneurs abandon viable ventures because they mistake discomfort for misalignment. Investors panic-sell during drawdowns not due to bad logic, but because they've emotionally exhausted their tolerance for ambiguity. Careers are derailed not by a lack of skill, but by a collapse of inner capacity at critical junctures.

Emotional capital acts as a shock absorber. It's the buffer that allows you to pause before reacting, to think longer-term, to choose the wiser—not just the faster—course. But just like financial liquidity, it can't be conjured out of thin air in a crisis. It must be accumulated deliberately in advance.

Where does this accumulation happen? In the small moments: the decision to sit with discomfort rather than self-medicate it, the choice to reflect rather than react, the ability to remain grounded when no immediate reward is forthcoming. These are not merely acts of character—they are deposits. Like compound interest, their effect grows quietly over time.

It is helpful here to borrow a concept from the world of finance: *risk-adjusted returns*. In investment, this refers to how much return you get relative to the amount of risk taken. The same logic applies to emotional capital. A high-output individual who performs well but at the cost of constant stress and burnout is delivering a low emotional return on effort. Conversely, a person who builds patiently, sustains momentum, and remains resilient through setbacks is generating a high emotional return with lower volatility. *Resilience is the emotional equivalent of a diversified portfolio: less glamour, more longevity.*

So why is emotional capital ignored? Partly because it is invisible. It doesn't announce itself with certifications or accolades. It's often misinterpreted as mere personality—some people are just "calm," we think. But more often, it's because we don't know how to value it. We are conditioned to overvalue output and undervalue stability. We praise risk-takers, but rarely honour the quiet consistency that holds complex systems together. We mistake temporary drive for sustainable capacity.

To shift this, we need new mental models. Emotional capital should be treated not as a luxury, but as infrastructure. In any high-stakes domain—entrepreneurship, leadership, investing, parenting—emotional infrastructure is what allows performance to persist through uncertainty. You would never build a skyscraper without accounting for wind, weather, and foundational stress. Why build a career or a company without equivalent inner scaffolding?

Consider also the social dimension. Emotional capital is contagious. Leaders with high reserves transmit calm, clarity, and confidence. They create environments where others can think rather than merely react. Conversely, emotionally depleted leaders amplify chaos. The same applies to families, teams, and communities. Your emotional capital is not only your private reserve—it is your contribution to the collective atmosphere around you.

Building emotional capital, then, is not a solitary exercise. It's a strategic commitment to both inner growth and outward impact. It requires boundaries—not as barriers, but as energy filters. It demands rituals that restore—sleep, reflection, focused time, physical movement. It involves *knowing your cost centres*: relationships, habits, or environments that consistently drain you beyond recovery. And it asks for the courage to protect what is invisible, long before the consequences become visible.

We must also normalise what building emotional capital looks like. Sometimes it means *doing less*. It means saying no not because you lack ambition, but because you're protecting a more important asset: your capacity to remain intact over time. It means choosing rest over reaction, reflection over performance, process over panic. These are not signs of slowness. They are indicators of *stability*, which is what makes speed sustainable in the first place.

It's time we placed emotional capital where it belongs: on the same level as financial capital, intellectual capital, and social capital. Because without it, all the others are at risk. A brilliant mind collapses under chronic anxiety. A well-funded project is derailed by ego-driven conflict. A powerful network becomes unusable when trust erodes. *Emotional capital is the quiet force that holds the visible parts of success together.*

In a culture that equates urgency with importance, reclaiming your emotional capital is a radical act. But more than that, it's a wise one. It ensures that you're not just performing well, but holding well. That you're not just executing, but enduring. And that the success you're building doesn't just impress others—but is actually sustainable for you.

This is the wealth most people overlook until it runs out. You don't need to be one of them. Emotional capital can be built. And when managed wisely, it's the most resilient form of wealth you'll ever own.

Chapter 2
The Emotional Economy of Decision-Making

We like to imagine that our most consequential decisions are the result of logic—that given the right information, we will weigh our options with care, forecast sensibly, and proceed along a rational path. It's a reassuring belief. And, more often than not, a mistaken one. What behavioural economists, neuroscientists, and anyone who has faced real-world complexity will tell you is rather more sobering: our decisions, particularly under pressure, are not neat calculations—they're emotional negotiations. We don't so much think through our choices as feel our way into them.

The cost of denying this truth is more than academic. In financial markets, it shows up as panic selling during downturns and euphoric overconfidence during rallies. In professional life, it manifests in sudden resignations, ill-timed career pivots, or the paralysing inability to exit a failing venture. In leadership, we see it in erratic moves born not of analysis but of ego, insecurity, or the fear of appearing indecisive. The through-line is clear: the outer action reflects the inner weather—not the data, but the emotional barometer beneath it.

This chapter introduces a concept that every adult navigating complexity ought to grasp: every decision carries an emotional cost basis. Just as investors assess assets based on intrinsic value and external context, we too must factor in emotional capital, cognitive bias, and the state of our internal climate. Without this lens, what we call "decision-making" is often little more than managed reactivity. And reactivity, though occasionally useful in a crisis, is a poor compass for long-term navigation.

Consider loss aversion—one of the most well-studied emotional biases in decision theory. Coined by Kahneman and Tversky, the term refers to our tendency to feel the sting of loss more keenly than the pleasure of equivalent gain. Losing £100 hurts disproportionately more than gaining £100 feels rewarding. But beyond this basic asymmetry lies a deeper behavioural consequence: this sensitivity warps our actions. Investors cling to losing stocks, paralysed by the thought of "realising" the loss. Entrepreneurs persist in flawed business models longer than prudence justifies. Professionals endure toxic workplaces, not because they're blind to the dysfunction, but because the imagined loss—of status, income, identity—feels heavier than the speculative gain of walking away.

The problem isn't the fear itself. It's that we rarely interrogate it. People don't avoid change because the logic doesn't add up—they avoid it because letting go feels too emotionally expensive. And yet, inaction is itself a choice. One that accumulates its own kind of cost. Over time, the burden of deferred decisions—each made in pursuit of temporary comfort—can outweigh the cost of decisive movement. The irony is painful: we cling to avoid discomfort, and in doing so, guarantee a larger reckoning later.

Another distortion arises from our tendency to conflate external volatility with internal instability. We mistake situational uncertainty for personal failure. When markets dip, when feedback falters, when a project lags—our emotional response is rarely confined to context. Instead, it invades the self. "Maybe I'm not cut out for this." "Maybe this was all a fluke." These are not technical reflections. They're emotional flares dressed up as self-doubt.

Here, the metaphor of the internal market cycle earns its place. Just as economies ebb and flow—booms followed by corrections, contractions followed by recoveries—our internal states follow a rhythm of their own. There are stretches of clarity and momentum. Then come the troughs: confusion, fatigue, fear. The error is in mistaking these dips for collapse. A wise investor doesn't liquidate a sound portfolio at the first sign of red. Likewise, an emotionally literate person doesn't abandon their calling because confidence took a dip. This kind of literacy—emotional, not merely intellectual—is foundational to enduring strategy.

Still, awareness alone isn't enough. It's one thing to know your emotional landscape; quite another to let that awareness reshape your decisions. What truly matters is the move from reaction to reflection. Reactivity is instinctive, fast, and fear-driven. Reflection is slower, values-led, and willing to sit in ambiguity. The space between these two modes is where most preventable errors reside.

Take, for example, a founder who receives blunt criticism from a major investor. The reactive mind—wired for survival—interprets threat. The body responds: adrenaline spikes, posture tightens, defensiveness rises. The founder might lash out, double down, or spiral inward. Contrast this with a reflective posture. The founder takes a beat. What's actually being said here? Is there truth in this? What fear has been activated? What decision—if any—ought to follow, and when? Reflection doesn't suppress emotion. It integrates it, positioning feeling as one data point among many—not the only voice in the room, but one that deserves to be heard and contextualised.

There are tools that can help make this transition more habitual. One is borrowed from consumer law: the cooling-off period. Before responding to high-emotion stimuli—an inflammatory email, a market shock, a confrontational comment—build in pause. Sleep on it. Go for a walk. Let the chemical dust settle so that clarity can rise. Another is the inner boardroom model: identify the emotional "voices" that show up—fear, pride, doubt, ambition—and let them speak. Then, critically, choose who gets the final vote. Not the loudest voice, but the one aligned with long-term principles.

What this chapter ultimately proposes is a shift in how we frame decision-making. Every choice we make, large or small, is shaped not only by external data but by internal sentiment. Just as market actors respond to liquidity, confidence, and perceived value, so too do we respond to energy, emotion, and belief—often subconsciously. We are not cool-headed machines that happen to feel. We are emotional organisms that occasionally think—and usually only after the fact.

To understand your own emotional economy—its reserves, its biases, its patterns—is to gain a strategic edge. You stop simply reacting to life and start designing your response to it. You become more consistent, more principled, less vulnerable to the passing moods that derail others. Over time, this steadiness becomes a differentiator. Because while others are pulled about by the tides of their inner weather, you are moving from something deeper, something anchored.

This chapter will map that anchoring process. We'll look more closely at how fear of loss distorts risk perception, how our emotional rhythms mirror broader market cycles, and how to shift from emotional volatility to grounded decision-making using practical mental frameworks. This is not an argument against emotion. On the contrary—it's a call to bring emotion back into the fold, not as an intruder, but as a guide. Because the best decisions aren't made in a vacuum devoid of feeling. They're made when clarity has been hard-won through stillness—and the noise has been allowed, for just a moment, to quiet.

Choices Are Emotional Before They Are Rational

The myth of the rational decision-maker is a persistent one—comforting, tidy, and misleading. Popular economic models still operate on the assumption of the "rational agent," a theoretical actor who weighs information, assesses risk, and selects the most beneficial option based on objective reasoning. But in real life, decisions—particularly financial ones—are rarely made in such a vacuum. They are shaped, guided, and often distorted by a far more influential force: *emotion.* We may rationalise our choices after the fact, but in the moment, it is usually our emotional state—not a spreadsheet—that drives our actions.

This is not a character flaw. It is a neurological and evolutionary reality. The brain's decision-making architecture is not led by the prefrontal cortex (the logical, analytical centre); it is governed, at least initially, by the limbic system, where emotions reside. When confronted with a decision—whether to buy a stock, accept a job offer, or invest in a new venture—the first response is affective. *Do I feel safe? Do I trust this? Does this match my values, fears, or needs?* The rational mind often arrives later, not to lead the process, but to justify what the emotional brain has already decided.

Consider the act of investing. Classic theory assumes investors are guided by utility-maximising logic. Yet countless studies from behavioural finance disprove this. People hold onto losing investments longer than is rational (loss aversion), they chase gains after a rally (recency bias), they overestimate their ability to predict outcomes (overconfidence bias), and they mimic others in times of uncertainty (herd behaviour). These are not minor deviations from logic; they are systematic, predictable patterns. The financial markets are not moved by pure data—they are moved by *emotionally charged narratives* that spread quickly and trigger collective responses.

This helps explain why economic bubbles—whether in housing, tech, or cryptocurrency—form in cycles that far exceed any objective valuation. Prices rise not simply because the fundamentals support it, but because the narrative becomes emotionally persuasive. People are not buying assets; they are buying *the feeling* of security, excitement, or belonging. This explains why even seasoned investors, trained in analysis, are not immune to collective emotional contagion.

Daniel Kahneman, Nobel laureate and pioneer in behavioural economics, famously said, "We're blind to our blindness. We have very little idea of how little we know. We're not designed to know how little we know." In his research with Amos Tversky, Kahneman showed that our judgments under uncertainty are riddled with shortcuts and gut-based estimations. His book *Thinking, Fast and Slow* distinguishes between System 1 (fast, intuitive, emotional) and System 2 (slow, deliberate, logical) thinking. Crucially, System 1 is always first to respond. By the time System 2 gets involved, we've often already made the decision—and are now in search of a rationale.

Real-world examples bring this to life. In 2008, as the global financial crisis unfolded, a study conducted by Professor Andrew Lo at MIT found that traders with higher emotional regulation—measured through skin conductance and heart rate variability—made better decisions under pressure. Their success wasn't due to more information, but *better internal regulation.* They could pause, interpret their emotional signals, and act from a place of composure rather than compulsion. The key variable wasn't knowledge; it was *emotional bandwidth.*

Outside of markets, the same principle applies. Consider a high-stakes career decision: accepting a promotion that comes with prestige but also more stress, relocation, or ethical compromise. On paper, the move may be logical. But something doesn't feel right. The discomfort is real, yet hard to quantify. Often, we ignore it—only to face regret later. Why? Because we overvalued external logic and undervalued internal cues. Emotions are not irrational. They are *informational.* The problem is not that we feel; the problem is that we haven't learned to decode what we feel.

In this context, emotion becomes not an obstacle to decision-making, but a critical data stream. Anger can indicate boundary violations. Fear may highlight risk perception—but also opportunities for growth. Envy might point toward values we haven't yet honoured. These signals are rarely precise, but they are always relevant. Ignoring them is like turning off a compass in the middle of a fog.

Importantly, not all emotions lead us astray. Some enhance judgment. Empathy, for example, can improve negotiation outcomes. A study from the Journal of Personality and Social Psychology found that negotiators who were emotionally attuned to their counterparts achieved more favourable deals—not by manipulation, but by recognising unspoken needs. In this way, emotional sensitivity became a *strategic asset.*

The mistake, then, is not in allowing emotion into the decision-making process. The mistake is allowing emotion to go *unexamined.* What's needed is not less emotion, but *more literacy.* Just as financial literacy helps us interpret markets, emotional literacy helps us interpret ourselves. It teaches us to ask, *What is this feeling pointing to? Is it a true signal, or a distortion?* Emotional awareness becomes a form of due diligence.

This reframing has significant implications for leadership and high-stakes environments. Leaders often pride themselves on being "objective," as though emotion contaminates judgment. But the most effective leaders understand that emotional signals—both their own and those of others—are essential to reading context, anticipating risk, and building trust. Emotional suppression is not stoicism; it's negligence. And it usually leaks out sideways through passive aggression, burnout, or poor morale.

One of the most powerful models in this domain comes from psychologist David DeSteno, who argues that emotions evolved precisely *because* they help us make better decisions in uncertain environments. Gratitude encourages long-term thinking. Compassion promotes cooperation. Pride, when grounded in genuine achievement, motivates persistence. These emotions are not cognitive errors—they are evolutionary strategies. When harnessed intelligently, they *outperform logic alone.*

And yet, despite all this research, our institutions remain skewed toward dispassion. Business schools teach case analysis but not emotional calibration. Investment firms assess risk but rarely assess reactivity. Start-up founders are encouraged to optimise metrics but not manage emotional volatility. The result is a form of institutional blindness—one where emotionally poor decisions are dressed up in spreadsheets, and emotional intelligence is still considered a "soft skill."

Correcting this doesn't require abandoning logic. It requires *integrating emotion into a broader model of intelligence.* This is particularly important in environments where stakes are high, timelines are long, and feedback is delayed. In such contexts, emotion often arrives *before* results do. The disciplined decision-maker learns not to be controlled by emotion—but to *listen* to it, interrogate it, and channel it with intention.

This chapter will guide you through that process. We'll explore stories from finance, business, and psychology to demonstrate how emotion quietly underwrites decisions we assume are rational. We'll examine how emotional states distort time perception, risk appetite, and confidence—and how to build awareness frameworks that recalibrate your internal decision compass. You'll learn how to identify emotional drivers beneath your most pivotal choices, and how to build systems that protect you from your own volatility.

Ultimately, the goal is not to strip decisions of feeling, but to *elevate the quality of feeling that informs your choices.* Because when you recognise that every choice is emotional before it is rational, you stop resisting emotion—and start using it as the sophisticated tool it was always meant to be.

Loss Aversion and the Panic Reflex

We are not wired to lose gracefully. In fact, we are not even wired to evaluate gains and losses on equal terms. A loss of £1,000 feels far more painful than the pleasure of gaining the same amount. This asymmetry, first codified by behavioural economists Daniel Kahneman and Amos Tversky in the late 20th century, is not a cognitive quirk—it is a structural feature of human psychology. *Loss aversion* describes our disproportionate sensitivity to potential loss and our tendency to take irrational, often damaging, actions to avoid it. And nowhere is this phenomenon more evident—or more costly—than in the domains of investing, career decisions, and long-range planning.

To understand the depth of loss aversion, we must first confront a critical truth: our decisions are not shaped in laboratories of pure logic, but in emotional environments. The moment we perceive something we value slipping away—be it money, status, opportunity, or identity—a powerful emotional response is triggered. This is the *panic reflex*. It is a biological survival mechanism rooted in the amygdala, the brain's threat detection centre. When activated, it shifts us out of reflective reasoning and into reactive mode. The result? We sell low. We walk away too early. We pivot too late. We conflate discomfort with danger and short-term pain with existential threat.

Take investing, where the emotional weight of loss is measurable in both individual and market-wide behaviour. During the 2008 global financial crisis, countless investors liquidated their portfolios at historic lows—not because the assets had lost long-term value, but because the emotional discomfort of holding them became unbearable. The same pattern repeated in March 2020 during the early phase of the COVID-19 pandemic. Investors rushed to cash as markets fell—only to miss the recovery that followed. These actions were not irrational in the sense of lacking motive; they were irrational in the sense of undermining long-term outcomes. *The decision to sell was driven not by strategy, but by emotional depletion.*

This pattern is not limited to financial assets. It shows up in career pivots, where individuals abandon stable but undervalued roles for ill-considered alternatives, simply to escape the discomfort of feeling stuck. It manifests in founders who pull out of ventures after an initial loss, misinterpreting early volatility as systemic failure. It occurs in professionals who remain in draining jobs for years because the idea of "starting over" feels like losing accumulated prestige. In every case, the fear of loss becomes more decisive than the logic of opportunity. We move not toward gain, but away from discomfort.

Kahneman and Tversky's *Prospect Theory* remains one of the most robust frameworks for explaining this bias. It suggests that individuals assign more weight to potential losses than equivalent gains when evaluating outcomes under uncertainty. This leads to risk-averse behaviour when facing potential gains—and risk-seeking behaviour when trying to avoid losses. Paradoxically, people will take bigger gambles to *avoid* a loss than they would to *achieve* a gain. This is why investors double down on losing trades ("it'll turn around"), and professionals stay too long in failed projects ("I've already invested too much"). The goal is not to win. The goal is to *not lose*—even if the path chosen increases the actual loss.

Neuroscience supports these findings. Brain imaging studies show that loss anticipation activates brain areas associated with fear and anxiety, particularly the insula and amygdala. The psychological stress of a loss—real or imagined—generates physiological responses akin to physical pain. This helps explain why people will go to extraordinary lengths to *avoid* even small losses, such as time, status, or perceived dignity. The emotional toll of loss is not hypothetical. It is embodied.

But the most damaging aspect of loss aversion is not that it makes us risk-averse. It's that it *narrows our time horizon.* When fear sets in, our capacity to think long-term is impaired. We discount future benefits and inflate immediate discomfort. This is the emotional equivalent of selling out of the market at the first sign of a downturn. You cut the arc short, misreading a temporary dip as a terminal decline. And this doesn't only affect capital—it affects momentum, conviction, and creativity.

Consider a founder whose product fails to meet its first traction target. Loss aversion doesn't just whisper that the idea might be flawed—it *shouts* that continuing would be reckless. Panic sets in. Pivot becomes euphemism for retreat. But was the idea flawed, or was the timeframe premature? Was the loss informational or terminal? These are strategic questions. But panic doesn't ask questions. It demands relief.

This is why emotional capital—our internal capacity to absorb discomfort without reacting—is so vital. Those with high emotional capital are able to *sit through the perceived loss long enough to reframe it.* They see setbacks not as verdicts, but as variables. This gives them space to act with reflection rather than compulsion. And that space is where better outcomes are born.

There are historical examples that drive this home. Amazon, widely considered one of the most valuable companies in the world, operated at a loss for nearly a decade. Shareholders who abandoned ship in those early years missed out on exponential returns—not because the company wasn't performing, but because the short-term losses eclipsed long-term vision. Likewise, Netflix was ridiculed when it split its DVD and streaming business in 2011. The backlash led to immediate subscriber losses and a 77% drop in stock value. But the leadership held. They absorbed the blow. Today, the decision is recognised as foundational to their global dominance. *Without emotional resilience, the decision would likely have been reversed—and the long-term outcome forfeited.*

So how can individuals resist the panic reflex? Not by eliminating emotion, but by *structuring around it.* This means building decision frameworks in advance—clear thresholds for action, pre-defined metrics for evaluation, intentional "cool-off" periods before irreversible choices. It means separating the signal from the sensation: *Is this pain instructive or merely uncomfortable? Is this volatility part of a broader pattern or a true inflection point?* These are questions the reactive mind cannot answer. Only a structured, reflective posture can.

It also means re-examining how we define loss. Not every decline is a defeat. Not every setback requires response. *Loss is not just a number—it is a narrative.* The story we attach to the event determines whether it becomes a breaking point or a building block. Reframing loss as information rather than indictment changes the emotional charge. It enables a shift from panic to perspective.

Finally, we must normalise the psychological experience of loss without moralising it. Too often, professionals treat discomfort as a sign of personal failure. They equate temporary downturns with long-term inadequacy. This self-judgment accelerates panic, narrows creativity, and leads to premature exits. But recognising loss aversion for what it is—a universal, predictable bias—frees us from its grip. It creates room for curiosity. And curiosity is the antidote to panic.

The work, then, is not to become fearless, but to become *fluent.* Fluent in recognising the emotional patterns that govern behaviour. Fluent in pausing long enough to interrogate the story behind the reaction. Fluent in sustaining clarity when the mind demands escape. That fluency is not only a psychological advantage—it is a strategic one.

Loss aversion is not going away. It is hardwired. But it can be accounted for, anticipated, and transcended. And those who do—those who can hold their ground when everything inside them screams to flee—are the ones who compound not just capital, but character. Because what we do in moments of perceived loss often defines the quality of what we're able to gain.

Time, Emotion, and the Inner Market Cycle

Markets move in cycles. This much is widely accepted across investing, economics, and systems theory. Booms lead to corrections, euphoria gives way to doubt, peaks are followed by troughs—and then, eventually, by recovery. Investors study these patterns with almost religious dedication, tracking indicators and constructing models in an effort to predict or survive the inevitable fluctuations. What is less acknowledged, yet just as critical, is that human beings move in cycles too. Internally, emotionally, psychologically—we expand and contract, ascend and regress, elate and despair, often in quiet synchrony with the volatility of the systems we inhabit. *Our inner state is not separate from the external environment; it reflects and amplifies it.*

This subchapter contends with a provocative premise: *that the volatility we observe in markets is mirrored—sometimes even magnified—by the emotional volatility we experience within ourselves.* The timing is rarely exact, and the causes may differ in mechanism. But the cadence, the oscillation between high confidence and low conviction, between forward momentum and anxious inertia, is remarkably consistent. Recognising this inner market cycle—and learning to navigate it with the same discipline we apply to financial cycles—is one of the most underdeveloped yet crucial skills in modern decision-making.

The first step in building that discipline is abandoning the myth of emotional linearity. Just as markets do not grow in a straight line, neither does personal development, focus, energy, or clarity. Yet the cultural expectation remains that high performance should be perpetual, that motivation should be self-sustaining, and that clarity should be constant. This expectation is not only unrealistic—it is damaging. It leads to self-judgement during inevitable downcycles, causes overextension during upcycles, and impairs the long-term decisions that require a wider temporal lens.

To draw the parallel more concretely: when a market enters a bear phase, seasoned investors do not panic. They assess fundamentals, reduce exposure where necessary, and prepare to deploy capital when conditions stabilise. But when individuals enter emotional drawdowns—moments of confusion, fatigue, self-doubt—they often do the opposite. They interpret the downturn as personal failure. They question long-held strategies. They abandon trajectories that, under stable conditions, still make sense. This is the *emotional sell-off*, and it is just as costly—if not more so—than a financial one.

Real-world examples reinforce the pattern. A founder experiencing team friction and funding delays begins to question not just their business model, but their identity as a leader. An investor navigating a market correction shifts from a disciplined strategy to reactive tinkering. A creative professional, mid-project and deep in the inevitable boredom of iteration, considers pivoting—not because the idea has lost merit, but because the emotional discomfort of the "middle" is misread as evidence of misalignment. These are not isolated lapses in logic. They are symptoms of an inner cycle out of sync with a broader perspective.

Psychology offers further validation. The work of Robert Thayer, a psychologist known for his research on mood and self-regulation, found that energy and tension—two core emotional dimensions—fluctuate rhythmically throughout the day and over longer periods. These shifts affect how we interpret information, assess risk, and perceive self-efficacy. When tension is high and energy is low, we are more likely to perceive neutral events as threatening and to default to protective behaviours. In contrast, high energy and low tension create states of optimism and expansiveness. These are not abstract moods; they are *decisional contexts*. They shape the very lens through which we perceive opportunities and threats.

The implication is profound: if you are unaware of your own inner market cycle, you will misprice your decisions. You will overvalue urgency when in a high-tension state. You will undervalue long-term plans when your emotional liquidity is low. And you will confuse temporary emotional contractions with permanent strategic flaws. *Emotional mispricing* is as real—and as dangerous—as financial mispricing.

This is where time re-enters the equation, not just as a background condition, but as an active variable. Most people do not misjudge outcomes because they lack intelligence or experience. They misjudge timing. They expect instant clarity during periods of inner fog. They push for external results when their internal system is in retreat. They withdraw at the very moment when holding steady would yield compounding benefits. Time is not just a metric—it is a medium through which cycles unfold. Without respecting it, we act prematurely or too late.

This connection between time, emotion, and decision-making is not merely theoretical. In ancient Stoic philosophy, time was seen as both a container and a teacher. Seneca wrote that "time discovers truth." Modern neuroscience echoes this in its findings on *emotional refractory periods*—the windows of time after an emotional event during which perception is skewed. During these periods, we interpret new information in ways that reinforce our existing emotional state. This is the cognitive equivalent of a market reacting to bad news with disproportionate sell-offs. Until the refractory period ends, data will be distorted. In emotional terms, *the signal is there, but the interpretation is wrong.*

To navigate this, we need a new form of literacy: *temporal-emotional literacy*. This is the ability to ask not just, *What am I feeling?* but *When am I feeling it?* And more importantly, *Is this the right moment to act on this feeling?* Timing, in this context, becomes a skill of restraint, not just execution. The best decisions are rarely made at the emotional peak or trough. They are made during the plateau—when clarity has returned and emotional volatility has cooled. Building the discipline to wait for that plateau is the mark of someone who understands the cost of impulsive action.

There are practical methods to support this kind of calibration. Emotional journaling, when done systematically, can reveal personal cycles over time. Pattern recognition enables better forecasting—not of feelings, but of when certain feelings are likely to arise and how they've historically influenced behaviour. Similarly, strategic sabbaticals—microbreaks from decision-making—can protect against ill-timed actions. Just as traders sometimes "go to cash" during periods of high volatility, individuals can opt for *emotional cash positions*: periods where no major commitments are made, no major reversals are allowed, and the primary task is observation, not correction.

None of this implies passivity. On the contrary, it implies a form of active patience—*the willingness to hold position, to preserve emotional capital, and to let time reveal what urgency conceals*. It is an approach grounded not in fatalism but in fidelity: faithfulness to one's principles even when the emotional weather shifts.

The emotional economy we all live within is not something to conquer. It is something to understand. And when we map our inner market cycles—our expansions and contractions, our volatility and stasis—with the same care that financial analysts map macroeconomic indicators, we begin to make decisions not only from intellect, but from *emotional integrity*. We don't eliminate volatility—we learn to price it in.

This subchapter offers a framework for doing exactly that. It shows how emotional patterns correspond to systemic fluctuations, how timing interacts with temperament, and how self-awareness—

tempered by structure—can prevent the premature liquidation of good ideas, relationships, and strategies. Because just as the best investors don't fear the cycle but work within it, the most emotionally resilient people don't resist fluctuation—they *learn when to act, and when to wait.* And that, more than insight or intelligence, is what sustains meaningful success over time.

From Reaction to Reflection

A single second can define the quality of an outcome. That second—between stimulus and response—is where human agency lives. And yet, for most people, that space is almost entirely consumed by reactivity. Someone criticises your work, and you respond with defensiveness. A project stalls, and you spiral into doubt. The market drops, and you sell in fear. These are not strategic moves; they are psychological reflexes. The difference between people who compound success over time and those who derail under pressure often comes down to *how well they use that second*—the space between what happens and how they choose to meet it.

This chapter addresses one of the most consequential shifts a person can make in their life and work: the shift from reaction to reflection. Not as a personality trait, but as a *trainable skill.* To be clear, reacting is not inherently wrong. It is evolutionarily efficient, and in certain contexts—emergencies, threats, high-speed decision environments—it is essential. But in complex domains like leadership, investing, relationships, and career development, reaction is usually too fast, too shallow, and too expensive. It favours immediacy over insight, impulse over alignment. *Reflection, by contrast, creates the conditions for deliberate, values-aligned action—even when under emotional pressure.*

Let's begin with the science. The brain's default operating system, particularly under threat or uncertainty, is not reason—it's survival. The amygdala, the brain's threat detection centre, scans for danger and cues the body for action: fight, flight, or freeze. This process unfolds within milliseconds, often before the prefrontal cortex—the seat of executive function and rational thinking—has had a chance to engage. It's efficient but crude. It was built to help us outrun predators, not navigate quarterly earnings, co-founder conflicts, or ambiguous feedback from a supervisor.

What makes this more challenging is that *threat is no longer defined by survival, but by discomfort.* Disagreement, delay, risk of embarrassment, loss of control—these now trigger the same circuitry as physical threat. Which means we're constantly being asked to make high-quality decisions in a neurobiological state that is fundamentally unfit for reflection. The result is a society saturated with reaction: tweets instead of dialogue, pivots instead of persistence, outrage instead of understanding. It's not just emotionally unsustainable. It's intellectually impoverishing.

So how do we disrupt the reflex? The answer lies in *mental frameworks that slow down cognition without paralysing action.* These are not mantras or affirmations, but structured ways of thinking that create a buffer between emotion and execution. One such framework is borrowed from Viktor Frankl, the psychiatrist and Holocaust survivor who famously wrote, *"Between stimulus and response, there is a space. In that space is our power to choose our response. In our response lies our growth and our freedom."* Frankl's insight was not poetic—it was profoundly neurological. He recognised that by expanding the space between event and action, we reclaim our agency.

Cognitive behavioural therapy (CBT), one of the most empirically supported psychological models, formalises this idea through a structure: situation → thought → feeling → behaviour. Most people collapse this sequence into situation → behaviour. But with training, individuals can identify the *thoughts and feelings* that occur in between and choose how to proceed. This is not a spiritual abstraction; it is a repeatable process. And those who internalise it gain a competitive edge—not just emotionally, but strategically.

Let's consider a real-world application. Imagine you are a team leader who receives negative feedback from a client. The reactive impulse might be to deflect blame, fire off an explanation, or make a rash internal change. But if you engage the reflective model, your first move is to *pause and decode your own reaction*: Is this anger, shame, fear? What is this emotion trying to protect? What part of this feedback is data, and what part is noise? What response would serve both the client relationship and the team dynamic best over the long term? That pause may take five minutes—or five hours. But the quality of action that follows will almost certainly outperform the knee-jerk response.

This is where *meta-cognition*—thinking about thinking—becomes essential. High performers across disciplines share one trait: they observe their thoughts as objects, not truths. They create a second-order awareness that allows them to act on intention, not just instinct. In the trading world, this is called "staying on strategy." In philosophy, it's called temperance. In psychology, it's called self-regulation. The language differs. The principle does not.

Crucially, reflection does not mean indecision. One of the most common misinterpretations of reflective behaviour is that it equates to slowness or inaction. But reflection is not the opposite of action; it is the *refinement* of it. Some of the most decisive people in history—Winston Churchill, Angela Merkel, Warren Buffett—are known not for impulsiveness, but for deliberative calm. Their strength lies not in the volume of decisions they make, but in the *clarity and timing* of those decisions. This is a discipline built over years, and it often flies in the face of cultural expectations that glorify speed.

To cultivate reflection as a baseline response, certain conditions must be created—both internally and environmentally. Internally, the nervous system must be regulated. It is nearly impossible to think clearly when physiologically dysregulated. Techniques such as controlled breathing, movement, or somatic grounding can bring the nervous system back to a baseline from which reflection is possible. Environmentally, space must be protected. The over-scheduled, hyper-notified calendar leaves no margin for thought. Reflection requires *buffer time*—moments in the day, week, and month where the primary task is not productivity, but perspective.

Another vital tool is the use of *decision journals*—structured records of high-stakes decisions, including context, emotional state, assumptions, and eventual outcomes. Over time, these journals reveal patterns: when you make your best decisions, when you tend to overreact, what emotional states distort your judgment. The value of such tracking is cumulative. It creates a feedback loop that builds emotional literacy and sharpens judgment.

It is also important to distinguish between *healthy reflection* and its counterfeit: rumination. Rumination is circular, unproductive, and emotionally draining. It fixates on the problem without moving toward resolution. True reflection is *directional.* It seeks understanding that leads to action. It is not about dwelling, but about *processing.* The litmus test is simple: does your thinking lead to clarity and intention, or to stagnation and doubt?

Organisations, too, can institutionalise reflection. After-action reviews, decision audits, and cross-functional retrospectives all serve as collective reflective practices. But they only work when psychological safety is present—when people can interrogate actions without fear of blame. In cultures dominated by reaction, such reviews become exercises in defensiveness. In cultures that value reflection, they become engines of learning.

Ultimately, the shift from reaction to reflection is not just a psychological upgrade—it is an economic one. It protects against impulsive exits, misaligned pivots, and reputational damage. It enhances the quality of relationships, the durability of strategy, and the consistency of outcomes. And it allows individuals to act not just from emotion, but with *emotional precision*—a skill that is increasingly rare, and therefore increasingly valuable.

The world will continue to offer provocations. Markets will crash. Clients will push back. Relationships will strain. Deadlines will move. The difference between those who are destabilised by these events and those who navigate them with composure is not intelligence, privilege, or even experience. It is this: *the capacity to insert reflection where reaction used to be.* That capacity is the cornerstone of mature self-leadership—and the foundation of durable, resilient decision-making.

Chapter 3
The Quiet Superpower: Defining Emotional Resilience

If strength made a noise, perhaps resilience would be easier to notice. But emotional resilience doesn't come thundering in with grand displays of confidence or sweeping, cinematic comebacks. It doesn't usually look heroic. More often, it resembles quiet composure. It's the choice to stay one more day when everything in you wants to flee. It's a withheld remark in a moment charged with emotion. It's a discomfort endured without drama, a pause held against the tug of escape. True resilience is subtle. It doesn't seek attention—and that's precisely why we so often overlook it. Yet in an era defined by distraction and volatility, it might be the most crucial psychological currency we have.

This chapter takes aim at a mischaracterisation that's become almost gospel in popular culture: that resilience is endurance wrapped in stoic denial. That to be resilient means to remain unaffected—untouched by grief, immune to fear, impervious to setbacks. This ideal persists because it flatters a certain fantasy of invincibility. But real resilience is not found in a person who "pushes through" at all costs. Rather, it lives in the subtleties—in the quality of response to difficulty, not in its suppression. The intention here is not to strip away the humanity of struggle, but to elevate resilience as something that can be cultivated, evaluated, and, importantly, practised.

Let's start by dismantling the myth that resilience is a static trait. It's not. It's better understood as a dynamic system—one that regulates and recovers, flexes and adapts. No one arrives at adulthood with a fixed stockpile. Like muscle, it builds with use. But unlike muscle, emotional resilience doesn't grow through sheer strain; it strengthens when we learn to work *with* stress, not merely against it. That nuance matters, because mistaking resilience for blunt force endurance leads to burnout disguised as discipline. This is not about gritting your teeth. It's about intelligent engagement.

Neuroscience offers a compelling reframe here. The concept of neuroplasticity—the brain's capacity to reshape itself based on experience—casts resilience in a whole new light. It's not just about character; it's about wiring. Research shows that consistent emotional regulation—not repression, but thoughtful engagement—actually enhances neural connectivity in regions tied to empathy, reflection, and self-control. This isn't theory. It's visible in scans. Resilience, then, is not an act of will so much as a physiological investment. The more we practise regulated responses under pressure, the more our brains learn to default to them when it matters most.

But if resilience can be built, it can also be depleted. Chronic exposure to stress without adequate recovery erodes the very capacities resilience relies on. Volatility without stabilisation, emotional suppression mistaken for strength—these are not badges of honour. They're warning signs. What may look like composure on the outside could well be a person running on empty inside, holding themselves together through habit more than health. Resilience doesn't mean simply withstanding impact—it means recovering from it, regenerating what's been spent.

And here lies the paradox: resilient people don't feel less. They often feel more. The distinction is that they've learned not to let those feelings steer them off course. The capacity to sit with sadness, anger, fear, or doubt—without immediately acting from it or fleeing from it—is not a flaw. It's a mark of strength. Emotional breadth is not a liability but a form of depth. Just as a diversified investment portfolio weathers storms more effectively than one built on a single bet, an emotionally diverse inner life is more resilient than one built on constant suppression or singular focus.

Too often, patience gets lumped in with passivity, which only adds to the confusion. This conflation, echoed in boardrooms and parenting philosophies alike, is misleading. Patience isn't about doing nothing. It's about knowing when *not* to act. It's a disciplined deferral, a space where observation is allowed to outpace impulse. Think of it as the psychological counterpart to avoiding a panic sell in turbulent markets. To wait, deliberately, is not weakness. It's timing. It's signal processing.

You see this most vividly in those who operate under relentless pressure—top-tier athletes, serial founders, long-view investors, trauma surgeons. People for whom chaos is not an event but a daily feature. What separates those who endure from those who flame out isn't just talent or intelligence—it's the quality of their responses over time. Resilience isn't what helps them bounce back after one crisis. It's what prevents them from crumbling under a cascade of them. It keeps the core steady while the surface shifts.

Take the entrepreneur navigating uncertain funding, unpredictable markets, and internal tension. A reactive leader might lurch from one tactic to the next, micromanage under the guise of "taking control," or burn bridges with impulsive calls. The resilient leader, on the other hand, absorbs the ambiguity, slows the pace, listens to emerging signals, and times their decisions. Their restraint is not hesitation. It's precision. Their silence in chaos? Not avoidance. It's calibration. The stillness is not empty—it's strategic.

And this raises a deeper question, rarely asked: resilience *for what?* It isn't inherently virtuous. It's only meaningful when anchored to something—purpose, principle, the long arc of a meaningful goal. Without direction, resilience can become little more than an endurance sport with no finish line. But tether it to something real, and it becomes transmutational. You're not merely withstanding life's battering—you're metabolising it into wisdom, clarity, and strength.

In this light, emotional resilience stops being a private virtue and becomes a public necessity. In a world beset by rapid change, information saturation, and widespread psychological strain, the capacity to remain anchored isn't just helpful—it's essential. Whether in the halls of government, corporate headquarters, classrooms, or dining rooms, the presence of resilient individuals has a stabilising effect. It softens conflict, prevents rash decisions, and expands our tolerance for ambiguity—one of the most valuable traits in uncertain times.

And yet, despite all its utility, resilience remains one of the most underdeveloped skills in formal settings. Schools rarely teach it. Workplaces mislabel it. Media romanticises it. What we need is not another inspirational soundbite, but a serious framework—something to dissect, study, and practise with intention. Not as a luxury skill, but as foundational infrastructure.

That, in essence, is the purpose of this chapter: to reimagine resilience not as a personal quirk or mythical gift, but as a system—one grounded in recovery, reflection, and psychological elasticity. We'll explore the power of patience—not as inertia but as a force of timing. We'll look at emotional range not as a threat to composure but as a tool for staying intact. And we'll build the case for resilience as the architecture of a well-regulated, purpose-driven inner life.

This is not a blueprint for becoming untouchable. Nor is it a glorification of suffering. What you'll find instead is a recalibration. A way to think about resilience as design—not armour, but scaffolding. Not a show of strength, but a quiet system of staying whole. Because in a world that burns hot and fast, the most resilient among us won't be the ones who run the hardest. They'll be the ones who remain—steady, clear, and unshakeably composed—long after the noise has passed.

Beyond Grit: What Resilience Really Is

It has become fashionable to idolise grit. In boardrooms, classrooms, and motivational seminars, it's the watchword of high achievers—the silent badge of those who push harder, endure longer, and persist where others fold. Grit, as popularised by psychologist Angela Duckworth, is defined as passion and sustained persistence toward long-term goals. It's compelling, intuitively appealing, and easy to celebrate. But as it gained cultural momentum, something critical was lost in translation: *persistence, on its own, is not always intelligent.*

A person can persist in a job that is depleting their health, in a market strategy that is structurally flawed, in a relationship that consistently erodes self-worth. Grit, without discernment, becomes stubbornness. And when blind persistence is mistaken for resilience, we risk reinforcing the wrong idea—that to be emotionally resilient is simply to keep going, regardless of what you're going toward.

True resilience is far more subtle. It is not mere tenacity or the capacity to tolerate discomfort indefinitely. It is *adaptive endurance aligned with purpose*. It means knowing *when* to hold the line and *when* to redirect, and doing both without collapsing under the weight of uncertainty. Resilience is not a reflex—it's a regulation system. It allows a person to endure difficulty not because they're impervious to pain, but because they've built the internal mechanisms to interpret, adjust, and act with precision under pressure.

Let's unpack the anatomy of this more sophisticated form of resilience. First, it begins with *awareness*, not willpower. A resilient person does not override their emotions—they register them. Emotional data is seen as a form of intelligence, not interference. From this base of awareness, they activate *agency*—the capacity to respond rather than react. This is where adaptive endurance diverges from brute perseverance: it *includes the flexibility to change course.* To persist in the same behaviour regardless of outcome is not strength—it's rigidity. Resilience requires an ongoing feedback loop between intention, effort, and recalibration.

A well-researched example comes from military psychology, where soldiers under high-stakes pressure are not simply trained to "grit their teeth." Instead, effective resilience training focuses on cognitive flexibility, emotional regulation, and situational awareness. A combat-ready mind is one that can detect fear without being paralysed by it, shift strategies under fire, and maintain purpose amid chaos. These are not passive qualities—they are skills. The most effective operators are not those who feel nothing, but those who can metabolise discomfort *into functional behaviour* without delay.

The same principle applies in high-stakes business environments. Consider a startup founder navigating investor rejections, product failures, and staff turnover. If their only tool is grit, they may persist with a flawed model far too long. But if they have built resilience—defined not by raw endurance but by adaptive response—they can absorb the setback, decode its signal, pivot if necessary, and stay grounded in the overarching vision. Their progress may still be slow, but it is informed and sustainable. *Resilience is what keeps the strategy intelligent when the environment is unstable.*

Importantly, this form of resilience is not uniform—it is shaped by context, culture, and personal history. People raised in environments where mistakes were punished rather than processed may have developed defensive persistence: they press forward not because they are resilient, but because they fear the consequences of stopping. Others may have inherited cultural narratives that glorify self-sacrifice, and thus equate burnout with virtue. In both cases, what looks like toughness is often a mask for unresolved fear or identity fragility.

That's why the language we use around resilience matters. When we frame it purely as "grinding through hardship," we obscure its most valuable component: *discernment under duress*. Resilience involves selecting your battles wisely, conserving energy when needed, and saying no with as much conviction as saying yes. It recognises that every act of persistence has a cost—and that the truly resilient are those who *budget their emotional capital* with strategic intent.

This brings us to a crucial but rarely explored distinction: the difference between *acute resilience* and *chronic resilience*. Acute resilience is your ability to withstand a sudden shock—a job loss, a health scare, a personal betrayal. It is tested in moments. Chronic resilience is what sustains you through extended ambiguity—building a career, raising a child, living with grief. The latter requires not just recovery from strain but continuity of purpose across fatigue, doubt, and delayed outcomes. This is where blind grit often breaks down. Without a deeper why, persistence curdles into martyrdom.

To cultivate chronic resilience, we must re-centre the role of *meaning*. Psychiatrist and Holocaust survivor Viktor Frankl observed that those who survived extreme psychological trauma were often those who could locate a purpose larger than their pain. Purpose provides context. It reframes suffering as tolerable, even productive, when tied to a coherent aim. And this isn't limited to extreme cases—everyday resilience benefits from the same logic. If you know why you're enduring difficulty, you're less likely to become emotionally fragmented by it.

This is not an invitation to glorify hardship. It is an argument for intentionality. Resilience becomes most valuable when it is *paired with purpose and governed by insight*. Otherwise, we fall into the trap of equating motion with meaning, or struggle with strength. The cultural idolisation of "pushing through"—fuelled by hustle media, self-help slogans, and performative work culture—has led many to exhaust themselves in service of hollow goals. This is not resilience. It is depletion masquerading as devotion.

A more accurate model views resilience as a cyclical process: stress, interpretation, response, recovery. The key is not to remain unbroken, but to recover faster and with greater clarity each time. Psychologists call this "stress-related growth"—the idea that adversity, when processed effectively, can leave you stronger and wiser than before. But growth is not automatic. It depends on the presence of reflection, support, and recalibration. Those without these supports may persist, but they won't evolve.

So what does this mean for practical living? It means that developing resilience is less about increasing your pain threshold and more about refining your mental architecture. It involves learning when to act and when to wait. When to seek help and when to self-resource. When to pivot and when to push. These are not traits—they are skills. And like all skills, they improve with practice, feedback, and patience.

Let's be clear: none of this implies that grit is obsolete. Grit has its place. But it must be *in service of something*, and it must be governed by wisdom. Without that, it is not a virtue but a liability. Adaptive endurance—resilience as we are redefining it—is not reactive effort. It is *responsive integrity*. It is knowing who you are, what you're building, and how to navigate obstacles without losing yourself in them.

If we are to build a world that rewards depth over performance, clarity over bravado, and longevity over spectacle, we must learn to distinguish between noise and signal—even in ourselves. Resilience is the quiet filter that helps us make that distinction. It is the subtle intelligence behind sustained progress. And it is the antidote to a culture that often mistakes loudness for leadership and burnout for commitment.

Resilience is not how loud you shout when things go wrong. It's how steadily you move when no one's watching. And it begins the moment you stop asking, *How do I push through this?* and start asking, *What am I actually moving toward—and why?*

The Elastic Mind: Bending Without Breaking

The mind's capacity to recover from disruption is perhaps the most underestimated determinant of long-term success. We are repeatedly told that stress is a threat, trauma a permanent scar, and failure a marker of inadequacy. Yet within the folds of modern neuroscience lies a more liberating truth: the brain is not fixed—it is *elastic*. And elasticity, not toughness, is the defining trait of emotional resilience.

At the centre of this elasticity is *neuroplasticity*—the brain's ability to rewire itself in response to new information, experiences, and environments. It's not simply a feature of childhood development, as once thought. It remains active, to varying degrees, throughout our lives. That means recovery is not a matter of stoicism or denial, but of *adaptive rewiring*. The same mental structures that hold pain can also be trained to process, reinterpret, and release it.

To understand this, we must first discard the idea that the mind operates like a brittle system that cracks under pressure. A more accurate metaphor is that of a suspension bridge: under load, it doesn't remain perfectly still—it flexes. That flexibility is engineered into its design. Likewise, the resilient mind is not a mind that resists movement, but one that integrates stress and restores equilibrium without shattering.

Neuroscientist Norman Doidge brought this concept to mainstream attention with his work on neuroplasticity in patients recovering from brain injury. Stroke victims, once thought to have limited cognitive restoration, demonstrated significant functional recovery through targeted mental and physical exercises. But neuroplasticity is not exclusive to trauma survivors. It is constantly at work in everyday life—each time we form a new habit, reframe a belief, or learn under pressure.

What distinguishes the resilient individual is not that they experience less adversity, but that their brains *learn more effectively from adversity*. This adaptation is cognitive, emotional, and behavioural. The brain doesn't just repair damage; it *assigns meaning* to it. This is where perception becomes powerful. A setback seen as failure embeds one kind of neural signature—one that may suppress action or confidence. But a setback framed as data triggers a different loop—encouraging curiosity, analysis, and recalibration.

Consider the example of post-traumatic growth (PTG), a psychological counterpart to PTSD. While PTSD centres on dysfunction following trauma, PTG involves enhanced psychological functioning—greater appreciation for life, improved relationships, clearer priorities. Studies show that individuals who engage in deliberate reflection, seek supportive dialogue, and reconstruct meaning from adversity are more likely to experience this form of growth. These are not passive responses—they are *neurologically active*. The brain restructures itself based on how we interpret difficulty.

This is where resilience training becomes both a personal and strategic pursuit. Whether you're a founder navigating business volatility, a clinician managing burnout, or a parent weathering emotional strain, the ability to *bend without breaking* is not innate—it's built. One of the most effective tools in building this capacity is *cognitive reappraisal*—the process of changing one's interpretation of a situation in order to reduce its emotional impact.

In neurological terms, reappraisal strengthens connections between the prefrontal cortex (responsible for rational thinking) and the amygdala (associated with threat detection and emotional reactivity). Repeated practice reduces the likelihood of disproportionate stress responses and enhances recovery speed. In simpler terms, the more you reframe, the less often you panic.

But reappraisal is only one tool. Another is *exposure with safety*. This concept, often used in trauma recovery and cognitive behavioural therapy, involves gradually reintroducing the individual to emotionally charged stimuli in controlled, supportive conditions. Over time, the brain learns that these stimuli are not fatal. The amygdala deactivates more quickly. Tolerance increases. It's neuroplasticity in action: the mind recalibrates its fear signature.

Resilience also depends on *habituation to ambiguity*. In a world increasingly defined by volatility—market shifts, social upheaval, professional instability—the ability to stay mentally agile amid uncertainty is non-negotiable. People with high tolerance for ambiguity display less anxiety, better decision-making, and more constructive problem-solving. And this tolerance is trainable. By consciously engaging in scenarios that challenge our control reflex—delayed decisions, fluid timelines, complex negotiations—we teach the brain to reduce its threat response to the unknown.

To be clear, elasticity is not the same as detachment. Some people cope with stress by numbing or disconnecting. This may resemble calm, but it's an illusion. True resilience is *responsive*, not avoidant. An elastic mind feels stress, processes it, and restores clarity—not by bypassing discomfort, but by metabolising it.

Take for instance elite athletes. Their performance under pressure is not a product of immunity to stress but of *neurological conditioning*. Mental toughness training in sports psychology is less about cheerleading and more about scripting the mind's response under specific, high-stakes scenarios. They visualise setbacks, mentally rehearse recovery, and wire their nervous systems to return to composure on command. The same principles apply off the field: if you train your brain to encounter, withstand, and move through emotional difficulty, you reduce its long-term scarring effect.

This brings us to one of the most overlooked aspects of resilience: *recovery speed.* In high-performance domains, success is less about avoiding dips in performance and more about reducing the time spent in recovery. Similarly, mental resilience is about *how quickly you can restore clarity and functionality after stress.* A delay is natural; collapse is optional. And the speed of that recovery is a direct function of the brain's plasticity.

Of course, neuroplasticity has its limits. Chronic stress, trauma, and repeated exposure to instability without support can degrade neural function. Cortisol—the body's primary stress hormone—at elevated levels can impair memory, decision-making, and emotional regulation. So, while the brain is adaptive, it also needs care. Sleep, nutrition, social connection, and meaningful engagement aren't luxuries—they're prerequisites for neurological health. Resilience is not built on suffering; it's built on sustained *conditions for adaptation.*

So how do we apply this practically? Start with *awareness of your recovery patterns.* When you face emotional strain, how long does it take you to return to composure? What supports that process—and what hinders it? Notice whether your stress becomes narrative ("I always fail") or data ("This didn't work—why?"). Cultivate micro-recovery habits: brief breathing resets, reflective writing, reframing conversations. These are not soft practices. They are neurological interventions.

Then, expand your ambiguity tolerance. Intentionally sit with unresolved issues. Tolerate slow feedback loops. Don't rush to fix what is merely uncomfortable. Discomfort is often the signal of new neural wiring in progress. The more often you let your brain complete this cycle, the stronger its architecture becomes.

Finally, integrate emotional feedback into decision-making. An elastic mind is not just reactive—it is *reflectively adaptive.* If something repeatedly drains your energy or clouds your judgment, it is worth investigation. Resilience is not about bouncing back to the same shape; it's about evolving into a stronger one.

The elastic mind is not a gift—it's a design feature that requires maintenance. It is how we evolve under stress without fracturing. It is what enables long-term patience without passive drift, and deliberate persistence without blind repetition. In a world that rewards speed but punishes fragility, the ability to stretch under pressure and reform with clarity is not just an advantage—it is a necessity.

And perhaps this is the most encouraging insight of all: *resilience is not a trait you either have or lack—it is a system you can train.* The brain is wired for it. The science supports it. And the future belongs to those who learn to bend with purpose—never snapping, never static, always expanding.

Patience ≠ Passivity

Why Stillness Is Not Inaction—But Strategic Strength

Patience is one of the most mischaracterised forces in modern culture. It is often confused with passivity, weakness, or lack of ambition. In a world obsessed with speed, output, and urgency, the person who waits—who pauses, who watches, who doesn't immediately leap—is misunderstood, sometimes even ridiculed. Yet this misunderstanding is both intellectually lazy and strategically expensive. Because *patience is not a lack of action; it is the discipline to act at the right moment.* It is not the avoidance of movement but the assertion of timing. And in high-stakes environments—whether in markets, leadership, relationships, or personal development—this kind of patience is often what separates enduring success from reactive failure.

The confusion arises from how our culture defines agency. Action is valorised in kinetic terms: productivity, disruption, hustle, execution. Stillness, on the other hand, is treated as suspicious—sometimes moralised as laziness, or pathologised as fear. But this dichotomy misses a third category altogether: *deliberate restraint.* Not inaction, but *strategic non-action.* This is where patience lives.

In behavioural psychology, the marshmallow test became a pop culture shorthand for delayed gratification. But what is often missed in retellings is that children who waited did not simply sit passively. They engaged in subtle forms of self-regulation: distracting themselves, imagining the marshmallow as a cloud, looking away, humming, thinking about rewards later. In other words, they *did something.* Their stillness was active. Their patience had tactics.

Likewise, in financial markets, the most successful investors are not those who trade most frequently, but those who understand when *not* to act. Warren Buffett once said that the stock market is a device for transferring money from the impatient to the patient. That observation is not merely philosophical—it is behavioural. Impatient investors often overreact to volatility, exit prematurely, or chase noise. Patient investors, by contrast, build frameworks that prioritise fundamentals over sentiment. Their advantage isn't apathy; it's timing. They don't miss the opportunity—they *wait until it matures.*

This applies far beyond money. In business, strategic patience often determines who survives. Consider Amazon's first decade: years of net losses, reinvestment, mocked business models, and deliberate delay of profits. That wasn't passivity. It was a form of conviction-driven endurance—an ability to hold course while the market caught up. Jeff Bezos didn't wait because he lacked ideas. He waited because he *knew which ideas needed time to scale.*

Yet even in the personal domain, this misreading persists. Patience in relationships is often mistaken for emotional disengagement. In reality, it may reflect maturity—the understanding that not every conflict requires an immediate resolution, that people grow unevenly, that trust compounds slowly. *The patient partner is not absent; they are present without panic.* Their restraint is emotional literacy in action.

What all of this suggests is that patience is not a dormant virtue. It is an *executive function.* It calls on attention regulation, emotional control, temporal reasoning, and goal alignment. These are not passive skills. They are high-level faculties that demand both training and effort.

And yet, the bias toward action runs deep in Western psychology and modern work culture. Productivity is rewarded more visibly than perception. As a result, there is a collective undervaluing of observation as a legitimate mode of agency. But observation is not neutral. It is information-gathering. It is environmental scanning. It is learning before leaping. And often, it is the difference between effective timing and catastrophic mistiming.

This distinction is perhaps most visible in emergency response environments. In military strategy, one of the first principles is to avoid reacting on first contact. Reconnaissance precedes engagement. In medicine, differential diagnosis requires *not rushing to treat the symptom* but understanding the whole system. In aviation, pilots are trained to pause—literally—to checklists during malfunction before taking action. Across all these domains, the lesson is clear: *when the cost of a misstep is high, patience is a form of intelligence.*

From a neurological standpoint, patience activates the brain's executive regions—particularly the dorsolateral prefrontal cortex, which governs planning and self-control. In contrast, impulsive action often comes from the limbic system, particularly the amygdala's fight-or-flight responses. What this means is that patience is not just a psychological preference—it is a *cognitive upgrade.* Choosing to wait when the system wants to react is a sign that the higher-order brain is engaged. And that engagement is predictive of long-term success across domains.

This should reframe how we think about leadership. The leader who doesn't speak first in a meeting isn't disengaged—they might be listening for signal through noise. The manager who doesn't respond to provocation might not lack authority—they might be processing implications beyond the moment. The founder who doesn't chase every trend might not be risk-averse—they might be risk-literate. *Patience, here, is not delay—it is discernment.*

But it's also important to be clear: patience does not mean perfectionism, paralysis, or avoidance. Those are their own dysfunctions. Patience is only healthy when paired with *readiness.* That is, you are not simply waiting because you're afraid to act—you are waiting because you're preparing to *act precisely.* The difference is not semantic. It's strategic.

Consider the Japanese concept of *ma*—the space between things. In traditional Japanese art, music, and even architecture, what is left unspoken or unplayed is as important as what is expressed. The pause has weight. The silence has form. This is a powerful metaphor for disciplined patience: *the capacity to allow space, without feeling the compulsion to fill it.* In high-noise environments, this becomes a superpower.

We are also learning that patience correlates with improved wellbeing. Studies in emotional regulation show that people who demonstrate higher delay of gratification tend to have better health outcomes, stronger relationships, and more stable career paths. Not because they are dull or unambitious—but because they are less reactive. Reactivity, by contrast, consumes bandwidth. It leads to overcommitment, decision fatigue, emotional whiplash. Over time, the cost of chronic reactivity erodes clarity and compounds stress. *Patience preserves both.* It is psychological compounding.

So how does one practise active patience? It begins with intention. You don't wait *by default*—you wait *on purpose.* You build decision thresholds. You learn your emotional triggers. You develop internal checklists for when to act and when to observe. And crucially, you communicate your patience. Because in fast cultures, uncommunicated waiting often gets misread. Clarifying *why* you're pausing—what you're assessing, what conditions you're observing—transforms patience from a mystery into a method.

Finally, you treat patience as a portfolio, not a personality trait. You don't need to be patient in all things. But you must be patient in the things that matter. Where the stakes are high, the noise is loud, or the feedback loop is long—*this is where patience belongs*. Not as retreat, but as calibration.

To think of patience as passive is to fundamentally misunderstand its architecture. Patience is kinetic restraint. It is the skill of aligning your energy with the right timing—not wasting it on the wrong one. It is a form of power that operates silently, often invisibly, but with enormous impact over time.

In a culture that moves faster than its own consequences, patience is not a relic—it is a revolt. A refusal to confuse haste with progress. A quiet form of control that sees further because it refuses to blink. And above all, it is a clarifying force. Because when you stop needing to act immediately, you can finally see clearly enough to act wisely.

Emotional Range as Resilience

Why Strength Requires Sadness, Fear, and the Capacity to Feel Deeply

Resilience is widely praised but poorly understood. It is often reduced to a caricature—stoic detachment, unflinching positivity, or the mental equivalent of muscle: unbending, ever-forward, unaffected. The imagery is seductive, but inaccurate. True resilience is not the absence of emotional disruption—it is the ability to *contain* it, to *integrate* it, and ultimately to *recover* with greater depth, not just greater speed. The strongest individuals are not those who suppress fear or bypass sadness. They are the ones who allow themselves the full spectrum of human emotion without becoming imprisoned by any single part of it.

This may seem counterintuitive, especially in cultures that reward control and punish vulnerability. But emotional range—the ability to feel widely and deeply without fragmentation—is not a weakness to overcome. It is a *structural asset.* To feel is not to falter; it is to engage fully with life's complexity. And it is in that engagement—not in avoidance—that long-term resilience is built.

To grasp why, we must begin with a misconception: that resilience is synonymous with emotional suppression. This view suggests that strength lies in pushing through without hesitation or reflection, as if tears, uncertainty, or fear somehow diminish our functional power. But neuroscience tells a different story. Emotional suppression is metabolically expensive and neurologically risky. Studies using functional MRI scans have shown that when people habitually suppress negative emotions, activity increases in the amygdala—the brain's threat detection centre—while connectivity with the prefrontal cortex (responsible for decision-making and regulation) weakens. In other words, suppression doesn't neutralise emotion; it deregulates it. *Over time, this creates fragility, not strength.*

Conversely, emotional labelling and expression—naming what is felt, rather than denying or dramatizing it—activate regulatory circuits in the brain, particularly within the ventromedial prefrontal cortex. These circuits help contain emotional intensity, preserve behavioural control, and reduce reactive decision-making. This is the crux: *resilience is not about keeping emotion out; it is about integrating it in a way that retains agency.*

This principle becomes vivid in trauma recovery. Those who heal most sustainably are not those who "tough it out," but those who learn to narrate their experience—who make space for grief, fear, guilt, or anger, not as intrusions to be eliminated, but as signals to be metabolised. The U.S. military's own resilience training protocols, including those developed for special forces, have shifted focus in recent years to include emotional agility, not just mental stamina. Reflection, vulnerability, and adaptive coping are now seen as mission-critical.

We also see this in the psychological literature on post-traumatic growth. The paradox is that many people report increased life satisfaction, purpose, and inner strength *after* significant emotional disruption—not in spite of it. This is not romanticising pain; it is recognising that the ability to move *through* pain with awareness creates a kind of emotional elasticity. That elasticity—*the capacity to stretch without breaking*—is the very definition of resilience.

There is also a false binary between emotions commonly labelled as "negative" (fear, sadness, anxiety) and the idea of progress. This binary implies that any deviation from calm optimism is a threat to forward motion. But that ignores the signal value of emotions. Fear can mark boundaries that matter. Sadness can signal loss and call for recalibration. Even despair, when held without collapse, can be clarifying—it strips away delusion and forces confrontation with core truths. *To cut oneself off from these signals in the name of resilience is to lose the very intelligence that resilience requires.*

Philosophical traditions have long recognised this. The Stoics, often misinterpreted as emotional minimalists, were in fact emotional realists. Marcus Aurelius did not advocate detachment from feeling, but alignment with reality, including the internal reality of grief, anger, and uncertainty. The goal was not to eliminate emotion, but to *train one's response to it*. In this sense, the Stoics weren't cold—they were precise. And emotional precision is a defining feature of true resilience.

In business, leaders who lack emotional range often misread team dynamics, mishandle crises, or make short-sighted decisions in pursuit of appearing unaffected. The appearance of stoicism can mask inner volatility, and that dissonance leads to poor trust and higher stress. On the other hand, emotionally intelligent leaders—those who can acknowledge uncertainty, express regret, or even show fear without surrendering authority—build trust and clarity. Their range allows them to adapt, not just persist.

This insight is particularly urgent in high-pressure sectors like healthcare, finance, and entrepreneurship. Professionals in these fields are often socialised to equate resilience with stoic impermeability. But this leads to burnout, moral injury, and ultimately poor judgment. As healthcare researchers have noted, "resilience without self-compassion is unsustainable." And self-compassion begins with the acceptance of emotional experience—not its denial.

Let us also consider the developmental perspective. Children who are taught to regulate emotion—not by ignoring it, but by naming and exploring it—develop higher executive function and stronger coping skills. They are less likely to be overwhelmed by stress as adults. This capacity is not innate; it is cultivated. And it is cultivated not by teaching them to *avoid* difficult emotion, but by teaching them how to *relate to it*.

The psychologist Susan David coined the term "emotional agility" to describe this phenomenon. It refers to the ability to move through emotional states with openness and flexibility, rather than being rigidly attached to or avoidant of them. Emotional agility requires acknowledging discomfort without judgement—and choosing values-aligned action anyway. This is not weakness. It is *mental dexterity under pressure.*

To define resilience, then, as a form of armour is to misidentify the nature of human strength. Resilience is less about defence and more about integration. A system that bends under pressure and reforms itself—one that accepts variation, disturbance, and repair—is more robust than one that resists all change. Biological systems, psychological systems, economic systems: the same principle holds. *Resilience is not rigidity; it is adaptability through complexity.*

This framing has important implications for how we train, reward, and assess resilience—in schools, in workplaces, in leadership programmes. Rather than asking whether someone remains cheerful under pressure or pushes through difficulty without complaint, we might ask different questions. Can this person *hold fear without panic*? Can they *acknowledge sadness without collapse*? Can they sit with ambiguity long enough to think clearly, rather than reactively?

If they can, they are resilient. Not because they are emotionally invulnerable—but because they are emotionally literate. Their range is not a liability—it is a toolset.

The broader truth is this: human beings are not designed for uninterrupted certainty. We are adaptive creatures. Our survival has always depended not on denying vulnerability, but on leveraging it as signal, feedback, and source of connection. Resilience, when correctly understood, is the maturation of this capacity. It is the quiet strength of those who feel deeply and remain standing—not despite what they feel, but because of what they've learned to feel fully and manage wisely.

To teach this—to embody this—is to evolve our definition of strength itself. Not as a mask, but as a container. One large enough to hold sadness, fear, uncertainty, and still move forward with clarity. That is resilience. That is range. And that is the emotional architecture of true inner wealth.

Chapter 4
The Patience Premium: How the World Rewards the Calm

There's a subtle lever—quiet, nearly imperceptible—that underpins most enduring success, yet it is so frequently ignored. Patience. Not the passive kind that merely loiters while time trudges on, but a more cultivated version: active, deliberate, and sharply attuned to context. The sort of patience that knows precisely what it's holding out for. In a world addicted to immediacy and caught in the gears of reaction, this form of patience is not only unusual—it's often misunderstood. Mistaken for hesitance or a lack of ambition, real patience doesn't drag its feet. It selects its moment. In boardrooms, creative studios, trading floors alike, the pattern is consistent: those who wait well, who wield restraint like a scalpel, quietly outperform.

Speed, of course, has long been conflated with intelligence—especially in business, finance, even romance. Sharpness is too often measured in quick reflexes. But take a step back and examine the arc of returns—monetary, creative, emotional—over time, and another shape appears. Those who consistently outperform are not reacting the fastest. They're the ones filtering signal from noise, discerning when not to act, and conserving their cognitive and emotional reserves with surgical precision. The real edge lies in their selectivity.

This isn't a moral argument, mind you. It's pragmatic. The ability to delay gratification, to resist reflex, to zoom out—these are traits that quite literally pay. Behavioural finance lays bare the evidence. Impulsive investors—those who chase trends, buy high and sell low, respond to headlines rather than fundamentals—habitually underperform. By a lot. Vanguard's internal studies routinely show that the average investor captures significantly lower returns than the fund itself, simply because of poor timing. It's not information that costs them. It's emotion.

And these patterns aren't confined to markets. They bleed into our careers, our relationships, our creative lives. Reactivity has a price—it just doesn't appear on a balance sheet. It shows up as squandered opportunity, fragmented focus, delayed clarity. There's a kind of psychological entropy at play—a hidden cost that gnaws away at our ability to think clearly and act wisely. Call it inner inflation. Like an undetected leak in a pipe, it drains your reserves, slowly and persistently.

By contrast, patience accrues compound returns—not just financially, but neurologically and emotionally. The patience premium is not an abstraction. It's tangible. It shows up in cooler heads, cleaner decisions, longer arcs of success. In environments like aviation, emergency medicine, and military strategy, patience isn't poetic—it's operational. Hesitating long enough to choose the *right* move rather than the fastest one is a matter of life or death. And intriguingly, the neurological circuits responsible for that kind of regulation? They're trainable. Interoception, impulse control, emotional self-regulation—these aren't traits you're either born with or not. They're capacities you can develop. Doing so, quite literally, becomes a form of capital.

And yet—here's the strange thing—patience has become oddly countercultural. We inhabit a world structured around immediacy. Ping. Swipe. Tap. Track. Same-day shipping. Instant updates. Every tool in the modern arsenal is designed to compress the distance between desire and fulfilment. As a result, we've developed an allergy to waiting. Stillness registers as stagnation. Silence feels like absence. If it's not happening now, it must not be happening at all. In such a context, choosing to invest in things that take years—relationships, businesses, inner growth—isn't just old-fashioned. It's almost rebellious.

This has systemic implications. Systems are healthier—markets, companies, communities—when they contain actors oriented toward the long view. Short-termists extract. Long-termists cultivate. And that orientation toward time has quietly become one of the most potent forms of strategic advantage. Precisely because it's become so rare.

The examples abound. Buffett and Munger aren't just revered for their intellects—they're praised for their behavioural discipline. Their genius lies not in volume, but in frequency: a small number of highly considered decisions made over decades. James Cameron disappears for years, only to return with something that reshapes the cinematic landscape. Patagonia's Yvon Chouinard famously ignored Wall Street's fixation on quarterly results, investing instead in values and ecosystems—only to produce financial returns that beat the benchmarks. These aren't paeans to slowness for slowness's sake. They are case studies in strategic delay.

Of course, delay can be a mask—sometimes for fear, sometimes for laziness. That isn't patience. That's avoidance. The difference lies in awareness. Real patience isn't vague or passive. It's keenly alert. It watches closely. It prepares. It sharpens the blade before the swing. And when the time to move arrives, it does so not tentatively, but with clarity born of waiting.

The ramifications ripple far and wide. In organisations, those who can absorb turbulence without flailing become stewards of continuity and judgement. In personal finance, those who resist the creeping tide of lifestyle inflation often find themselves freer, earlier. In emotional life, those who learn to sit with discomfort without fleeing toward distraction or numbness typically gain the deepest insights. They also, not incidentally, tend to suffer less over time—not because they avoid pain, but because they metabolise it differently.

Still, the cultural drumbeat continues: hustle, optimise, disrupt, scale. The algorithm rewards not depth but velocity. Those who "perform" certainty and output dominate feeds, win clicks, earn applause. But underneath, many are fraying. Effort isn't what's lacking—equilibrium is. And equilibrium doesn't arise from doing more. It comes from knowing when *not* to do. To be unhurried in an environment built on urgency isn't failure—it's a form of sovereignty.

This chapter is, in some ways, a provocation. A reconsideration of tempo as a metric. It will delve into the economic costs of reactivity, the neural architecture of restraint, the philosophical frameworks that help re-enchant waiting—not as resignation, but as design. It offers a posture shift: from relentless pursuit to deliberate positioning. And it asks what kind of success is truly worth chasing—one measured by speed, or by longevity?

Because at the end of the day, the world doesn't always reward the swiftest hand. More often, it honours those who can master their timing. Those who know when to hold, when to move, when to let the noise pass. Those who have trained themselves to remain still not because they're paralysed—but because they've learned something most people haven't.

That in the space between impulse and action lies a kind of power. And the few who can wield it? They tend to win—not loudly, but definitively.

Compounding Calm

There is a form of wealth that cannot be tracked by bank statements or investment dashboards. It accrues invisibly, but powerfully—often at the pace of trust, insight, and self-mastery. It does not spike with short-term wins or vanish in downturns. Instead, it builds, quietly and relentlessly, over time. This wealth is calm. And like compound interest, its rewards multiply exponentially when left undisturbed.

The idea of "compounding calm" challenges modern economic metaphors. We are taught to think of productivity as acceleration, output, hustle. But what if the greatest leverage wasn't in doing more, but in *reacting less*? What if the most valuable outcomes in our lives—decisions made, relationships preserved, health maintained—originated not in clever tactics, but in composure under stress? Emotional stability is not a soft trait. It is an economic asset. And, when practised consistently, its returns are cumulative, self-reinforcing, and scalable.

The evidence is compelling. Begin with the Marshmallow Test—a psychological experiment first conducted by Walter Mischel in the 1970s, which tracked children who delayed eating a marshmallow in exchange for a promised second one later. Follow-up studies revealed that those who managed to wait tended to have higher academic scores, better social skills, and greater overall life satisfaction. Critics have since pointed out socioeconomic and environmental limitations in replicating these findings. But the deeper insight remains: the ability to *wait well* correlates strongly with long-term outcomes. Not because waiting is magical—but because it demonstrates impulse control, perspective, and tolerance for discomfort. These traits, over time, underpin everything from financial prudence to conflict resolution.

In financial markets, the math of compounding is well understood. What is less appreciated is that calmness—defined here as the capacity for emotional regulation during volatility—functions in much the same way. Investors who panic at downturns, sell prematurely, or constantly rotate strategies degrade their long-term gains. Data from DALBAR's annual studies of investor behaviour consistently show that individual investors underperform the very funds they invest in—not because of the assets themselves, but because of *their behaviour*. Emotional reactivity erodes performance, while disciplined stillness preserves and amplifies it.

But this principle is not limited to money. Consider interpersonal dynamics. A manager who reacts sharply in tense meetings may get compliance in the moment, but lose trust over time. A parent who cannot regulate stress transmits anxiety to their child, shaping a worldview rooted in instability. A founder who shifts direction at every market signal may exhaust their team and confuse their stakeholders. By contrast, the individual who maintains composure in complexity earns reputation equity. That equity—trust, credibility, reputational leverage—does not come with an app or KPI, but its value is undeniable. And like capital, it compounds.

This compounding occurs because calm is not just a momentary state—it is a developmental skill. Neuroscience supports this. The prefrontal cortex, responsible for executive function and self-regulation, can be strengthened through mindfulness, cognitive behavioural techniques, and reflection-based practices. The more you practise staying calm under pressure, the more your brain learns to interpret ambiguity not as threat, but as data. Over time, this rewiring shifts your entire orientation to challenge. You no longer burn cognitive resources fighting every fire; you conserve energy for strategic action. The net effect: *you make fewer mistakes, miss fewer opportunities, and build more credibility—all without increasing your effort.*

The paradox is that this form of growth is often invisible until it isn't. Calm rarely produces viral metrics. It doesn't look like the loudest voice in the room, the fastest mover in the market, or the first response in the inbox. But in environments of chronic uncertainty—and we are undeniably in one—the most resilient players are those who don't exhaust themselves trying to control what can't be controlled. They direct their energy inward, toward stabilising their own lens of interpretation. They compound not by chasing, but by *protecting their signal-to-noise ratio.*

Take the example of Naval Ravikant, the entrepreneur and investor who has become an emblem of this mindset. In interviews and essays, Ravikant speaks not just about capital accumulation, but about *equanimity* as leverage. His approach is deceptively simple: reduce inputs, increase clarity, act with intent. He views calm as a form of competitive advantage—especially in domains where most players are caught in reactive loops. What makes his insights powerful isn't novelty—it's the refusal to be swept up by the performative urgency that dominates so much of modern decision-making.

In psychology, this approach echoes Viktor Frankl's work in *Man's Search for Meaning*, where he identifies the space between stimulus and response as the most powerful locus of freedom. This is where calm lives—not in the absence of emotion, but in the mastery of choice. The ability to *respond instead of react* is what distinguishes the impulsive from the wise, the amateur from the mature. And it is this discipline of pause, more than any other, that accumulates quietly into extraordinary resilience.

Importantly, compounding calm is not the same as suppression. Emotional numbness does not lead to wisdom. In fact, the effort to avoid emotion altogether creates a form of inner volatility that often erupts under pressure. Calm is not the absence of feeling—it is the capacity to feel fully *without being hijacked.* To stay with discomfort, to witness fear or anger without collapsing into it, is not just psychological fitness; it's practical leadership. In boardrooms, classrooms, negotiation tables, and family dinners alike, the ability to hold composure without suppressing truth changes outcomes. People trust those who can feel without flinching.

It also enables better timing. In fast-moving environments, those who stay grounded are better positioned to recognise inflection points. They don't burn themselves out on false positives. They're not constantly chasing the next surge of excitement or validation.

They're *present.* And presence—true, non-anxious presence—is often the decisive factor in high-stakes decisions. It allows you to *see* what others miss because they're looking through fog.

This brings us to a final, crucial observation: calmness is not just a personal asset—it is a collective one. Teams, companies, and societies that reward knee-jerk behaviour breed fragility. Those that honour thoughtful restraint cultivate durability. In a world over-leveraged on urgency, the ability to model calm becomes a kind of cultural corrective. It reorients attention from instant outputs to meaningful inputs. From short-term optics to long-term integrity.

The calm individual doesn't just suffer less; they *compound more.* Their relationships deepen, their ideas mature, their timing improves, and their outcomes—financial, social, existential—gather force over time. Calm scales. Not loudly. Not immediately. But consistently.

And in the end, it is consistency—not charisma—that compounds into something unshakeable.

The Market Pays the Patient

There is a quiet pattern running beneath the noise of high-frequency trading floors, quarterly performance reviews, and entrepreneurial blitz-scaling. It's not a secret. It's observable, documented, and well understood by those who choose to look beneath the surface: *the market rewards patience—not speed.* Whether in finance, business, creativity, or reputation-building, those who adopt a long horizon—who make fewer, more strategic moves and resist the dopamine lure of instant validation—tend to outperform. Not by inches, but by orders of magnitude.

The idea seems almost heretical in a culture that idolises urgency. Founders are praised for rapid pivots, investors for timing exits, creators for chasing the next trend. And yet, when the data is clear and the dust settles, the disproportionate returns almost always flow to those who *waited well.*

Let us begin with what may be the most iconic example in modern investing: Warren Buffett. The so-called "Oracle of Omaha" has long been held up as the paragon of value investing. But it's not simply his talent for picking stocks that made him one of the wealthiest individuals in history—it's *his relationship with time*. The bulk of Buffett's net worth was accumulated *after* his 60th birthday. Why? Because compounding is nonlinear, and Buffett allowed his capital, and his discipline, to ride the full curve. In his own words, "Time is the friend of the wonderful business, the enemy of the mediocre." The subtext is equally vital: *Time is the friend of the emotionally stable investor.*

Buffett's business partner, Charlie Munger, was even more direct: "The big money is not in the buying or selling, but in the waiting." That one word—*waiting*—encapsulates the discipline most market participants lack. When volatility hits, they exit. When the news cycle shifts, they chase. When fear rises, they sell. And in doing so, they abandon not just their positions, but their potential.

This principle holds true far beyond financial markets. Consider the trajectory of creators and intellectuals who have opted for *deep work over fast output.* J.K. Rowling wrote the first Harry Potter novel over the span of several years, in relative obscurity and without the leverage of social media. The global franchise that followed—books, films, merchandise—was not the result of chasing virality, but of building patiently, iterating thoughtfully, and holding to a clear creative standard.

Similarly, the Japanese concept of *ikigai*—roughly translated as "a reason for being"—is not built around speed, but alignment and longevity. In Okinawa, where people live longer and often report higher life satisfaction, the practices associated with patience—gardening, craftsmanship, community-based decisions—are not considered indulgent, but essential. They reflect a culture that understands the difference between activity and progress.

In entrepreneurship, the pattern remains. Jeff Bezos built Amazon with a 10-year horizon, explicitly prioritising long-term customer trust over short-term profit. In his shareholder letters, he repeatedly returned to the idea that the company's success would be determined not by quarterly results, but by its ability to think in decades. "We are willing to be misunderstood for long periods of time," he once wrote. That willingness—so rare in publicly traded environments—is a psychological moat. It filters out those who cannot tolerate ambiguity or deferred reward.

Critically, this is not passivity masquerading as wisdom. The long-term thinkers we admire—Buffett, Bezos, Rowling, and many others—are not static. They *act.* But they do so *strategically and sparingly.* The patient investor studies deeply, buys selectively, and holds through storms. The patient founder tests hypotheses but doesn't pivot at every breeze. The patient artist discards 99 drafts to arrive at one timeless piece. In each case, what looks like slowness is actually *precision.*

There is also a deeper psychological principle at work: *The ability to delay gratification is often a proxy for internal coherence.* People who operate on longer timeframes have usually done the inner work required to tolerate uncertainty, manage anxiety, and decouple self-worth from external validation. They are less reactive because they are more integrated. And from that integration flows consistency—a trait the world eventually rewards.

Behavioural finance confirms this repeatedly. Studies in behavioural economics—most notably by Daniel Kahneman and Amos Tversky—reveal that humans are chronically short-term in their thinking. We overvalue immediate outcomes, underweight long-term consequences, and panic at perceived losses. These biases—loss aversion, recency bias, and others—lead to self-defeating behaviours, especially under pressure. Patience, then, is not simply an asset; it is a *counter-bias.* A cognitive skill that mitigates against the distortions of fear and greed.

And yet, despite its advantages, patience is perennially undervalued—precisely because it lacks spectacle. It does not announce itself. It doesn't trend on social media. It isn't energising in the short term. But its returns, financial and otherwise, accumulate beneath the surface until they are impossible to ignore. A reputation earned quietly over ten years is more enduring than one manufactured in ten months. A customer base built slowly through trust is more resilient than one acquired through hacks. An investment thesis executed with discipline often survives cycles that obliterate trend-chasers.

One might ask: what makes patience so difficult? Beyond the neurological pull of dopamine and the cultural glorification of immediacy, there is a subtler challenge: *patience requires an internal locus of control.* You must believe that your efforts, compounded over time, will matter—*even if no one sees them today.* That belief is existential. It speaks to your philosophy of action, your tolerance for solitude, your ability to steward attention without applause.

The market—whether we define it as financial, reputational, or creative—does not simply reward patience randomly. It *selects for durability.* And durability, in turn, is the consequence of choosing depth over speed, signal over noise, direction over momentum.

Of course, patience without clarity is just inertia. Strategic patience is active. It involves evaluation, filtering, and alignment. It asks: Is this worth holding through the storm? Is this action, idea, or habit consistent with my long-term vision? It is not about being passive, but about *being deliberate.*

This is why the best investors don't just have diversified portfolios—they have *disciplined minds.* The best creators don't just have talent—they have *editorial restraint.* The best entrepreneurs don't just chase product-market fit—they build with *conviction beyond hype cycles.* All of them share one thing: a willingness to *miss out temporarily in order to compound meaningfully.*

Patience, when paired with strategy, becomes exponential. It allows time to do the heavy lifting. It removes you from the tyranny of now. And it opens the door to asymmetric gains—not because you moved quickly, but because you moved *correctly and consistently.*

The market pays the patient. Not always in the way they expect. But always in a way that endures

Inner Inflation: The Cost of Emotional Reactivity

It is easy to track the price of petrol or the rising cost of groceries. We have names for those phenomena: inflation, recession, volatility. But what do we call the less visible, internal cost we incur when our emotional state erodes our judgement? What term describes the hidden premium we pay for reactivity—for stress-fuelled decisions, for panicked exits, for sleepless nights that leave our thinking dull and defensive? This chapter introduces a rarely discussed but deeply consequential form of inflation: *inner inflation.* It is the psychic tax we accumulate when we live at the mercy of our emotional impulses rather than in partnership with them.

The modern world is exquisitely engineered to provoke and exploit reactivity. News is delivered with urgency, interfaces are designed to grab attention, and algorithms reward outrage. In this landscape, maintaining calm is not merely a matter of personal well-being—it is an economic strategy. Because when inner costs rise, outer outcomes degrade. You don't just feel worse—you do worse. The job you quit too soon, the investment you sold in fear, the relationship you severed in haste: each carries a hidden toll that compounds over time. Emotional reactivity doesn't just cloud our view; it depreciates our assets—financial, relational, and cognitive alike.

Stress, for example, is not merely a feeling. It's a neurochemical event with downstream consequences. Chronic stress elevates cortisol, which in turn impairs memory, reduces risk tolerance, and distorts temporal perception. You become more short-termist, less imaginative, and more drawn to immediate resolution—even at great cost. When researchers at Harvard and Princeton studied the effects of financial stress on cognitive function, they found that subjects under economic pressure lost the equivalent of 13 IQ points—roughly the same impact as going a full night without sleep. The mind under pressure narrows. It trades nuance for certainty. It stops investing in possibility and starts hoarding control.

This is the architecture of emotional inflation: your mental resources—attention, clarity, patience—become scarcer under pressure, and the cost of effective decision-making rises. It's not just that you're more irritable or tired; it's that your cognitive capital is depleting, and the decisions you make under that depletion come with compounding consequences.

Take investing. The market punishes those who panic. Countless studies across behavioural finance have shown that individual investors underperform the very funds they invest in, simply because they jump in and out at the wrong times—buying high, selling low, and acting from fear rather than principle. DALBAR's annual reports consistently show this gap. One particularly damning statistic: over a 20-year period, the average investor earned just over 4% annually—less than inflation—while the S&P 500 delivered over 9%. The difference? Behaviour, not information. Reactivity, not access. Inner volatility, not market volatility.

The same pattern holds in professional settings. Emotional reactivity often masquerades as decisiveness. But fast decisions made under emotional duress often cost more in the long run. A leader who cannot tolerate uncertainty may prematurely abandon a promising strategy because early indicators fluctuate. A founder obsessed with instant validation might pivot away from a long-term vision in favour of metrics that rise quickly but hollow the brand over time. These are not tactical errors—they are psychological expenses dressed as operational decisions.

And yet, the costs are rarely accounted for. Unlike credit card debt or business losses, there's no monthly statement tallying the price of panic, the bill for burnout, or the depreciation of your focus. But the erosion is real. Left unexamined, emotional reactivity becomes an invisible drain on your decision-making economy—a silent tax on every conversation, investment, and commitment.

It's not that emotions are the enemy. Far from it. Emotions are signals—data points, not directives. But when we fail to distinguish between feeling something and obeying that feeling, we surrender autonomy. This is the true risk of inner inflation: we don't just pay more—we become less free.

The antidote is not detachment or stoicism for its own sake. It's *disciplined emotional literacy*: the capacity to observe one's own emotional weather without being blown off course by it. This requires training. Just as a trader learns to read market signals without panic, or a surgeon learns to operate under pressure without haste, we can learn to process emotional activation without translating it into impulsive action. This is emotional resilience at its most strategic: not a denial of feeling, but a refusal to mortgage the future in service of immediate relief.

Patience, then, is not passivity. It is the capacity to bear momentary discomfort in service of a longer-term aim. It is the wisdom to recognise when doing nothing is more powerful than doing something. And it is the courage to let clarity arrive on its own schedule, rather than forcing certainty before it's due.

This form of patience pays. It reduces the frequency and severity of bad decisions. It preserves optionality. And over time, it compounds—just like capital. Those who master emotional regulation accrue not just better choices but a quieter mind, more aligned relationships, and a more durable sense of self. They gain what markets reward and what modern life too often discourages: the ability to hold steady when the world tilts.

There's a paradox at the core of emotional reactivity that often goes unnoticed: the more we act to escape emotional discomfort, the more we entrench the very conditions we hoped to avoid. A reactive decision may offer immediate psychological relief—saying yes to a deal to avoid conflict, quitting a position to escape anxiety, sending a sharp email to discharge tension—but that temporary solace is usually bought at the cost of long-term clarity, influence, or momentum. What feels like control in the moment often becomes constraint in hindsight.

In behavioural economics, this is often referred to as *present bias*: the tendency to overvalue immediate rewards at the expense of future outcomes. Yet what's rarely appreciated is how much this bias is amplified by emotional volatility. Anxiety collapses our sense of the future. Sadness makes future rewards feel unreachable. Anger demands immediate restitution. Under such conditions, our time horizons shorten. Patience becomes inaccessible not because we lack time, but because we lose the emotional scaffolding that allows us to value deferred outcomes. The future, in short, ceases to feel real enough to plan for.

This isn't a metaphorical problem. It's physiological. Research in affective neuroscience has shown that strong emotional states alter the function of the prefrontal cortex—the brain region responsible for future planning, impulse control, and complex decision-making.

When we are flooded by emotion, activity shifts toward the amygdala, which prioritises survival-based responses: fight, flight, or freeze. In such states, nuance is a luxury. Trade-offs disappear. What remains is a stark binary: escape or endure. This is the crucible in which poor decisions are forged—not from ignorance, but from a narrowing of cognitive bandwidth in the grip of unregulated feeling.

The implications of this dynamic ripple through nearly every high-stakes domain. Consider entrepreneurship. Founders often operate under constant stress—burn rates, shifting markets, investor demands. Those who thrive tend to have a discipline around emotional regulation that is as robust as their strategic thinking. Take Jeff Bezos, for example. Whatever one thinks of his broader ethics, his decision-making style is notably calm and delayed. He's spoken at length about making "high-quality, high-impact" decisions slowly, and being extremely cautious about decisions that are irreversible. This is not a personality trait—it's a cultivated orientation toward time. It is a refusal to be emotionally rushed into suboptimal actions under the illusion of urgency.

In contrast, consider the often-discussed "founder's panic" that leads to premature pivots or ill-conceived product launches. These are not business errors, in the strictest sense. They are emotional failures—instances where the discomfort of uncertainty becomes intolerable, and a decision is made not because it's wise, but because it ends the anxiety. The decision becomes an anaesthetic. But as with all numbing agents, the relief is short-lived, and the underlying complexity remains unresolved.

This same phenomenon plays out in personal finance. One of the least discussed realities about financial stress is that it's not always caused by objective scarcity. Often, it's the result of *perceived* instability amplified by emotional reactivity. A market correction feels like a personal crisis. A minor income disruption triggers catastrophic thinking. People liquidate retirement accounts to "feel safe" or take on high-interest debt to "feel stable"—even when the numbers don't justify the panic. Over time, the cumulative cost of these emotionally charged micro-decisions adds up to what could be termed a "reactivity penalty"—a stealth tax on long-term wealth.

The health domain offers another illustration. Emotional reactivity is closely correlated with poor health behaviours: stress eating, substance misuse, skipping workouts, inconsistent sleep routines. Each of these may appear trivial in isolation, but over time, they lead to the very conditions—obesity, fatigue, chronic illness—that compound emotional volatility in a vicious feedback loop. The internal cost rises invisibly until it manifests externally in doctor's visits, missed workdays, and diminished quality of life. The inflation is not just in healthcare bills, but in daily cognitive wear: a fog that thickens, choices that shrink, a self that no longer feels sovereign.

There is, however, a different way to account for our internal economy. Just as savvy investors track the hidden costs of fees, taxes, and opportunity costs, emotionally intelligent individuals begin to audit their reactions. They become attentive to the real cost of saying yes too fast, of speaking without pausing, of planning under pressure. They begin to invest in practices that *buffer* against volatility—mindfulness, journaling, therapy, deep conversation, exercise—not because those are trendy habits, but because they slow the feedback loop between stimulus and response. They give the system breathing room. They reintroduce *margin.*

Margin, in this context, is not idle time. It's emotional liquidity. It's the difference between reacting and responding, between living on the brink and making decisions from centred ground. Without that margin, even minor disruptions feel existential. With it, even major setbacks can be met with poise.

To view your inner world as a kind of economic engine is not to reduce emotion to finance—it is to elevate emotional stewardship to the level of strategic mastery. Just as we prize compound interest for its quiet power, we can begin to value calmness not merely as a virtue, but as an asset. The calm mind spots better opportunities. It recognises false urgency. It negotiates more effectively. It listens longer. It waits for better prices—on everything from homes to partnerships to ideas. This is not abstract wisdom. It is concrete advantage.

But if calmness is such a powerful force multiplier, why is it so rare?

The answer lies, in part, in cultural misvaluation. Our dominant economic models reward speed, scale, and volume. Platforms are optimised for immediate reactions—likes, retweets, trades, purchases—not for thoughtful pauses. In leadership, reactivity is sometimes mistaken for responsiveness. In markets, constant motion is often equated with competence. And in personal life, the ability to "do something" quickly is confused with decisiveness. In this climate, stillness can look like neglect. Reflection is misread as uncertainty. Restraint is dismissed as hesitation.

Yet the most formidable decision-makers—whether in diplomacy, capital allocation, or creative direction—tend to operate on what could be called a *delayed emotional loop*. They don't trust the first impulse. They allow themselves time to metabolise internal volatility before externalising it as action. It's not that they don't feel. It's that they've learned how to *contain the signal* until it becomes intelligible. And they know something most people don't: reacting quickly may feel powerful, but responding *wisely* is what moves the needle.

In psychological terms, this capacity is supported by the development of what researchers call "meta-cognition"—the ability to observe one's thoughts and feelings without being immediately consumed by them. It's the difference between *being angry* and *noticing that one is angry*. That space between stimulus and response, to borrow from Viktor Frankl's famous insight, is where all human freedom resides. And yet, in the economics of attention and productivity, that space is systematically eroded. Our calendars are saturated. Our feeds are endless. Our cortisol levels spike by mid-morning. In such a context, sustained calm becomes not just difficult—but subversive.

It's also essential for long-term excellence. The idea that emotional reactivity erodes performance isn't merely a philosophical proposition—it's an empirically validated fact across domains. In elite athletics, for example, clutch performance is strongly correlated with emotional regulation. The athlete who can breathe under pressure outperforms the one who panics, even if the latter is technically stronger. In high-stakes negotiations, those who can remain composed under provocation routinely secure better terms. In medicine, surgeons who stay internally regulated during high-risk procedures are more likely to maintain accuracy. Across all these fields, *inner calm converts directly into outer impact.*

This is where the metaphor of "inner inflation" gains real explanatory power. Emotional volatility doesn't just make life harder. It makes everything *more expensive*—in energy, opportunity, trust, clarity. It introduces drag into our relationships, friction into our planning, distortion into our vision. And like economic inflation, the damage often compounds quietly. By the time it's visible, it's already embedded. A fraught decision made under pressure may take months to unravel. A reactive outburst in a professional setting might take years to repair. A pattern of emotional volatility in personal life may shape reputations that prove difficult to reverse.

What, then, does emotional anti-inflation look like?

It begins with pattern recognition. Noticing which emotions tend to hijack your decision-making—whether it's urgency driven by anxiety, overcommitment fuelled by guilt, or avoidance linked to fear. Then, it requires insertion of a reflective gap: journaling before replying, walking before committing, breathing before responding. These aren't acts of avoidance; they are acts of optimisation. You're not pausing because you don't know what to do—you're pausing because you care about doing it *well.*

Second, it demands that we normalise calm—not as a luxury, but as a default. This may sound idealistic, but it is possible. Leaders can begin to model it. Cultures can begin to incentivise it. Individuals can train for it. Mindfulness-based cognitive therapy (MBCT), for instance, has been shown to decrease emotional reactivity and improve long-term emotional resilience. Cognitive behavioural tools can help reframe intrusive thoughts before they calcify into impulsive decisions. And regular physical practices—like yoga, weightlifting, or even deliberate cold exposure—have measurable effects on emotional regulation capacity.

Lastly, it requires reframing the narrative around calmness. This is not about becoming passive or emotionally indifferent. On the contrary, the calm individual is often more attuned—precisely because they are not overwhelmed. They can detect subtle shifts in team dynamics, sense unsaid tensions in partnerships, recognise emerging patterns in markets. Emotional calm is *not the absence of feeling*. It is the presence of clarity *in spite of feeling*. It's not stoicism in the detached sense, but the ability to hold complexity without capitulating to it.

The true cost of emotional reactivity, then, is not just that it disrupts our plans. It distorts our *perception of time, value, and consequence*. It blinds us to nuance. It accelerates us toward suboptimal decisions under the illusion of necessity. And unless we learn to regulate that internal volatility, the external world will continue to feel like a perpetual emergency.

Calmness is not an accessory to intelligence—it is its amplifier. And in a society that monetises your attention, inflames your urgency, and profits from your stress, learning to regulate your inner economy is no longer just a personal benefit. It is an act of sovereignty.

That sovereignty is not loud. It doesn't posture. It doesn't demand to be seen. But over time, it pays. Quietly, powerfully, and exponentially.

Delayed Gratification as a Radical Act

To delay gratification in today's world is to swim against a riptide engineered to keep you impulsive. The culture we inhabit doesn't merely encourage immediacy—it is structurally dependent on it. Algorithms favour short engagement loops. Financial markets reward quarterly performance. Social media timelines are designed to reset every hour. We are surrounded by technologies and systems that monetise our impatience and pathologise our stillness. In this context, the act of waiting—not out of passivity, but out of intentional discipline—becomes a quiet form of rebellion.

Patience, when stripped of its caricatured associations with dullness or indecision, is not resignation. It is resistance. It is the refusal to let your behaviour be dictated by someone else's urgency. It is the self-governed act of recognising that speed does not always correlate with wisdom, and that gratification earned later often holds greater compounding value—psychologically, economically, and relationally—than that seized now.

But to practise patience in a culture of hyper-speed is psychologically taxing. It requires active friction with your own neurobiology. The default setting of the human brain is to value immediate rewards over distant ones. This is not a moral failing—it is a remnant of our evolutionary past. Dopamine, the neurochemical associated with desire and motivation, spikes not when we receive a reward, but when we anticipate it. The shorter the loop between stimulus and satisfaction, the more reliably that reward system is reinforced. This makes instant gratification not just pleasurable, but *addictive.* Each scroll, swipe, or notification serves as a micro-hit of affirmation. Waiting, by contrast, feels like deprivation.

This is where delayed gratification earns its radical edge. It is not just an exercise in willpower—it is a neurological and philosophical counter-programming. It requires you to extend your time horizon, override your limbic impulses, and expand your capacity to hold tension without resolution. To wait—consciously, deliberately—is to cultivate a rarer form of sovereignty: *agency over your attention, over your impulses, and over your timeline.*

In behavioural science, this capacity is known as "temporal discounting"—the tendency to devalue rewards that are further in the future. Numerous experiments, from the classic Stanford marshmallow test to more nuanced longitudinal studies, show that people who can delay gratification tend to experience more favourable life outcomes: better academic performance, more stable relationships, improved health, and stronger financial wellbeing. But what is less often explored is the psychological cost of this deferral in a world that does not reward it quickly. The person who delays gratification must contend not only with internal cravings but also with a world that constantly suggests: "Why wait when you can have it now?"

To delay gratification today is to endure social dissonance. You say no to a weekend of consumption to invest in your long-term goals, while others spend and post. You decline the dopamine rush of reactive outrage to preserve mental clarity. You build slowly and deliberately in a marketplace that celebrates viral speed. The world calls it hesitance. But underneath that restraint is *strategic defiance*—a refusal to allow one's trajectory to be dictated by short-term optics.

Consider the investor who holds a position for decades, enduring years of unremarkable returns for an exponential payoff. Consider the artist who releases their first public work only after thousands of private iterations. Consider the entrepreneur who builds infrastructure instead of hype, knowing that brand equity outlasts attention metrics. These are not passive individuals—they are *active delayers*. They understand that enduring value is rarely built on immediacy. And they accept the psychological solitude that often accompanies that long arc.

In this way, delayed gratification is not about abstinence—it is about *alignment*. It is the deliberate choice to match your actions to your highest values rather than your lowest cravings. It requires a long-term lens, not just on goals, but on identity. Who are you becoming by the things you repeatedly choose to wait for? What is being strengthened—not just achieved—in the space between desire and its fulfilment?

This reframing elevates delayed gratification from a discipline of denial to a philosophy of construction. You are not merely resisting temptation; you are *investing in your future self*. Every postponed impulse is a vote for a more composed, capable, and strategically autonomous version of you. In this way, delayed gratification ceases to be a personal virtue alone—it becomes a collective necessity in a culture drifting ever closer to attention bankruptcy.

Patience, when operationalised as delayed gratification, is not merely a character trait—it is a learned behavioural protocol in direct conflict with the dominant economic incentives of our time. In most consumer environments, immediacy is equated with efficiency, convenience with superiority. But convenience can be a corrosive comfort. It trains us to expect results without investment, returns without resilience. That expectation silently erodes not just discipline, but discernment.

To understand the radical nature of delayed gratification, we must first locate it within the broader architecture of economic decision-making. Consider financial markets: short-term traders move in and out of positions within seconds, their behaviour gamified by algorithmic platforms and hyper-volatile price feeds. In contrast, long-term investors like Warren Buffett or Charlie Munger make only a handful of high-conviction decisions each year, and sometimes none at all. Their wealth, however, is not a function of hyperactivity—it is the cumulative result of *inactivity with insight.* What sets them apart is not intellect, but temporal orientation. They possess the emotional steadiness to let time do its compounding work.

This principle generalises far beyond finance. In the realm of personal development, one of the most powerful growth accelerators is not relentless action, but the refusal to switch goals prematurely. The modern professional is tempted by opportunity overload: pivot to a new career, pursue a new certification, launch a side hustle, change platforms, change cities. While agility can be an asset, chronic pivoting often reflects a deeper discomfort with slow, silent progress. The radical act, in such a case, is to *stay.* To stay in the discomfort of plateau, to stay with a project beyond its honeymoon phase, to stay long enough for delayed returns to materialise.

Psychologically, delayed gratification rewires our sense of time. When we reduce our relationship with time to a race against deadlines or a countdown to rewards, we orient ourselves around scarcity. We become reactive, impatient, and prone to tunnel vision. But when we view time as an ally—an active multiplier of value rather than a mere limiter of capacity—our internal tempo shifts. We begin to favour strategy over speed. We learn to distinguish movement from progress.

Yet this shift is deeply counter-cultural. From 24-hour delivery to rapid-fire content, every signal in modern society reinforces the belief that faster is better. Even educational institutions are often structured to reward output over depth, deadlines over durability. Within such a framework, the individual who defers gratification is not simply unusual—they are structurally disadvantaged in the short term. They earn less attention, receive fewer immediate affirmations, and must endure the silent labour of unseen effort. That, precisely, is what makes their path subversive. It privileges *long-term alignment over short-term applause.*

This subversion becomes especially relevant in the creative and intellectual domains. Writers, researchers, and thinkers often work for months or years with little or no external validation. The reward structures are slow-moving, sometimes non-existent. In this context, delayed gratification is not just a psychological skill—it becomes a moral stance: a willingness to serve truth, craft, or clarity over visibility. The artist who refuses to chase virality, the scholar who labours over precision instead of publishing frequency, the technologist who builds infrastructure instead of hype—each exemplifies patience as a force of principled rebellion.

But if delayed gratification is so powerful, why is it so rare?

Because it hurts. It requires sitting with unmet desire. It demands confidence in outcomes you cannot yet see and control over urges you can instantly satisfy. It offers no immediate dopamine, only the slow-burning validation of internal coherence. That discomfort is precisely what gives it developmental power. Like resistance training for the psyche, the act of waiting—intentionally and with awareness—strengthens emotional bandwidth, meta-cognition, and long-term planning capacity. In short: it builds *emotional resilience.*

Ironically, the very discomfort that deters people from delaying gratification is what makes it valuable. In a culture where ease is the default, effort becomes a signal of distinction. The ability to delay gratification becomes a source of competitive asymmetry—not just in external metrics like income or influence, but in internal metrics like clarity, calm, and conviction. It allows individuals to navigate crises without panic, to build assets that last, and to live lives that are not dictated by every ping, pull, or panic of the surrounding world.

This is not to say that immediacy is always wrong. There are contexts—emergency medicine, security alerts, live trading—where quick action saves lives and protects value. The problem arises not from the existence of urgency, but from its *over-application.* When the operating tempo of life is always accelerated, we confuse speed with intelligence, and activity with effectiveness. Delayed gratification, then, becomes the recalibration—the counterweight that restores equilibrium between the urgent and the important.

To practise it well, one must develop systems. Not all delayed gratification is sustainable by raw willpower. It needs reinforcement through identity (Who am I becoming by waiting?), through structure (How do I reduce exposure to unnecessary temptation?), and through accountability (What does long-term success require of me today?). This is why elite performers—across disciplines—routinely structure their environments to favour discipline. They automate savings. They time-block deep work. They pre-commit to projects with high exit barriers. In doing so, they transform patience from an aspiration into an ecosystem.

And herein lies the most profound shift: *delayed gratification is not deprivation—it is design.* It is the architecture of a life built on purpose rather than impulse. It creates space for values to take precedence over cravings, for wisdom to surpass whims. In a marketplace that incentivises reactivity, such a life is not just radical—it is rare.

To choose patience is to choose power. Not the power of control over others, but the deeper sovereignty of control over self. It is a quiet rebellion that does not announce itself loudly, yet leaves unmistakable traces—in your choices, your relationships, your legacy.

And those who learn to delay well, *compound quietly*

Chapter 5
Breaking Point: How People Snap—And Why You Won't

There comes a moment—often unspoken, yet unmistakably felt—when a person's internal elasticity gives way. It doesn't always arrive with fanfare. Sometimes it's just a sentence in a meeting that unravels you, or an innocuous email that lands with the weight of an avalanche. A minor setback becomes a crushing blow. Not because it is objectively catastrophic, but because it is the final abrasion in a long, silent erosion. This is not ordinary exhaustion. It is something more acute. A threshold. That invisible tipping point where resilience no longer holds, and reflex takes over. Yet—and this is crucial—not everyone unravels. So what makes the difference?

To understand why some withstand pressure and even seem to expand under it, while others collapse, we need to move beyond the crude archetypes of toughness still romanticised in our culture. The caricature of "mental toughness"—that cold, stoic ideal of pushing through pain with clenched teeth—is outdated at best, harmful at worst. It confuses suppression for strength, and denial for mastery. But mounting evidence from neuroscience, behavioural research, and long-term performance data tells a different story. The truth? Emotional resilience is not about being unaffected by pressure. It's about building the internal infrastructure to process it, metabolise it, and—sometimes—transform it.

This chapter begins with a blunt but necessary premise: no system—biological, emotional, intellectual, professional—is infinitely expandable. Even the most capable individuals have limits. Just as overheated financial markets self-correct, so too do human beings. Overreach invites regression. Ambition without cycles of recovery begets burnout. And unprocessed emotional overload tends to show up in sabotage—abrupt decisions, rash withdrawals, emotional tailspins that ruin what reason once built. But here's the subtle truth: collapse is almost never sudden. It's cumulative. It's rarely the final straw that breaks us. It's the weight of all the unnoticed ones before it.

To fully grasp this, we must rehabilitate our understanding of stress. Stress, in itself, is not inherently toxic. It's a signal. A form of intelligence. A flare from the nervous system saying: your resources are stretched, your attention is split, your inputs and outputs are misaligned. But when stress becomes chronic—when it lingers without being metabolised—it begins to corrode. It narrows your field of vision. It reduces optionality. And it shortens the space between stimulus and reaction. That's how people who are otherwise intelligent and composed end up derailing themselves—quitting abruptly, lashing out unnecessarily, or abandoning something meaningful midstream.

So how do we build toward resilience that holds? This chapter proposes three keystone frameworks: the stress buffer, the trigger audit, and the patience plateau.

Let's begin with the stress buffer. Not some vague lifestyle balance trope, but a deliberate accumulation of practices that expand your emotional bandwidth. Think of it as a psychological savings account. Just as financial buffers protect against market swings, stress buffers insulate against emotional volatility. These are built not through grand gestures but through steady, almost invisible disciplines—adequate sleep, deliberate boundaries, routines that restore coherence, rituals of reflection. The result isn't invincibility—it's latency. A lag between provocation and reaction. And that delay? That momentary gap? That's where better decisions live.

Then there's the trigger audit. This is where things get intimate. Under pressure, we don't rise to the occasion—we fall to our level of programming. Which means if you haven't examined your triggers, your patterns, your emotional blind spots, then you're navigating with a faulty compass. Whether it's criticism that stings too sharply, uncertainty that hijacks your judgment, or perceived rejection that activates your worst instincts—these are not minor glitches. They are stress multipliers. This chapter will guide you through a systematic inventory: where your reactivity lives, how it operates, and how to create distance from it. Because what you can name, you can navigate. And what remains unnamed will, eventually, own you.

And then we arrive at what might be the most underestimated terrain of all: the patience plateau. That long, dull middle stretch of any meaningful pursuit. It's not dramatic. It creeps in. You're no longer energised by novelty, nor yet buoyed by results. You're slogging through the dry centre. This is where self-doubt multiplies, motivation wanes, and premature exits masquerade as smart pivots. But make no mistake: this is the proving ground. The patience plateau is not a detour—it's the crucible where sustainable growth is forged. Behavioural data and case studies alike bear this out: those who can remain steady through this uninspiring middle tend to outperform—not occasionally, but repeatedly.

Let's be clear. This chapter will not deal in superficial "mindset hacks" or commodified self-care. What it will offer are systems—tools grounded in psychology, behavioural science, and real-world performance. These are not about pretending pressure doesn't exist. They're about equipping you to meet it on your own terms. To extend your stress threshold not through sheer will, but through structural redesign: of how you think, recover, act, and self-regulate.

At heart, this chapter is an invitation—to construct a version of yourself that doesn't shatter under strain. Not by becoming emotionless, but by becoming fortified. To build a foundation that doesn't rely on external calm, but generates internal clarity even amid external chaos. Because the world is not slowing down. Complexity will not wait for your comfort. But you can become someone who holds steady regardless.

And therein lies the edge. While others react, you calculate. While others spiral, you stabilise. While others retreat, you reassess and re-engage—deliberately, not impulsively. This isn't resilience as theatre. It's resilience as architecture. Designed. Reinforced. Built to last.

Let's begin the build.

The Tipping Point of Tolerance – Why People Quit Just Before Breakthroughs

There is a specific kind of despair that arrives not at the beginning of an effort, but near its apex—when you're closer to progress than you realise, but too exhausted, disoriented, or disheartened to see it clearly. At that point, many quit. Not because they lack the ability to continue, but because their *tolerance*—emotional, psychological, financial—has quietly been depleted. And yet, this quitting often occurs just before meaningful change would have taken root. The tragedy isn't failure; it's premature abandonment.

Breakthroughs are not events. They are culminations. They rarely arrive with fireworks or applause. More often, they occur in silence—an unseen click of compounding effort, a convergence of accumulated skill, a final inch of emotional durability that shifts the entire trajectory. The problem is that this final inch demands the most of us—often after we've already spent everything we thought we had. *The tipping point of tolerance*, then, is less about limits and more about perception: the mistaken belief that nothing is working, when in fact, something is about to.

To understand this dynamic, we must first examine how human tolerance functions—not as a static limit, but as a fluctuating emotional resource influenced by context, feedback, expectation, and identity. Whether in a volatile market, a faltering relationship, or a high-stakes creative endeavour, the decision to quit is almost never made in rational isolation. It is made in the presence of psychological fatigue, amplified by uncertainty and distorted by cognitive bias. It is not willpower alone that fails. *It is the erosion of meaningful belief that continuing will be worth it.*

Take entrepreneurship as a starting point. The "valley of disappointment" is a well-documented psychological phase where results lag far behind effort. This is not due to inefficiency, but due to the nonlinear nature of compounding. As James Clear notes in *Atomic Habits*, the most powerful outcomes of any enduring effort are delayed by default. In early phases, feedback is minimal and external validation is rare. You're building infrastructure that no one can see—developing a skill, establishing trust, refining systems. But the modern mind, conditioned by rapid gratification, reads this lack of visible progress as failure. It assumes flatlines mean futility. *What it cannot see, it doubts.* And doubt, unchecked, becomes disengagement.

This is not limited to professional pursuits. In long-term relationships—romantic or otherwise—the tipping point often manifests not as one large fight, but as a slow attrition of emotional bandwidth. Tolerance is tested when conversations feel circular, when affection feels effortful, when small irritations eclipse shared purpose. But again, it is often just before renewal that people leave. Why? Because the discomfort of confronting emotional stagnation feels harder than the imagined relief of exit. What's missed is the potential that *the very friction they're experiencing is a signal of growth trying to emerge.* Intimacy, like endurance, often deepens only after it fractures—when both parties are forced to rebuild not out of convenience, but conviction.

Neuroscience offers a further lens. The prefrontal cortex—home to planning, reasoning, and delayed gratification—is frequently overruled by the limbic system under chronic stress. This is particularly true in volatile environments: a job with no clear metrics of success, a creative process with no guaranteed payoff, or an emotional relationship with erratic feedback. When clarity diminishes, the brain shifts into short-term self-preservation mode. It looks for relief, not reward. And quitting—at least momentarily—*feels* like relief. It gives the illusion of control. But the cost is hidden: all the unseen progress forfeited, all the sunk resilience discarded, all the momentum quietly erased.

It's not just individuals who struggle with this. Organisations, teams, and even entire cultures are susceptible. Consider the history of some of the world's most influential innovators—Walt Disney, whose first company collapsed; Sara Blakely, who sold fax machines door-to-door for years before launching Spanx; or even Thomas Edison, whose repeated failures weren't just technical—they were emotional. The thread between them isn't genius. It's a capacity to *tolerate* the psychological ambiguity that precedes external success. And this capacity is built, not born. It is *trained* through practice, perspective, and structural support.

So why don't more people push through? Because pushing through, in its popularised form, has been romanticised into a kind of blind persistence. But *persistence without recalibration* becomes self-sabotage. The real skill is not to never quit. It is to know *when* to hold, *why* to hold, and *how* to hold intelligently. Emotional tolerance is not stubbornness. It is the capacity to differentiate between discomfort worth enduring and signals worth heeding.

One key variable is narrative coherence. If people lose the thread of *why* they're doing something, they misinterpret fatigue as futility. Viktor Frankl, in *Man's Search for Meaning*, made this point with piercing clarity: a person who has a *why* can tolerate almost any *how*. But if meaning dissolves, even a relatively mild adversity can become intolerable. This is why recommitting to purpose—especially during prolonged plateaus—is not indulgent reflection. It is strategic maintenance. It restores coherence, which in turn restores tolerance.

There is also the phenomenon of *failure fatigue.* This is different from burnout. It is not caused by overwork, but by under-reward. Repeated small losses or stalled progress degrade confidence and shorten one's ability to wait. Financially, this can manifest in panic-selling just before markets rebound. Emotionally, it can surface as abandoning therapy just as breakthroughs are around the corner. Creatively, it often leads to abandoning a project in the final stretch of refinement—not because the project failed, but because the creator's tolerance for imperfection ran out. What's needed in these moments is not more intensity, but *strategic patience*—the discipline to pause, adjust, and stay.

There is a physiological parallel worth noting: the "pain gate theory" in neurology. It posits that the nervous system modulates how we experience pain based on psychological factors—attention, expectation, and prior experience. Emotional thresholds work similarly. A person's ability to endure stress, ambiguity, or delay is not fixed. It is shaped by *how they frame the experience* and whether they perceive it as meaningful. In this light, *tolerance is not purely endurance—it is interpretation.*

Practically, then, the path forward is not to simply "tough it out." It is to *architect conditions* that increase staying power. That means:

Regularly reconnecting with your original motivations.

Tracking non-obvious forms of progress—skills gained, emotional composure, feedback loops improved.

Setting default rules for quitting (e.g., "I never make exit decisions in a valley") to depersonalise momentary doubt.

Reframing rest not as weakness, but as strategic refuelling.

Surrounding yourself with people who recognise the invisible labour of tolerance—and mirror it back to you with respect, not pity.

In a world that rewards speed and visibility, we often mistake patience for passivity and quitting for intelligence. But the deeper truth is that *the point of maximum doubt often overlaps with the point of maximum potential.* The people who move past it don't do so because they feel certain. They do so because they're *prepared to feel uncertain* and continue anyway.

If there is a final insight here, it is this: breakthroughs are not dramatic—they are cumulative. And most are missed not because the opportunity didn't arrive, but because the person left too early. The tipping point of tolerance, then, is not a personal flaw. It is a predictable threshold. And like any threshold, it can be moved—if you build the structure to hold yourself one moment longer.

Because often, *one moment longer is enough.*

Building a Stress Buffer – Expanding Emotional Bandwidth Before Burnout

Stress is not inherently the enemy. The capacity to face pressure, manage challenge, and respond to complexity is central to any meaningful pursuit—be it a business, a relationship, or an inner transformation. What breaks people is not stress itself, but *the absence of a buffer.* It's the difference between a system with slack and one running at full capacity with no margin for error. A well-designed bridge can handle weight far beyond its average load—because it was built with tolerances. Human resilience works the same way. The question is not "How do I eliminate stress?" but rather *"How do I create structural slack so I don't collapse under it?"*

In today's context, that slack—emotional, cognitive, physiological—is rapidly vanishing. We live in environments optimised for immediacy and reaction. Notifications fragment

anxiety," or "This is a control reflex") rather than becoming it. This subtle shift builds space. And space is buffer. Practising metacognition regularly—through journaling, mindfulness, cognitive defusion, or structured coaching—doesn't eliminate stress. It *recontextualises* it. That recontextualisation is everything.

Equally essential is emotional granularity. This refers to how precisely one can identify and label internal states. People who distinguish between "disappointment," "frustration," and "resentment" (rather than just saying "I'm stressed") are better at self-regulation. Studies by Lisa Feldman Barrett and others in affective neuroscience show that emotional precision correlates strongly with better decision-making, lower cortisol levels, and increased resilience in high-pressure environments. The clearer your emotional vocabulary, the more nuanced your stress response becomes. And nuance is a buffer.

Beyond self-awareness, buffers are also built through environmental architecture. Where you work, how you work, and who you work with shapes your emotional resilience more than willpower does. Open-plan offices that prioritise speed over depth deplete focus. Team cultures that valorise urgency over clarity induce reactive decision-making. Even something as mundane as lighting or noise level can increase cognitive load and lower stress thresholds. This is not micromanagement. It is *stress ergonomics*. High-functioning individuals and systems are those that reduce unnecessary friction—and preserve cognitive energy for high-leverage thinking.

If metacognition provides the lens, and emotional granularity sharpens the resolution, then *rituals* form the scaffolding that holds the buffer in place. Emotional bandwidth is not only a function of the mind; it is built through behaviour. And behaviour, particularly under stress, defaults to habit. This is why rituals—structured, intentional, repeatable practices—are essential for buffering. They create predictability where life offers none. They signal to the nervous system that not everything is in chaos, even when chaos surrounds.

For example, consider the case of Ray Dalio, founder of Bridgewater Associates, one of the most successful hedge funds in history. Dalio attributes his decision-making clarity not to financial acumen alone, but to his twice-daily practice of transcendental meditation. This ritual, simple but non-negotiable, allows his cognitive and emotional system to reset amidst staggering volatility. Likewise, elite surgeons report lower burnout when they engage in ritualised pre-surgery routines—not merely for procedural accuracy but because it calms the body, centres the mind, and delays reactive spirals. These aren't luxuries. They are *performance buffers.*

In environments where pressure is non-negotiable—military combat zones, air traffic control towers, emergency medical units—buffers are not left to chance. They are institutionalised. Debriefing sessions, timeouts, and shift rotations aren't bureaucratic features. They are psychological pressure valves. In contrast, in civilian life, many professionals operate as if endurance were a proxy for worth. The irony is clear: those in the *most dangerous jobs* are often given *more tools* to protect their bandwidth than the average corporate executive or freelance creator.

This brings us to a difficult truth: many people don't lack resilience—they lack permission. They don't feel authorised to build buffers because rest is interpreted as laziness, boundaries as selfishness, and emotional needs as weakness. This cultural conditioning is not accidental. It is the legacy of industrial models of productivity grafted onto post-digital life. In that model, humans are machines. Downtime is lost output. But humans are not machines; we are biological systems governed by ultradian rhythms, emotional cycles, and cognitive limits. When we ignore that reality, we break—not all at once, but slowly, through attrition. A missed meal here. A skipped walk there. A blurred line between "urgent" and "important" until you can no longer distinguish fatigue from failure.

To build a stress buffer, then, is to reclaim sovereignty over one's mental ecology. This involves not just daily habits, but *strategic pattern recognition*—understanding when your system begins to fray and intervening early. One of the most underutilised tools here is the personal stress inventory. This is not about logging stress after a breakdown. It's about regularly auditing one's friction points: Where does my energy consistently drain? Which relationships deplete rather than restore? What types of tasks trigger urgency over clarity? These insights become signals, not threats. And in turning signals into structure, one begins to anticipate and absorb life's impact more effectively.

Let us take an example from organisational psychology: Google's Project Aristotle. In examining what made the most effective teams perform better, Google found that psychological safety—far more than intelligence or skill—was the defining variable. Teams that had space to speak openly, admit uncertainty, and acknowledge emotional friction without punishment outperformed more technically gifted teams that lacked that buffer. The takeaway? *Resilience at scale is collective.* It's not just about how you regulate your own state, but about how your ecosystem helps absorb and distribute psychological pressure.

This applies to personal relationships as well. In emotionally mature partnerships—whether romantic, familial, or professional—people don't avoid conflict. They simply build buffers into their communication: designated times for check-ins, agreed-upon protocols for disagreement, even shared language for emotional states ("I'm not angry—I'm overstimulated"). These buffers act as shock absorbers. They reduce the violence of emotional misinterpretation and preserve connection through difficulty. Without them, relationships don't fail because of stress. They fail because there is *nowhere for that stress to go.*

Still, one might ask: how much buffering is too much? Doesn't too much emotional insulation lead to avoidance, stagnation, or fragility? This is a valid tension. A stress buffer is not a cocoon. It is not an escape from difficulty, but a conscious modulation of it. It's what allows one to engage with complexity *more fully*, not less. In this sense, the real skill is *titration*—the art of dosing intensity so that it strengthens rather than overwhelms. Just as a skilled trainer doesn't push an athlete to failure every session, a skilled mind-builder doesn't force emotional breakthroughs without recovery. Growth requires challenge, but sustained growth requires buffering that prevents collapse.

This distinction brings us back to the deeper logic of resilience: *it is not about tolerating more; it is about recovering faster.* And recovery is a function of system design, not just grit. Grit without repair becomes stubbornness. Drive without rest becomes erosion. Which is why high-functioning individuals protect their stress buffers with near-religious discipline. They know that to have more emotional range, more impact, and more clarity in the long run, they must resist the short-term illusion that urgency equals importance.

To close this subchapter, consider this framing: buffering is not about becoming less involved, but more deliberate. It is the ability to choose when to lean in, when to step back, and how to maintain coherence in the face of chaos. It is not about being unbothered. It is about being *unbroken*. In a world that valorises immediate reaction, building a stress buffer is an act of long-term rebellion. And that rebellion, when sustained, becomes resilience.

The Trigger Audit – Mapping Emotional Hot-Buttons, Patterns, and Predictive Reactions

In any high-functioning system—financial, operational, or biological—knowing where volatility is likely to spike isn't optional. It's fundamental. You don't wait for the bridge to buckle before reinforcing the weak beam. You don't wait for a wildfire to spread before charting drought zones. Likewise, in emotional resilience, *you don't wait for the outburst, the breakdown, or the self-sabotage to understand your triggers*. You map them in advance.

The process is neither indulgent nor therapeutic fluff. It is a strategic, cognitive exercise that belongs as much in boardrooms and trading floors as it does in clinical practice. A trigger audit is not about what *happened to you*—it is about understanding how your *system interprets stimulus*, anticipates threat, and executes rapid, often unconscious behavioural responses. This is not about blame. It's about *pattern literacy*.

What qualifies as a "trigger"? Not just extreme trauma, although that certainly counts. In this context, a trigger is any stimulus—external or internal—that reliably provokes *disproportionate reactivity*, bypassing rational decision-making. It is the invisible override switch that yanks you out of the calm, considered self and into fight-flight-freeze patterns. These triggers are not universal. They are highly specific, historically conditioned, and context-sensitive. And most people have no formal map of them.

Take the case of a senior executive who finds themselves inexplicably enraged when asked to justify a project's budget line items. The content of the question is benign. But the subtext—*being questioned, being doubted, being perceived as incompetent*—lights up an old neural pathway. That surge of cortisol, that narrowing of attention, that need to dominate or withdraw, is not about the budget. It is about a personal trigger—perhaps an early pattern of being micromanaged, ignored, or held to unfair standards. Without a trigger audit, the executive will assume the reaction is valid. With one, they can interrupt it.

In neuroscience terms, what's happening is simple: the amygdala hijacks the prefrontal cortex. But this elegant phrase conceals a complex reality. The amygdala doesn't act without a reason. It acts based on its memory. It has seen this before. It has filed it away. And the file isn't labelled "budget query." It's labelled "threat to worth." When we don't perform regular audits of these files, they run in the background like malware—draining processing power, compromising performance, and making us reactive rather than reflective.

A trigger audit, properly done, requires structured attention across three dimensions: *content, context, and consequence.* Content is the surface stimulus: what was said or done. Context refers to the environment, the power dynamics, the time of day, even your physical state (sleep-deprived, hungry, overstimulated). Consequence is the behavioural result—what did you do immediately after? How did it feel in the body? How long did it take to return to baseline? These audits must be written, not just contemplated. Our minds are masters of narrative distortion. Paper reveals patterns.

Let's ground this further. Suppose someone notices that every time a peer receives public praise, they feel an internal jolt—envy, defensiveness, withdrawal. The surface story might be that the colleague is manipulative, favoured, or superficial. But a well-executed audit may reveal a deeper belief: *"I only matter when I outperform."* That belief is the real trigger—not the applause itself. And that belief often stems from earlier conditioning—parental dynamics, early workplace hierarchies, even cultural myths of meritocracy. Once revealed, it can be challenged. Not by positive affirmations, but by evidence and repetition. If the person deliberately begins noticing instances where cooperation led to better outcomes than competition, the neural map slowly redraws itself.

The most valuable audits are not reactive; they're *proactive.* Instead of waiting for the next emotional blow-up, high performers begin to pre-identify likely hotspots. These include:

Situational triggers: deadlines, public speaking, being interrupted, ambiguity

Relational triggers: criticism from authority, perceived rejection, being outshined

Internal triggers: shame, fatigue, hunger, insecurity, overexertion

Each category has physiological signatures. Stress doesn't arrive abstractly—it arrives somatically. Your jaw tightens. Your breathing shallows. Your chest compresses. Learning to *notice before you narrate* is one of the most powerful skills in building resilience. Because once you tell yourself the story—*they're undermining me, I always fail, no one listens*—you're already downstream.

This is why elite coaches, therapists, and resilience trainers teach *interruption techniques*. These are not distractions. They're circuit breakers. A deep breath isn't a gimmick—it's a down-regulation signal to the nervous system. A well-placed question ("What else could this mean?") isn't denial—it's cognitive reappraisal. A 10-minute walk isn't procrastination—it's restoration of prefrontal engagement. And over time, these practices reinforce a fundamental truth: *you are not your first reaction.*

From a philosophical standpoint, trigger auditing echoes the Stoic tradition. Marcus Aurelius wrote: "If you are pained by any external thing, it is not this thing that disturbs you, but your judgment about it." But this is not a call to suppress feeling—it's a call to examine it. Judgement is not something to delete; it's something to refine. Emotional reactivity is not weakness. It is information. And trigger audits are the process by which that information becomes insight.

In team settings, the value multiplies. Psychological safety increases when members understand not only their own triggers but signal them clearly. A project manager who says, "I tend to get defensive when timelines are questioned without data—just flagging that so I can manage it better," is not indulging emotion. They are preventing escalation. This kind of clarity is rare. It requires self-awareness and systems thinking. It is also the mark of emotional intelligence that moves from concept to culture.

The point is not to become triggerless. That would require becoming humanless. The point is to become *trigger-literate.* To know which wires are exposed, which patterns are outdated, and which emotional software needs patching. We don't fault a car for having a dashboard—we use it. Likewise, we should not fault ourselves for emotional signals. We should build better dashboards. A trigger audit is the beginning of that process.

To summarise—not to conclude—here is the transformation we are aiming for: from reacting blindly to recognising patterns, from pattern to conscious pause, from pause to choice. That is the terrain on which patience grows—not as waiting, but as sovereignty over one's attention. And the more sovereignty you have, the less likely you are to be derailed by someone else's urgency, chaos, or provocation. That is not avoidance. That is mastery.

Failure Fatigue and the Patience Plateau – Normalising the Boring Middle Where Nothing Seems to Work

Progress has a marketing problem. It's too often sold as linear, exciting, and instantly validating. We are shown the dramatic arc—the before and after, the origin story and the climax, the underdog and the trophy. But in the real world, most transformation happens not in lightning bolts of insight or meteoric rise—but in the *flat, tedious, uncertain space in between.* That space has a name. *The Patience Plateau.*

The plateau is not where most people begin. Nor is it where most people end. It is where most people *quit.* The idea didn't go viral. The business didn't scale. The weight wouldn't drop. The manuscript stayed half-written. You showed up, again and again, and the universe seemed unimpressed. In modern terms, it's what venture capitalists call the "trough of sorrow." In psychological terms, it's the testing ground of identity. And in this chapter, we argue that learning to endure this plateau—*without losing clarity, integrity, or energy*—is one of the rarest and most essential components of emotional resilience.

But to understand this phase, we first need to deconstruct a powerful myth: that success is primarily the result of short-term brilliance or brute force persistence. It is neither. More often, it's the ability to *persist intelligently when there is no applause.* And that ability is consistently eroded by a modern condition we might call *failure fatigue*—a subtle exhaustion that accumulates when reality fails to reward effort at the expected tempo.

Let's be precise. Failure fatigue is not laziness. It is not burnout in the clinical sense. It is not even about dramatic setbacks. It is the quiet, creeping demoralisation that arises when feedback loops are absent or delayed. When the energy going in begins to feel disconnected from results coming out. And it's at this point—far more than at moments of crisis—that most people unconsciously scale down their ambition, reduce their risk appetite, or retreat entirely. Not because the goal was impossible. But because *their nervous system no longer felt safe or sane continuing to pursue it.*

This, incidentally, is where emotional resilience diverges sharply from mere toughness. Toughness says: double down, push through, silence the voice of doubt. But resilience—real resilience—is more adaptive. It doesn't silence the voice. It listens to it, interrogates it, and then decides whether the voice is forecasting truth or simply echoing discomfort. It allows for recalibration without surrender. *Resilience isn't rigid—it's discerning.*

Consider the example of James Dyson, who developed 5,126 prototypes of his cyclone vacuum cleaner before one worked. Or more modestly, the independent author who writes for six years before earning meaningful royalties. Or the investor who holds an unpopular position for a decade before the market catches up. These are not tales of overnight success. They are illustrations of people who were willing to live in the space where results were ambiguous, timelines were stretched, and public validation was absent.

Neuroscience provides part of the explanation. The brain's dopamine system is built on feedback. Progress—even imagined progress—creates chemical reward. But when action is met with silence, the reward loop short-circuits. This makes plateaus not just conceptually hard, but biochemically difficult. That's why sticking through the plateau is not a matter of willpower alone. It requires architecture—routines, reflections, support systems—that compensate for the absence of immediate reward.

In cognitive psychology, this intersects with the concept of *learned helplessness*—where repeated lack of perceived control over outcomes leads to emotional shutdown. But the inverse is also true. When people are *taught to interpret* plateaus as natural, even necessary, they develop a psychological immunity to the illusion that "nothing is happening." In reality, a great deal is happening. Skills are compounding. Identity is maturing. Conditions are quietly aligning. The seed is germinating beneath the surface.

In entrepreneurship, this is often called *the grind*. But that word carries too much baggage—too much glorification of suffering. A more accurate term might be *the incubation period*: a time when patience is not passivity, but active alignment with process over impulse. And in almost every field of excellence—music, athletics, research, leadership—this period lasts far longer than most people anticipate.

Philosophically, the plateau challenges the modern obsession with speed. We are a culture addicted to momentum. "Moving fast and breaking things" is treated as gospel. But wisdom traditions across centuries—from Taoist thought to Stoic reflection—emphasise the inverse: stillness as power. The capacity to stay composed in the absence of signals. The discipline to hold a long view without guarantee. It is no coincidence that the best investors, creators, and thinkers are often those who are *least reactive to short-term noise.*

One powerful illustration of this can be found in the history of breakthroughs. The painter Georgia O'Keeffe produced some of her most significant work in her fifties, after decades of experimentation. The physicist Peter Higgs waited nearly fifty years for the scientific community to verify his proposed particle. Even in technology—where innovation is expected to move fast—some of the most transformative products, from the iPhone to ChatGPT, were the result of *patient iteration*, not sudden flashes of genius.

But how does one *practically* endure the patience plateau?

First, by **redefining progress**. If progress only means external outcomes—profit, followers, milestones—you're hostage to conditions you don't control. But if progress includes *internal mastery*—calmer decision-making, clearer thought, stronger ethics—you always have traction. This is not semantic spin. It's a shift in metrics.

Second, by **building emotional granularity**. Research by Dr. Lisa Feldman Barrett suggests that people who can label their emotional states with precision—rather than defaulting to vague descriptors like "stressed" or "tired"—have more adaptive nervous systems. The better you understand what you're feeling during the plateau, the less likely you are to confuse discomfort with failure.

Third, by **normalising boredom**. The plateau is often less about struggle than it is about tedium. Systems aren't breaking; they're just slow. And in a world that rewards novelty, being able to *remain consistent through monotony* becomes a radical form of maturity.

And fourth, by **anchoring to purpose, not outcome**. If your effort is only worth it when it produces what you expected, you are setting yourself up for chronic disenchantment. But if your effort is aligned with values—craftsmanship, contribution, excellence—the plateau becomes less of a purgatory and more of a proving ground.

There is no guarantee that every plateau ends in breakthrough. Some ideas need to be abandoned. Some paths *do* require pivoting. But the ability to *discern wisely between a signal to quit and a signal to endure*—that is what separates impulsive exit from strategic patience.

And so, what we call "failure fatigue" is not a personal defect. It is a natural response to an impatient culture. But it can be rewired. And when it is, the boring middle stops being a place of despair—and becomes the laboratory of endurance, where emotional resilience compounds, slowly but unstoppably, into something that looks very much like lasting success.

Chapter 6
The Stoic Investor

There are moments—quiet, easily missed—when the most intelligent move in a market or in life is to do nothing. Not out of apathy or paralysis, but because discernment has prevailed over noise. In such moments, restraint proves sharper than reaction. Focus, more potent than frenzy. And it is clarity—not clever manoeuvring—that quietly becomes the investor's sharpest edge.

This chapter explores an increasingly rare temperament in an age addicted to overstimulation and leverage. We call it The Stoic Investor—not a fixed strategy, but a mental orientation. It is not about cold detachment, nor is it about blunting emotion. Rather, it is about disciplined perception. A method of thinking that insulates you from the chaos you cannot control, while sharpening your influence over the few things that truly matter.

We begin with a truth so widely repeated that it risks becoming ornamental: you cannot control outcomes—only inputs. But this is no empty aphorism. It is, properly grasped, a scalpel for clarity. It draws a line between illusion and responsibility, between the futile and the vital. Markets, like life, are unpredictable not because they are unknowable in principle, but because they are driven by an ever-shifting web of externalities—prices, policies, pandemics, sentiment. And yet, many respond by doubling down on illusion: refreshing dashboards, tweaking allocations, absorbing headlines, acting in haste. Mistaking the buzz of movement for the presence of mastery.

The Stoic Investor chooses differently. They don't attempt to outsmart the market—they aim to outgrow its noise. Their concern isn't with forecasting volatility, but with managing their own. Because more than anything, investing is emotional theatre. And the investor's experience becomes a kind of mirror, reflecting not spreadsheets, but character: how you handle ambiguity, how long you can remain bored, and whether discipline holds in moments of surplus.

This concept is not some modern invention. Epictetus, nearly two millennia ago, offered a frame that remains strikingly relevant: "Some things are up to us and some are not." He wasn't managing a portfolio—but he might as well have been. The core of his thinking maps neatly onto the central findings of behavioural economics: humans, by and large, are poorly wired for probabilistic environments. Our decisions are stories before they are statistics, and those stories are guided less by fundamentals than by feeling.

Which brings us to a second insight: emotion is not merely noise in markets—it is the market. Not just the frenzy of others, but your own internal tremors. Markets are, in the end, collective sentiment rendered as price. Every spike and slump reflects a shared psychological rhythm—fear, greed, hope, denial. Misreading this rhythm is easy. Confusing it with fundamental value is easier still.

The untrained eye sees volatility as danger. The Stoic sees it as signal—though not necessarily a signal to act. They read moods without absorbing them. They expect exaggeration. They plan for distortion. They treat headlines with suspicion and urgency with caution. In a world engineered to provoke, their refusal to be provoked becomes an unusual—and therefore valuable—asset.

Let's be clear: this is not passivity masquerading as wisdom. Stoicism is often misinterpreted that way. But the classical Stoics were anything but inert. They advocated decisive action—within reason, within bounds. The Stoic Investor is not someone who blindly clings to a "buy-and-hold" orthodoxy. They observe. They respond. But their actions are chosen—not triggered. Their edge lies not in doing more, but in acting better. Not just once, but consistently.

Warren Buffett is the archetype most reach for, and for good reason. He didn't make his fortune through constant reinvention. He did the same thing repeatedly, with fewer interruptions than most. And while his intelligence is often credited, what's more instructive is his emotional restraint. His success is less about discovering new tricks and more about applying old truths for a very long time. Compounding works. But only for those who don't get in their own way.

This is where the modern investor struggles. Not because they lack access to tools, data, or advice, but because they are overloaded by them. Algorithms hum. News cycles churn. Opinions multiply. In this cacophony, signal is drowned by spectacle. And yet, those with the greatest edge are often not those with the best models, but those with the cleanest attention. They know what to ignore. They guard their focus like capital. They treat mental bandwidth as scarce and precious.

In this chapter, we'll unpack three foundational ideas that make up the Stoic Investor's inner infrastructure:

Controlling the Controllables – A cognitive discipline that separates the essential from the irrelevant. You'll learn how to conserve energy by refusing to wage psychological war against the unknowable. Historical case studies and modern examples will illustrate how this mindset converts confusion into composure.

Emotion as Market Noise – A deeper dive into how collective psychology—not hard data—drives short-term movements. We'll examine mania, crashes, and investor regret through a psychological lens. And you'll discover why emotional neutrality, though rare, is an extraordinary advantage in cycles of overreaction.

Fortune Follows the Focused – Profiles of investors and thinkers who chose depth over breadth, and precision over performance. You'll see how fewer decisions, made under greater clarity, often outperform frenetic decision-making. And why, in a reactionary world, focus has become a kind of superpower.

But this isn't just a manual for portfolio management. It is, at its heart, a guide for navigating complexity. Because markets, for all their mystique, are mirrors of other systems: relationships, careers, aspirations. All are subject to the same fluctuations in perception, emotion, and narrative. The traits that define resilient investors—emotional poise, strategic patience, internal clarity—are the very same traits that define resilient people.

The Stoic Investor, then, is not merely someone who reads financial statements. It is someone who reads the world with equanimity. Who understands that noise is part of the game, but not the game itself. Who holds steady—not by pretending chaos doesn't exist, but by refusing to be seduced by it.

This chapter is an invitation. Not to withdraw from the world, but to enter it more wisely. To be emotionally informed, but not emotionally led. To reframe uncertainty not as a threat to control, but as a context for presence. Because in the final analysis, markets will do as they please. Circumstances will shift. The world will remain unpredictable. But how you respond—that remains yours.

And that is the real trade. Not between stocks or sectors, but between reactivity and reason. The Stoic Investor makes that trade deliberately. And wins accordingly.

Why Markets Reward the Philosophical

It is not intellect alone that differentiates enduring investors from erratic ones, nor merely technical skill or access to superior data. Time and again, what separates those who prosper through market cycles from those who panic at the first sign of volatility is something far more ancient and underappreciated: philosophy. Specifically, the kind of enduring, practical philosophy that the

Stoics of antiquity championed—one that governs emotion, embraces uncertainty, and seeks composure not in the absence of pressure but in the mastery of response. What modern finance repeatedly proves, and what behavioural economics is now beginning to quantify, is that *the psychological posture of the Stoic investor maps astonishingly well onto the demands of long-term market participation.*

Consider for a moment what the Stoics actually taught—not the caricature of cold indifference, but the structured pursuit of equanimity in the face of events outside one's control. Marcus Aurelius wrote in his private meditations, "You have power over your mind—not outside events. Realise this, and you will find strength." For the investor, the relevance is immediate. Markets move with unpredictable force. Economic news surprises. Algorithms trigger flash crashes. Political events reshape sectors overnight. What remains controllable—what is always controllable—is the individual's internal response: how they allocate attention, how they tolerate discomfort, how they refrain from acting on impulse. In this light, Stoicism is not simply a philosophical ornament but a direct strategic advantage.

One of the core ideas in Stoic philosophy is the dichotomy of control: the division between what is up to us and what is not. Epictetus, the former slave turned philosopher, stressed that our judgments, desires, and actions lie within our power; everything else—including reputation, market movement, and outcomes—does not. This principle dovetails precisely with what disciplined investors learn over time: that obsessing over outcomes derails process, and that chasing certainty in an uncertain domain leads only to stress and misjudgement. *Long-term performance depends not just on what one knows, but on what one resists doing when emotions flare and the herd stampedes.*

In practical terms, philosophical thinking inoculates against the most costly behavioural biases. Loss aversion, for instance—the tendency to feel the pain of losses more intensely than the pleasure of gains—leads to premature selling and risk aversion just when markets may be turning. Stoic thinking invites the practitioner to *observe such emotional reactions without fusing with them*, to treat discomfort as information rather than instruction. The disciplined investor begins to recognise fear as part of the system, not a sign to exit it. Likewise, FOMO—the fear of missing out—is nothing new. Seneca warned of the dangers of envy and emotional contagion long before financial media turned every upward tick into a dopamine trigger. To borrow his wisdom: "It is not the man who has too little, but the man who craves more, that is poor." The market rewards those who can delay reaction in favour of reflection—those who can examine a spike in sentiment and ask, "Is this noise, or is this signal?"

This is not abstract theory. Consider Warren Buffett, whose annual letters read more like essays in practical wisdom than conventional finance reports. Time and again, Buffett has described temperament as more important than IQ in successful investing. His famous line, "Be fearful when others are greedy, and greedy when others are fearful," is not a trading tip—it's a Stoic stance. It requires calm in chaos, confidence in disapproval, and detachment from the emotional temperature of the crowd. Likewise, Ray Dalio's principle of radical open-mindedness echoes Stoic humility: to act effectively, one must acknowledge how much one doesn't know. The market is a machine for humbling overconfidence. The philosophical investor pre-empts that humility by making it a daily practice.

Furthermore, philosophical investing resists the tyranny of immediacy. In a financial culture saturated with real-time updates and short-term incentives, Stoic principles restore perspective. They encourage a shift in time horizon—from what is urgent to what is essential, from daily fluctuations to generational trends. This reorientation is no small matter. It allows the investor to tolerate underperformance in the short term in exchange for compounding over the long term. It's what allows someone to hold an unpopular position not for weeks, but for years, and to reap disproportionate gains when the market eventually realigns with reality. Patience, here, is not passive—it is philosophical courage.

To be clear, Stoicism is not synonymous with detachment from results or the romanticisation of pain. It does not instruct one to be inert or disengaged. Rather, it is a discipline of clarity—*an emotional audit that prioritises process over outcome, preparation over prediction, and resilience over reaction.* It asks not that we be perfect, but that we recognise our reactions, question our assumptions, and practice restraint where others indulge urgency. In this sense, Stoicism is less about suppression and more about alignment—a system for harmonising action with principle under pressure.

In moments of panic, philosophical investors do not reach for hacks or heuristics. They reach for habits of mind. They pause. They review first principles. They ask: *What do I control here? What does reason, not emotion, suggest? What decision will I be glad to have made in five years, not five minutes?* This framing is not theoretical; it's behavioural armour.

Interestingly, many of the modern disciplines now studied under behavioural finance—from prospect theory to confirmation bias—merely provide empirical backing for what philosophers have long known: *that without deliberate cultivation, the human mind is a poor investor.* It reacts, extrapolates, overweights recent events, and seeks safety in numbers. Philosophy trains precisely the muscles that counteract this: awareness, discipline, self-command. It's not about escaping emotion, but governing it.

A curious tension arises here: while markets reward rationality, they are composed of irrational participants. This is not a contradiction; it is an opportunity. As Benjamin Graham, mentor to Buffett, famously put it, "In the short run, the market is a voting machine, but in the long run, it is a weighing machine." The philosophical investor does not waste energy trying to predict when the votes will shift. They concern themselves with weight—with intrinsic value, with process integrity, with staying power. Over time, this philosophical patience creates a competitive edge that few can replicate.

Philosophy also restores ethical depth to financial decision-making. In a world increasingly driven by algorithmic speed and impersonal transactions, Stoicism reminds us that investing is, fundamentally, a human practice. It is an expression of trust—in time, in value, in one's judgment. It is shaped not only by external events but by internal character. A philosophical approach foregrounds questions not just of return, but of responsibility: What do I stand for? What will I not compromise? What does it mean to win, and at what cost?

Ultimately, the philosophical investor is not one who rejects data, models, or analysis. Rather, they insist that such tools be used in service of clarity—not confusion. They treat market turbulence not as a threat to their plan, but as a test of their preparation. They do not confuse activity with progress. And they never forget that in the financial world, as in life, *the most important decisions are often emotional, not technical.* Philosophy sharpens that awareness. It offers, in place of panic, a posture of prepared calm.

Markets may be ruled in the short term by sentiment, but over decades, they reward principle. That is why the philosophical investor endures—not by being louder, faster, or luckier, but by being wiser. And wisdom, unlike market timing, is not a gamble. It is a daily practice. It is the ultimate unfair advantage.

Controlling the Controllables

One of the most significant cognitive errors humans routinely make—especially under stress—is conflating influence with control. We believe that with enough effort, intelligence, or determination, we can bend complex systems to our will. The truth is more sobering, and more liberating: *most variables in our lives are not within our command.* This is not a reason to surrender agency. It is the foundation of true power. In investing, business, health, and personal development, success is less about mastering everything and more about mastering the distinction between what can be shaped and what must be absorbed. *Those who thrive sustainably are not those who try to control the uncontrollable, but those who allocate their energy to the controllable with extraordinary precision.*

This principle is not new. The Stoics framed it as the dichotomy of control. Epictetus taught that external events lie beyond us, but our choices, values, and judgments do not. It is this internal locus of control that defines the resilient thinker—the one who stays steady in crises not because outcomes are guaranteed, but because they never built their stability on outcomes to begin with. Modern psychology affirms this. Research on locus of control, especially by Julian Rotter and his successors, shows a strong correlation between perceived internal control and psychological well-being. When people believe they can influence their responses, their behaviours, and their priorities, they become more adaptive and less reactive—even in situations of genuine uncertainty.

In the context of high-stakes domains like investing or entrepreneurship, this insight becomes operational. Markets move. Policies shift. Competitors emerge. Trends change. You cannot dictate these forces. But you *can* define how you position your capital, how you interpret volatility, how you build in redundancy, and how you define success over long arcs instead of short thrills. *Control is a narrow path; but walking it with rigour yields exponential calm.*

Consider how elite decision-makers function. Jeff Bezos popularised a distinction between "Type 1" and "Type 2" decisions—irreversible versus reversible. But the most critical framing beneath this classification is the acceptance that *one cannot control outcomes—only inputs, processes, and probabilities.* The best decision-makers structure their thinking to minimise regret over controllables, not to eliminate uncertainty. Similarly, successful investors such as Howard Marks and Ray Dalio often return to this central wisdom: managing risk is not about prediction; it's about preparation. You cannot control the storm, but you can control whether you've built a seaworthy vessel.

One of the most practical applications of this mindset is attention management. In today's economy, attention is currency—and most people spend it poorly. Emotional bandwidth is squandered on headline noise, on comparisons with others, on speculation and outrage over events no individual can influence. *The disciplined mind protects its attention like an asset.* It doesn't overexpose itself to information it can't act on. It doesn't allow itself to spiral in the presence of ambiguity. Instead, it returns, again and again, to the handful of levers it can actually pull.

In this sense, controlling the controllables is not merely an act of prioritisation—it is a form of psychological governance. It requires consistent metacognition: the ability to step outside one's thoughts and evaluate, *Is this within my sphere of influence?* And if not, *what is?* This skill has practical implications in domains far beyond finance. In health, it means focusing on sleep, diet, and exercise rather than fixating on outcomes like weight or aging. In relationships, it means committing to how one listens and responds, not trying to change the other person. In leadership, it means focusing on clear expectations, feedback loops, and cultural clarity—not the emotions or loyalty of others, which cannot be forced.

A common objection arises here: what about ambition? What about striving to influence systems bigger than oneself? The answer is both philosophical and tactical. *There is no contradiction between high ambition and radical clarity about control.* In fact, the latter strengthens the former. When you cease wasting energy on variables beyond you, you reclaim enormous bandwidth to improve what is within your domain. The difference lies in *influence without attachment.* You play to win—but you don't hinge your identity on the score. You move the needle—but you don't collapse when the dial doesn't turn as expected. This is what separates resilient achievers from fragile high performers.

It also helps explain the emotional instability of many intelligent people. The smarter you are, the more you may *expect* to control things—because you've often succeeded through effort. But the complexity of the world doesn't scale neatly with your intelligence. Markets don't respond to willpower. Other people don't follow logic. Outcomes don't always reflect merit. The more one understands systems thinking, the more one sees that most environments are influenced by feedback loops, randomness, and lag time. *To stay grounded, the intelligent mind must learn humility—not as a virtue, but as a practice of efficiency.*

In behavioural finance, this maps to the distinction between internal and external benchmarks. Novice investors tie their emotions to performance against others: did my portfolio outperform the index? Am I wealthier than my peers? Experts tie their emotions to fidelity to process: *Did I execute my strategy with discipline? Did I avoid emotional trades? Did I manage risk well?* The first mindset invites volatility of mood; the second fosters sustainable confidence.

In practical terms, controlling the controllables requires deliberate architecture. It means designing your environment to reduce temptation. It means tracking leading indicators rather than lagging ones. It means crafting routines that insulate you from reactive spirals. For example, great thinkers and investors often have rituals of daily review—not to fix the world, but to reset their attention on what they can influence today. They write, not because writing will change the market, but because clarity in thought precedes clarity in action. *Discipline is not rigidity. It is a system of self-respect.*

There is also a political and social dimension to this idea. Many modern frustrations stem from a misallocation of control. People rage against institutions but neglect their habits. They obsess over election outcomes but ignore local civic engagement. They fret over corporate greed but make no adjustments to their own consumption. The Stoics, again, offer a mirror: to be politically aware without becoming politically consumed, one must begin by ruling oneself. *The most impactful activism starts with stewardship of your own mind.*

To be clear, controlling the controllables does not mean shrinking from life. It is not apathy. It is *precision in engagement.* You conserve your emotional energy for what matters. You relinquish illusion so you can act effectively. In this way, it is one of the most freeing disciplines a person can adopt—freeing not because it reduces responsibility, but because it aligns responsibility with reality.

The paradox is this: *when you stop trying to control everything, you gain more actual control.* You stop flailing against uncertainty. You start executing with calm. You stop blaming conditions. You start refining strategies. The result is not just better performance—but better composure, better relationships, better sleep, better use of time.

In a world addicted to urgency, controlling the controllables is a radical act of focus. It says: I will not waste my life rehearsing worst-case scenarios. I will not outsource my peace to outcomes. I will not confuse force with effectiveness. *I will do what I can, fully—and release what I can't, completely.* That is not just discipline. It is liberation.

Emotion as Market Noise

On 19 October 1987, the Dow Jones Industrial Average plunged more than 22% in a single trading day—still the largest one-day percentage drop in Wall Street history. No single geopolitical event or economic data point could explain it. Instead, it was a cascade of panic, driven not by fundamentals but by emotion, speculation, and herd behaviour. To this day, analysts still debate the technical triggers. But the psychological mechanism is clear: *markets don't always behave rationally because humans don't either.*

This is not a historical anomaly. It is a structural feature of markets. Behind the numbers, tickers, and asset classes, every market is ultimately an arena of collective belief. Prices are not just a reflection of value—they are a reflection of sentiment. In the short term, fear and euphoria often overwhelm analysis and logic. *Emotion becomes noise, and the noise moves billions.*

Understanding this is not merely a theoretical exercise. For the thoughtful investor—or indeed anyone navigating a volatile system—the ability to distinguish signal from noise is a competitive edge. The signal is composed of durable, often unsexy truths: cash flows, competitive advantage, macro conditions. The noise is emotional: headlines, social contagion, recency bias. One informs; the other distorts.

Modern behavioural economics has devoted decades to studying this tension. Daniel Kahneman and Amos Tversky, pioneers of prospect theory, showed that people fear losses more than they value equivalent gains—a phenomenon known as loss aversion. This leads to irrational sell-offs, risk-averse hoarding, and poor timing decisions. Likewise, confirmation bias—the tendency to seek out evidence that supports one's existing beliefs—drives investors to double down on flawed theses long after the facts change. These are not isolated errors. *They are predictable patterns of human misjudgement, baked into the very structure of the market.*

Take the tech bubble of the late 1990s. The fundamentals of many internet startups were abysmal—no revenue, no business model, only hype. Yet markets inflated these companies to billions in valuation. Why? Because the narrative of a "new economy" captured the collective imagination. People weren't buying earnings; they were buying hope, momentum, and the fear of missing out. And when the illusion broke, trillions vanished.

Or consider the pandemic of 2020. As COVID-19 spread globally, markets collapsed at a pace faster than any prior crisis. Within weeks, indices had fallen by 30% or more. But within months—despite ongoing deaths, lockdowns, and uncertainty—markets rebounded dramatically. Again, emotion led and lagged reality. Many who exited in fear missed the recovery entirely.

None of this is an argument against investing. It is an argument against *emotional investing*. The Stoics of ancient Rome taught that emotions cloud judgment not because they are inherently bad, but because they distort our perception of what matters. Epictetus advised: “It’s not things that upset us, but our judgments about things.” This principle applies with unsettling precision to financial markets.

Today, emotional narratives are more potent than ever—not because people are more irrational, but because the environment amplifies reactivity. Social media platforms reward extremity and immediacy. Financial news cycles blur into entertainment. Alerts ping constantly. Every headline feels urgent. In this ecosystem, staying rational is not just difficult—it is countercultural.

What makes this worse is that the market rarely penalises you immediately for being emotional. In fact, some emotional bets pay off—at least for a while. A retail investor hears that a stock is “going to the moon” on a forum, buys in, and doubles their money. The outcome reinforces the behaviour. But over time, *repeatedly acting on emotion instead of principles leads to underperformance*. The occasional win does not offset the systemic risk of poor decision-making.

The antidote is not cold detachment but emotional literacy. Investors must learn to feel their fear without obeying it. They must learn to notice hype without being pulled by it. This is a skill—like reading a balance sheet or understanding a valuation model—and it can be cultivated. Awareness of one’s own biases, routines to slow decisions, and deliberate exposure to contrary information all help build immunity to market noise.

Professional investors institutionalise this wisdom. Firms like Bridgewater build entire cultures around radical truth and process discipline. Howard Marks warns against "second-level thinking"—the habit of asking not just what's true, but what others *think* is true, and how they're likely to act on it. Warren Buffett's famous aphorism, "Be fearful when others are greedy, and greedy when others are fearful," is not a call to be contrarian for its own sake—it's a call to detach from the mood of the crowd and return to fundamentals.

This does not mean emotion has no place in markets. Emotion drives innovation. Passion drives entrepreneurial risk. Visionaries don't calculate everything—they feel possibilities others don't. But when it comes to *allocation of capital*—when stakes are high and uncertainty is pervasive—emotion must be a data point, not a driver. As the historian Yuval Noah Harari notes, Homo sapiens dominate the planet not because we are the smartest species, but because we are the most cooperative—and *cooperation is often driven by shared stories, not shared spreadsheets.* To succeed in markets, then, one must learn to discern when the story is moving the price more than the substance.

This insight is especially relevant during bubbles and busts. Every cycle has its own narrative: tulip mania, subprime mortgages, cryptocurrency revolutions. The underlying assets change, but the emotional arc does not. Exuberance builds. Skeptics are mocked. Price rises justify themselves. Then—often suddenly—confidence cracks, and the herd stampedes in the opposite direction. *Those who've trained themselves to listen for noise can sidestep the stampede—not always by predicting it, but by refusing to run with it.*

It's also worth noting that emotional noise doesn't just come from others. It comes from within. Investors bring their life stories into every trade: childhood lessons about money, cultural scripts about success, unconscious associations with risk. These internal narratives shape perception in ways we rarely examine. The investor who panics at a 10% dip may not be responding to the market at all—but to a deeper fear of loss, failure, or shame. *Until those emotional templates are understood, they will act like noise in the system—masking signal, distorting intent, and clouding judgment.*

This is why great investors are often not the most brilliant, but the most self-aware. They know their own patterns. They know when they are prone to overconfidence, to fear, to overtrading. They don't fight emotion by pretending it doesn't exist. They factor it in. They build systems—automated rules, diversification, journaling practices—that absorb their tendencies without letting them dictate outcomes. In this way, they build *emotional anti-fragility* into their portfolios.

To navigate markets intelligently in the modern age, one must become a kind of emotional minimalist. Strip away noise. Observe your reactions without identification. Refuse to outsource your convictions to collective panic. Accept that markets will always include irrationality—but that your edge lies in not joining it.

In the end, emotion is not the enemy of reason—but it is a poor substitute for it. When emotion becomes the loudest voice in the room, it drowns out the data, the context, and the perspective needed to make sound decisions. The disciplined investor listens to the emotion but acts on principle. That is not detachment. That is maturity. And in a world awash with noise, maturity is an asset that compounds.

Fortune Follows the Focused

At first glance, the modern world seems designed to reward those who are agile, constantly pivoting, and plugged into every signal. Markets fluctuate by the minute. News updates arrive by the second. Algorithms reward hyper-responsiveness. In such a context, the virtues of stillness, focus, and patience can appear outdated—quaint relics in a culture addicted to immediacy. And yet, the data consistently reveals a paradox: *the most resilient investors, entrepreneurs, and thinkers are not those who chase complexity, but those who master the discipline of consistency.*

Consider Warren Buffett, a name almost synonymous with long-term investing. His genius is not in secret algorithms or high-frequency trading. It is in choosing a handful of businesses he understands, buying them at reasonable prices, and doing... nothing. The overwhelming majority of Buffett's wealth was accumulated after the age of 50, not because of new techniques but because of uninterrupted focus. As Buffett famously quipped, "The stock market is a device for transferring money from the impatient to the patient." What's often overlooked is the mechanism behind that patience: *he isn't trying to predict every movement—he's trying to avoid unnecessary ones.*

The principle scales beyond finance. Take the example of author James Clear, whose book *Atomic Habits* became a global bestseller not because it offered radically new content, but because it articulated the immense power of repeating small behaviours over time. Clear didn't build his influence by writing across multiple niches or following trends. He wrote about human behaviour with relentless focus—publishing a newsletter on the topic for years before his work gained mass attention. It's a pattern worth studying: *focus creates trust, and trust compounds.*

In start-up culture, too, there's a widespread myth that success comes from moving fast and breaking things. Yet many of the most enduring companies—Apple, Amazon, Google—were built not through constant pivots, but through an obsessive commitment to a core vision. Jeff Bezos repeated the same mantra to shareholders year after year: "It's still Day One." He focused Amazon not on short-term profit, but on customer obsession, operational efficiency, and long-term infrastructure. The result? A company that not only survived multiple downturns but redefined entire industries.

Why does this work? In part, because *focus reduces friction.* Every time we switch priorities, abandon strategies, or chase novelty, we incur a hidden cognitive cost. Economists call this "switching cost," and it applies not only to markets but to minds. The more you focus, the fewer decisions you must remake. The fewer remade decisions, the more energy is available for depth, refinement, and execution. Complexity may look impressive on the surface, but consistency wins underneath.

Psychologically, focus also shields us from emotional reactivity. When we lack clear commitments, every fluctuation feels personal, every setback existential. But when we are grounded in a long-term frame, we stop interpreting volatility as failure. Instead, we see it as noise. This framing shift is a kind of psychological compound interest: *the longer we remain focused, the more immune we become to the irrationality of the crowd.*

There is also a strategic dimension. Focus creates a filter. It tells us what to ignore, which is increasingly valuable in an age of information overload. The Stoic investor doesn't just resist distraction; they engineer their environment to *avoid exposure* to unnecessary inputs in the first place. That's not passivity—it's design. In practical terms, this may mean turning off notifications, restricting portfolio checks, or precommitting to decision thresholds. But the deeper commitment is philosophical: *to not confuse movement with progress, or speed with insight.*

Historical examples reinforce this. Charles Darwin didn't publish *On the Origin of Species* until two decades after formulating his theory of natural selection. Why? He was meticulously gathering evidence, refining arguments, and anticipating objections. In that time, others raced to publish theories of evolution, many now forgotten.

Darwin's impact endures not because he moved first, but because he moved precisely. *He won through focus, not frenzy.*

Likewise, the legendary investor John Templeton was known for his contrarian but disciplined approach. He bought 104 stocks trading below $1 during the Great Depression—companies no one else wanted. Most survived. Some thrived. He held many of them for years, ignoring headlines and sentiment. His method was not complex. It was brutally consistent: *buy low, hold long, avoid noise.*

Contrast this with the average retail investor, who often underperforms the market not due to lack of intelligence but because of excess reactivity. Studies by Dalbar and others show that over decades, average investor returns lag behind index performance—largely due to panic selling during downturns and euphoric buying at peaks. The lesson? *Even intelligent people lose to the market when they abandon consistency for excitement.*

Focus is not just a personal virtue. It's a signal. In a world where everyone is chasing the next thing, those who persist with the same thing stand out. This is true in creative fields, professional development, and even relationships. Consistency builds credibility. Credibility attracts trust. Trust opens doors. It is the compounding mechanism of reputation.

There is, of course, a caveat. Focus must be *disciplined*, not dogmatic. Stubbornness masquerading as strategy is a common trap. What distinguishes productive focus from blind rigidity is reflection. The best investors revisit their theses periodically, not reactively. They don't jump ship at the first sign of turbulence—but they also don't cling to sunk costs. In this way, *focus is not the absence of change—it is the result of intentional choice.*

In practical terms, the implications are stark: fewer trades, not more. Fewer priorities, not more. Fewer commitments, more deeply honoured. The investor who tracks 50 metrics is rarely as effective as the one who tracks five—and does something meaningful with each. The entrepreneur with a dozen side projects often fails to master one. The thinker with a thousand open tabs seldom finishes a paragraph that matters. *Concentration is not a constraint. It is a multiplier.*

The modern world whispers the opposite. It tells us that diversification equals safety, that options equal freedom, that complexity equals sophistication. But as any seasoned operator will tell you, *you don't rise by doing more—you rise by doing less, better.* The hard part is not learning this. It's remembering it when everything around you encourages forgetting.

In the end, fortune does not simply favour the bold. Nor does it favour the gifted, or the connected, or even the informed. *It favours those who stick—through doubt, through boredom, through volatility—because they've committed to something larger than short-term validation.* In markets, in work, and in life, the truly rare skill is not genius. It is perseverance applied with precision. And that skill, cultivated over time, quietly becomes a form of wealth.

Chapter 7
Inner Wealth and the Invisible ROI

Mention the word "wealth" and watch how quickly the mind narrows. For most, it conjures images of account balances, stock portfolios, or assets neatly listed under management. It's hardly surprising—modern culture has spent decades conditioning us to equate success with the visible and value with the quantifiable. But not all forms of wealth are made to be seen. Some accumulate quietly, almost secretly. They don't show up in quarterly reports or glossy profiles, but they matter more—far more—than we tend to admit. These are the forms of wealth that shape how well we think under pressure, how clearly we see in chaos, and whether we remain whole when the world fractures. This chapter is concerned with that deeper stratum of wealth.

Unlike its louder, flashier counterpart, inner wealth cannot be granted, inherited, or displayed. It is not tied to job titles, social metrics, or applause. It is constructed, slowly and deliberately, through the cultivation of discipline, emotional composure, and the quiet refusal to let external turbulence dictate internal decision-making. And, as with all forms of capital, it is not immune to depletion. You can fall into emotional debt just as you might financial debt—only the former tends to announce itself more subtly, and often more destructively. You won't see it in a spreadsheet, but you'll feel it: in your irritability, your fractured attention, your reflexive cynicism, your dwindling energy. Emotional overdrafts exact a steep price—in clarity, in steadiness, in the ability to hold yourself together.

This chapter begins by inviting a small but potent shift in framing: to view emotional experience as a kind of personal economy. Some behaviours generate emotional income—habits that restore clarity, replenish calm, reinforce dignity. Others become liabilities:

attention-leaking obligations, corrosive comparisons, and the digital white noise that leaves the mind scattered and brittle. As in finance, it's not necessarily about how much you make emotionally—it's about how well you manage the outflow. Inner wealth emerges when we begin to treat our psychological reserves with the same seriousness we usually reserve for financial planning.

But this metaphor is merely the opening act. What unfolds next is a deliberately unconventional exploration of value creation—specifically, the kind that eludes public recognition. Consider this: what if being unseen is not a curse, but a kind of superpower? In a world increasingly addicted to exposure, visibility, and performance, the ability to work—quietly, steadily, without external affirmation—may be one of the most underutilised advantages available. History, if one cares to examine it, is scattered with examples. Scientists whose breakthroughs emerged from decades of private thought. Entrepreneurs who founded enduring companies during downturns, far from the spotlight. Artists who shunned brand-building in favour of craft. These aren't stories of obscurity out of fear—but of voluntary invisibility, chosen precisely because it protects the work from dilution.

The argument, then, is not that invisibility must be endured, but that it can be wielded. There is something deeply resilient about value that does not require validation. Confidence that grows in quiet environments—free from applause or scrutiny—doesn't just survive adversity; it thrives on it. When your worth is not tethered to performance metrics or public perception, you become remarkably difficult to manipulate. You are less reactive to trends, more deliberate in your choices, and far more capable of investing in long arcs of growth.

That brings us to a distinction worth drawing: reputation versus resilience. These two concepts are often used interchangeably, but they are fundamentally different. Reputation lives in other people's minds. It is fluid, subject to misinterpretation, exaggeration, and even slander. It can be built or destroyed by circumstances entirely outside your control. Resilience, on the other hand, is personal property. It is acquired through discomfort, sharpened in boredom, and forged in places no one sees. To chase reputation at the expense of resilience is to surrender your sovereignty. But when you reverse the equation, you start building something no rumour or downturn can shake.

None of this is framed as a moral prescription. This is a practical blueprint. Because in volatile environments—be they economic, relational, or existential—the people who focus on appearances tend to overreach. They optimise for optics, not outcomes. They burn out chasing proximity to prestige. But those who prioritise durability—those who reject the pressure to constantly perform—tend to outlive the hype cycles. They don't flash. They endure.

Throughout this chapter, we'll probe into the nuances of inner wealth: how it's cultivated, how it's drained, and—critically—how it can be protected. We'll explore the architecture of emotional cash flow as more than analogy; we'll treat it as a decision-making model. We'll examine why stepping out of the limelight can, paradoxically, sharpen your influence. We'll investigate how the pursuit of external validation often carries hidden opportunity costs. And we'll ask a difficult but necessary question: is the currency you're chasing actually worth anything?

Make no mistake—this path is not easy. It requires the very quality the Stoics once prized above all: indifference to indifferent things. It demands a kind of inner reckoning, the ability to like yourself for reasons no one else sees or celebrates. It asks you to decouple success from spectacle. But those who manage it acquire a kind of fortitude that is unusually difficult to erode. Because when your identity isn't reliant on attention, you stop spending energy trying to keep up appearances. You become the kind of person who can quietly outlast.

If earlier chapters in this book taught you how to widen your emotional aperture—to hold more complexity, to absorb more chaos—this chapter narrows the lens. It asks: what's worth carrying? Where is your attention best spent? What truly deserves your bandwidth? It makes the case that the deepest forms of wealth are the least visible, the most consistent, and often the hardest won. That progress, when done right, makes very little noise. And that the true yield on your internal investments is not what others see, but what remains intact—unshaken, undiminished—when the noise eventually fades.

Peace as Profit – Argues that peace of mind is not a byproduct of success—it's the precondition."

Peace of mind is often spoken of as a reward—something to be earned after the hard work is done, after the risk has paid off, after the reputation has been established. It is framed as the dessert of a successful life. But this framing is backwards. *Peace is not the outcome of strategic mastery; it is the condition under which strategy becomes sustainable.* It is not what follows clarity—it is what enables it.

This chapter examines a quiet but powerful reversal: what if peace isn't a luxury afforded by the successful, but rather the prerequisite that makes success meaningful and repeatable?

To understand why this matters, one must first interrogate the prevailing model. In high-performance environments, particularly among professionals and entrepreneurs, the dominant belief is that peace of mind must be sacrificed in the short term in service of long-term wins. That stress, overcommitment, and chronic urgency are simply part of the cost structure of ambition. That comfort is the enemy of achievement. This trade-off model is seductive because it aligns with capitalism's most aggressive scripts: optimise, accelerate, scale. But the real cost is often unaccounted for.

Burnout doesn't merely limit capacity—it distorts judgment. Anxiety doesn't just feel bad—it lowers one's tolerance for ambiguity, which in turn leads to reactive decisions, short-term thinking, and missed opportunities for compounding growth. When the nervous system is perpetually hijacked by cortisol, *the brain defaults to survival mode*, narrowing its focus to risk-avoidance and emotional self-protection. Under these conditions, creativity is throttled, perspective collapses, and strategic patience evaporates. In financial terms, chronic stress is a silent tax on long-term returns.

It's worth noting that peace is not the same as comfort. Nor is it passivity. Peace is not the absence of challenge—it is the presence of *stability amid challenge*. Peace is a form of preparedness. It grants the mental spaciousness to think beyond the noise, to resist the impulse to act just because others are. In volatile environments—markets, negotiations, career pivots—*peace becomes a performance enhancer.*

Consider how this manifests in investing. The most consistent outperformers are rarely the most anxious or reactive. They are the ones who stay in the market when others are scrambling, who hold cash when others are rushing in, who know when to wait and why. Their edge is not insider information or technical brilliance—it's temperament. Warren Buffett's oft-quoted line, "The stock market is a device for transferring money from the impatient to the patient," is less about market mechanics than psychological posture. His success is not merely intellectual—it is emotional. *He protects his peace as rigorously as he protects his capital.*

This principle holds true outside markets as well. In creative work, the quality of output is rarely proportional to the number of hours worked. It is more tightly correlated to *depth of attention*, and depth of attention is impossible without emotional quiet. A mind in chaos cannot access flow. A distracted brain cannot do high-leverage thinking. Every unfinished loop, every ambient worry, every unresolved social pressure—all these act as open tabs in the mental browser, consuming RAM and slowing performance.

In this sense, peace of mind is not a soft concept. It is operational infrastructure. It determines what kind of decisions you are capable of making under pressure. It influences how quickly you recover from setbacks, how much feedback you can integrate without defensiveness, how well you can calibrate your behaviour to long-term outcomes rather than short-term relief. *Without peace, even the most brilliant ideas will be executed poorly. With peace, even modest ideas can be refined into powerful leverage.*

The ancient Stoics understood this well. Marcus Aurelius wrote, *"Nowhere you can go is more peaceful—more free of interruptions—than your own soul."* His prescription for leadership was not aggression or hyperactivity, but interior clarity. In a similar spirit, the philosopher Epictetus reminded his students that power begins with self-command: *"No man is free who is not master of himself."* Peace, then, is not retreat. It is *strategic inner stability*. It is the ability to remain undisturbed in the face of provocation—not from apathy, but from clarity about what matters.

Modern psychology has caught up to this wisdom. Studies on emotional regulation and decision-making show that people with higher baseline calmness have a greater capacity to evaluate risk accurately, avoid impulsive behaviour, and maintain attention under pressure. In organisational psychology, leaders who exhibit emotional steadiness are rated as more trustworthy, more competent, and more adaptive. Not because they react faster, but because they *react less*. They have cultivated a bias for considered action over habitual motion.

It is not difficult to spot the inverse. Hyperactivity disguised as productivity. Urgency masquerading as importance. People building impressive systems that are secretly held together by anxiety. Individuals who look successful but are internally bankrupt—living in cognitive overdraft, borrowing energy from tomorrow to meet today's appearances. *The external machinery of achievement running on fumes of inner turmoil.*

This is the invisible cost structure of modern ambition—and it is unsustainable. It's why so many high-achievers eventually plateau, not because they lack skill or opportunity, but because their internal systems collapse under the strain of unmanaged complexity. They optimised everything but themselves.

This brings us to a radical reframing: peace as profit. Not as a reward, not as an indulgence, but as *a condition for enduring returns.* Imagine treating peace not as a byproduct, but as an asset class—something you invest in, protect, and compound. What would change?

You might say no to more things—not from fear, but from clarity. You might give fewer explanations—not from arrogance, but from self-possession. You might pursue fewer projects but finish more of them. You might upgrade your habits not to impress others but to preserve your inner state. You might measure wealth not just in financial terms but in the number of decisions made from calm, not chaos.

There are, of course, structural and social factors that complicate this. Not everyone has the privilege to optimise for peace in the same way. Economic insecurity, systemic pressure, and personal trauma all distort access to emotional sovereignty. But even within these constraints, *the pursuit of peace remains a powerful axis of control.* And crucially, it is one of the few forms of wealth that cannot be faked. You can't manufacture peace through branding. You can't perform it into existence. It either lives in your nervous system or it doesn't.

Which is precisely why it's such a potent advantage.

To operate with peace in a culture built on noise is to reclaim a form of sovereignty that transcends the metrics others use to define success. It is to build not just a career, but a life that is internally congruent—where your outer choices don't betray your inner needs. It is to do difficult things without being driven by desperation. It is to grow without distortion.

Peace is not a luxury. It is the original arbitrage. The rare, compounding asset that too few recognise—until they've paid the cost of its absence.

Emotional Cash Flow – Introduces the concept of 'emotional income and debt.

We often measure our well-being through external accounts—bank balances, net worth, income streams. But rarely do we audit the more critical system running behind the scenes: our *emotional cash flow.* Just as a financially solvent person may still collapse under poor liquidity, many high-functioning individuals carry emotional insolvency masked by achievement. They look functional on the outside, but they're financing today's composure with tomorrow's stability.

To thrive over time—especially in a fast-moving world that taxes our attention, identity, and energy—requires more than managing money. It requires *managing mood.* Emotional cash flow is the unseen balance sheet that determines whether our lives are sustainably powered or silently depleting.

This chapter introduces and expands the concept of emotional cash flow: the balance between what replenishes and what drains your internal reserves. When this balance is consistently negative, you're living in *emotional debt.* When it's positive, you're operating from surplus—creative, clear-headed, patient. Like financial liquidity, emotional liquidity gives you margin: the space to navigate difficulty without defaulting into reactivity.

What is Emotional Income?

Think of emotional income as the inner equivalent of earnings—psychological dividends that replenish your energy, improve your outlook, and reinforce your resilience. It's composed of the habits, relationships, and experiences that restore your emotional equilibrium.

Emotional income is generated by:

High-quality relationships where you are seen, not managed.

Creative expression without pressure of performance.

Time in solitude that doesn't demand productivity.

Engaging in work aligned with personal values—not just compensation.

Moments of aesthetic nourishment: beauty, music, deep reading.

Maintaining integrity between thought, word, and action.

This is not self-care in the performative sense—it's not spa days and scented candles unless those things create true psychological restoration. *It is self-structure.* Activities that restore your emotional bank not because they look healthy, but because they align with your specific wiring.

Importantly, emotional income compounds. A single instance of rest might produce marginal benefit, but consistent replenishment builds cognitive reserves, emotional range, and attentional control. Over time, the individual becomes more patient under stress, more discerning in choice, more enduring in pursuit. These are long-term returns rarely acknowledged but deeply felt.

What is Emotional Debt?

By contrast, emotional debt is what you owe your nervous system when you continually operate beyond your recovery threshold. It accumulates slowly—then suddenly. And like credit card interest, it compounds at the worst times.

Emotional debt is incurred when you:

Say "yes" out of guilt and "no" out of fear.

Work past fatigue as a default, not an exception.

Engage in relationships that demand self-abandonment for harmony.

Internalise external expectations until you no longer know what you want.

Let unresolved stress become the backdrop for every decision.

Substitute distraction for rest, and hypervigilance for focus.

Over time, this debt creates distortions: you react too quickly, trust too slowly, interpret feedback as threat. You begin optimising your behaviour not for excellence but for exhaustion management. What should be strategic becomes reactive. What should be thoughtful becomes anxious.

At scale, emotional debt manifests in burnout, cynicism, emotional detachment, and self-sabotage. Like any unsustainable system, it eventually collapses—or demands intervention.

The Invisible Cost of Emotional Leverage

What's particularly insidious is that modern professional culture often rewards those who run on emotional debt. People who sacrifice sleep, suppress emotion, and power through discomfort are praised as "dedicated," "resilient," and "indispensable." The cost, however, is passed onto the future self. It is paid in the form of degraded focus, impaired judgment, relational disconnection, and eventually, lost clarity.

This is where the metaphor of cash flow becomes more precise than mere "mental health." It's not just about crisis—it's about *liquidity.* A person can be mentally functional but emotionally overleveraged. They can appear in control but lack access to creativity, patience, or perspective.

High performers often mistake adrenaline for capacity. But adrenaline is emotional credit. It can fuel short bursts, but not long-term systems. The body and mind demand repayment—with interest.

Tracking Your Emotional Ledger

One of the most practical implications of emotional cash flow is that it can be tracked—not with spreadsheets, but with reflective honesty. The question is not whether you *feel okay* today. The question is: *Are you drawing from reserves or replenishing them?*

Ask:

Which people in your life are net emotional income—and which are net expense?

Which parts of your work are giving you meaning versus extracting energy?

Are you building routines that return you to clarity, or just help you survive the day?

When you rest, do you actually recover—or just escape?

Is your ambition built on replenished energy or borrowed urgency?

These questions do not offer binary answers. Some days you will be in the red. That is natural. The goal is not to feel good all the time. The goal is *to stop normalising permanent emotional overdraft.*

Emotional Resilience as Return on Investment

Once you begin framing your inner world through the lens of cash flow, a powerful shift occurs: you stop treating peace of mind as decorative. You start treating it as *essential capital.* You build systems that protect your capacity. You become more discerning with inputs, more patient with outputs, and more deliberate with commitments.

Resilience, then, becomes less about powering through and more about designing for sustainability. Emotional bandwidth is not just the ability to handle more pressure—it is the ability to recover *faster* and decide *wiser* under stress. This agility—born from surplus, not scarcity—is what gives emotionally solvent individuals their edge.

They are less likely to chase distraction. Less likely to overreact. More likely to pause, wait, and act from signal, not noise.

The Strategic Implications

This concept is not just personally useful—it's strategically transformative. Teams and organisations that understand emotional cash flow begin to manage performance differently. They look beyond output metrics and ask: *What is the emotional infrastructure supporting this team?* Leaders begin to assess not just performance, but *recovery systems*. Culture is no longer measured only in perks, but in emotional architecture.

The world is becoming faster, noisier, and more cognitively demanding. People are not burning out because they're weak. They're burning out because the system assumes *emotional liquidity is infinite*. It is not. And those who ignore this truth will suffer the compound effects of neglect—first in judgment, then in execution, and eventually in direction.

Closing Insight

There is no shame in emotional debt—only in refusing to acknowledge it. And no status is worth holding if it comes at the cost of inner solvency. Emotional cash flow is not soft. It is structural. It is the mental accounting that decides how long you can play the game—and at what cost.

The most enduring form of wealth is the kind that leaves your mind clear, your focus sharp, and your soul unencumbered. That begins with living inside your means—not just financially, but emotionally.

Don't just earn more. Spend wiser. Replenish faster. Invest where your emotional return outpaces the draw. That's the architecture of true resilience—and quiet power.

The Value of Staying Unseen – The Underrated Power of Being Underestimated, Low-Profile, or Working in Silence

Visibility has become the default metric of worth in the modern age. To be known, followed, endorsed, or recognised feels like evidence that one is on the right track. Platforms reward presence. Algorithms favour noise. And we've internalised a belief—often unconsciously—that what isn't broadcasted doesn't matter. But this belief is not only flawed; it's counterproductive to deep work, authentic growth, and long-term resilience.

There is compounding value in being underestimated. Not because one is incapable, but precisely because the world is too distracted by spectacle to notice the slow, deliberate build happening offstage. This subchapter explores a principle that defies the logic of attention-driven culture: sometimes, the greatest strategic advantage is found in remaining low-profile.

The Illusion of Signal

The pressure to be seen often leads to performative urgency. Projects are published before they're polished. Opinions are shared before they're formed. The appearance of progress overtakes the substance of it. Yet visibility, when pursued too early, distorts feedback loops. Instead of refining ideas in quiet, we seek validation in public—and the market responds not to depth but to dopamine.

This dynamic parallels Daniel Kahneman's notion of *substitution*: when people can't measure what matters, they substitute what is measurable. In today's landscape, visibility becomes the measurable proxy for competence. But *signal isn't always insight.* Noise can masquerade as relevance. The most important developments—personally and professionally—often happen in silence.

Underestimation as Strategic Asset

Being underestimated has advantages that high-visibility players often forfeit. The underestimated are not subjected to the same scrutiny, expectation, or interference. They are free to experiment, recalibrate, and fail quietly. They can be underestimated because they are in early stages, or because they have deliberately cultivated ambiguity around their capabilities. Either way, this asymmetry becomes a source of leverage.

Consider Warren Buffett in the 1950s. While other investors rushed to make noise on Wall Street, Buffett operated from Omaha, quietly accumulating value in companies the market had mispriced. His low-profile positioning was not a limitation—it was insulation. It gave him the clarity and autonomy to think long-term without having to manage the distractions of constant external commentary.

Or take the example of author Elena Ferrante, whose global literary acclaim has never been accompanied by public appearances or personal exposure. By choosing anonymity, Ferrante reclaims control of narrative. Her work speaks louder because her presence remains silent. In a culture that equates authorship with personality, she redefines authority as mastery, not identity.

To be unseen is not to be inactive. It is to be strategically protected from the noise that corrodes precision.

The Diminishing Returns of Constant Visibility

Attention is finite. What we give attention to inevitably shapes our internal state. But what's less often discussed is that *being the object of attention is also metabolically expensive.* Research in neuroscience shows that performance anxiety—especially when paired with perceived surveillance—triggers the brain's threat circuitry. Over time, this compromises creativity, problem-solving, and emotional regulation.

Visibility also invites distortion. As public profile increases, so does the likelihood of being misinterpreted. You're no longer simply refining your craft; you're managing perception. You're curating content, anticipating backlash, and adjusting tone. The cognitive load increases while the signal-to-noise ratio decreases.

Moreover, excessive visibility often locks people into identities they've outgrown. A coder becomes an "influencer." A thinker becomes a "thought leader." These labels, however lucrative, can become cages. The unseen are spared this rigidity. They can pivot, reinvent, and deepen their focus without having to announce it.

Staying unseen, then, is not withdrawal. It's choosing depth over performance, clarity over applause.

Why Silence Builds Substance

There is something essential about building without the need to explain. When an artist paints without a gallery in mind, or a founder iterates before pitching to the market, or a scientist experiments before publishing, they are reclaiming a form of internal sovereignty. Their attention is aimed at refinement, not response.

This echoes the Stoic idea of *eudaimonia*—the pursuit of excellence aligned with inner virtue, rather than public acclaim. Marcus Aurelius, despite being Emperor of Rome, wrote privately to himself in *Meditations*, not for fame but for personal clarity. He understood something deeply countercultural: *not everything important needs to be broadcast.*

From a psychological perspective, staying unseen allows for cognitive incubation. Studies on creativity consistently find that periods of quiet, undistracted focus are essential for original insight. The frontal cortex needs room to make novel connections, and that room is often eroded by constant reactive engagement with external stimuli.

Silence is not absence—it is bandwidth reclaimed.

Cultural Pressure vs Individual Strategy

The modern economy rewards exposure. Careers in media, entrepreneurship, or advocacy often require public platforms. Yet even in these fields, the most effective practitioners build leverage privately before deploying it publicly. The mistake is not in being visible—it's in being prematurely visible, or in believing that visibility equals value.

There is a difference between *being known* and *being ready*. One is a marketing strategy. The other is a form of maturity. And maturity can't be fast-tracked by metrics. It must be earned through sustained, unglamorous practice. This is why some of the most enduring creators, leaders, and investors remain invisible until their work is undeniable.

The psychological dimension here is equally crucial. Resilience isn't merely about grit—it's about reducing unnecessary friction. Public validation may feel good temporarily, but it rarely protects against long-term fatigue. What does protect is the ability to create from a space of inner alignment, unpolluted by premature external judgment.

Resilience scales with invisibility, not performance. The more unseen your process, the more unshakeable your foundation.

Reframing the Metrics

What happens if we recalibrate our metrics of success? Instead of reach, we consider retention. Instead of clout, we prioritise clarity. Instead of response, we value refinement. These metrics are harder to measure, but infinitely more durable.

In economics, we speak of *lagging indicators*—metrics that confirm success only after the fact. Quiet progress is one such indicator. By the time someone is publicly celebrated for mastery, the real work has long been completed, often in obscurity.

This applies not just to careers, but to character. The most trustworthy people are often not the loudest. They are the ones who operate with consistency whether or not anyone is watching. They are not chasing exposure, but cultivating integrity.

And in doing so, *they become the kind of person whose absence is noticed more than their noise.*

Conclusion: The Invisible Advantage

To stay unseen is not to opt out—it is to opt in to a different kind of game. One where attention is a resource, not a reward. One where strategy precedes spectacle. And one where the deepest returns—creative, emotional, intellectual—are accrued not in the spotlight, but in the shadows.

In a culture that rewards the loud, the consistent quietly win.

Because in the long run, the most powerful people are not those constantly proving their worth—but those too focused to need to.

Reputation vs Resilience – Challenging the Idea of Chasing Status or Visibility as Validation

Reputation is seductive because it promises stability. The social currency of being admired, applauded, or recognised creates the illusion of security: that if enough people validate us, we become insulated from failure, doubt, or insignificance. Yet beneath this illusion lies a fragile structure. *Reputation is externally granted; resilience is internally earned.* One fluctuates with perception. The other endures with integrity.

This subchapter challenges the pervasive idea that visibility is a proxy for value—and proposes instead that *the most formidable kind of strength is built in the absence of applause.*

The Mirage of Status

Status is a positional good. Its value increases not by what it is, but by what others lack. Social media and digital platforms intensify this dynamic. Visibility becomes gamified: followers, likes, rankings. But these metrics are not objective indicators of worth—they are social mirrors, often warped, reflecting more about the context than the individual.

The chase for reputation subtly distorts behaviour. Individuals begin optimising for appearance rather than substance. The writer tailors their words for virality instead of clarity. The leader chooses consensus over courage. The entrepreneur pivots not for strategic necessity but for market optics.

This shift is not always conscious—but it is corrosive. The more one depends on external validation, the less freedom they have to think, act, or evolve independently.

Reputation, in this frame, becomes a fragile asset: valuable, yet volatile. Resilience, by contrast, is antifragile—it strengthens under pressure.

What Resilience Actually Looks Like

Resilience is often mistaken for mere endurance. But at its core, resilience is *adaptive integrity*. It's the capacity to remain grounded in one's principles, even when outcomes are uncertain and recognition is absent. It is not loud. It doesn't self-promote. It operates on a different axis entirely.

This distinction is exemplified by figures like Angela Merkel, whose chancellorship was marked by restraint, rationality, and unflashy consistency. She was not driven by soundbites or spectacle, but by long-term stewardship—a resilience of thought, not just temperament. Her reputation, ironically, grew because she didn't chase it.

Or consider James Clear, the author of *Atomic Habits*, who spent years building a reputation not through virality but through quiet consistency—writing newsletters, refining his craft, and only publishing a book once the material had been tested, matured, and internalised. He focused on being useful, not visible.

Resilience asks: are you doing the right thing even when nobody is watching? Reputation asks: are you being seen doing the right thing by the right people?

The Psychology of External Validation

From a psychological perspective, reputation taps into a core human need: belonging. We are social creatures. Approval historically meant survival. But this need, when hijacked by modern performance culture, becomes dysregulated. The line between *authentic contribution* and *curated identity* begins to blur.

Psychologist Carl Rogers made a critical distinction between *organismic valuing* and *conditions of worth*. The resilient person develops internal standards for evaluating progress, while the reputation-chaser becomes dependent on external signals for self-worth. Over time, the latter becomes a hostage to perception.

This dependency leads to risk aversion. When one's identity is entangled with status, experimentation becomes threatening. Mistakes must be hidden. Questions must be rehearsed. Vulnerability becomes a liability. The irony, of course, is that true growth—the kind that sustains success—requires exactly those things: error, ambiguity, and risk.

Resilience makes space for failure. Reputation punishes it.

Long-Term Consequences of Status Dependence

Chasing reputation is not just emotionally draining—it's strategically limiting. Careers built on perception can rise quickly, but often collapse under the weight of unmet substance. Think of high-profile entrepreneurs who flame out after hype outruns product. Or public intellectuals whose ideas ossify once they prioritise applause over rigour.

Moreover, reputation dependence leads to *decision distortion*. Leaders who fear backlash compromise clarity. Creators who obsess over their brand dilute originality. Investors who crave peer validation ignore asymmetric opportunities. The more visible one becomes, the more one's choices are constrained by what others expect.

By contrast, resilient individuals cultivate a longer time horizon. They can endure obscurity, contradiction, or disapproval in service of a principle or a vision. They don't need to be agreed with immediately—because they are playing for something more durable than applause.

Reputation bends toward consensus. Resilience bends toward conviction.

Visibility Without Attachment

This is not an argument against visibility. Public presence can be useful, even necessary. But there is a difference between *leveraging visibility* and *needing it to feel real.* The key is detachment.

The Stoics called this *indifference to externals.* One might accept reputation when it arrives, but does not define oneself by it. As Marcus Aurelius wrote, "It is not things themselves that disturb us, but our interpretations of them." To be known and respected is not a problem. To crave it as a substitute for resilience is.

The question becomes: *Can you build in public without being built by the public?*

This orientation protects mental clarity. It allows one to operate with focus in an environment that incentivises distraction. It also guards against burnout. Because when you're no longer performing for status, energy returns to its rightful domain: the work itself.

Legacy vs Optics

One of the most overlooked ideas in modern work culture is the distinction between *momentum* and *trajectory*. Reputation often tracks momentum—short bursts of attention, rapid gains in status. But resilience builds trajectory—a steady arc toward meaningful contribution, regardless of whether it is noticed in real time.

This is why some of the most influential thinkers, scientists, and builders spend the bulk of their lives unrecognised. Their reputations are posthumous. Their resilience, however, was consistent throughout.

In investment terms, resilience compounds silently. Reputation spikes. One is cumulative; the other volatile. The resilient person often looks less impressive day to day—but they are the ones still standing when the market cools, the trends shift, or the spotlight moves on.

Legacy is not crafted by perception but by endurance.

Choosing Your Metrics

What if, instead of chasing status, we tracked internal coherence? What if our progress was measured not in shares or applause, but in the quality of our attention, the rigour of our thought, the integrity of our decisions?

This reframing doesn't negate external recognition. It simply places it where it belongs: downstream of substance, not upstream. It protects us from overvaluing what others think and undervaluing what we know to be true.

Ultimately, *the most resilient people are not the ones who have escaped doubt or pressure—they are the ones who have trained their attention away from noise and toward alignment.*

They do not wait for permission to proceed. They are not auditioning for credibility. They are building it—quietly, precisely, on their own terms.

Chapter 8
Training the Resilience Reflex

Resilience, as it's commonly spoken about, has been oddly mischaracterised. It's paraded as a triumph-over-adversity tale, glorified in the rearview mirror, or mistaken for raw grit—a kind of mental bravado masquerading as virtue. But in truth, resilience isn't reactionary and it certainly isn't performative. It doesn't shout. It doesn't posture. Real resilience is cultivated—a quiet, often invisible discipline. And in an era that mistakes speed for strength and spotlight for substance, perhaps it's time we redefined it: not as a rebound, but as a baseline. A built-in readiness. A stance, rather than a scramble.

This chapter doesn't present resilience as a moment of dramatic comeback. Instead, it offers it as a reflex—somatic, cognitive, and strategic—that can be trained like any other. Because here's the deeper premise: those who possess emotional wealth don't merely recover from setbacks. They've constructed the internal scaffolding to make collapse far less likely in the first place. The way a well-tuned immune system neutralises threats before symptoms show, psychological resilience works upstream. It buffers strain. It metabolises disruption before it metastasises into chaos. And the reason it works isn't mystical—it's methodical.

This is not a chapter about motivational slogans or aesthetic rituals. It's about mechanics. Breathwork, reframing, narrative reengineering—these aren't just passing wellness trends. They are infrastructure. Emotional infrastructure. The same way a strong economy needs liquidity buffers, a healthy mind requires stress buffers—bandwidth, pacing, and pause. What most consider "bouncing back" is often just the visible end of a much quieter process of readiness.

Let's begin, rather deliberately, with breath—the most underused tool in the entire resilience toolkit.

The general association most people have with breathwork is far from helpful. It conjures images of incense, yoga mats, and desperate attempts to self-soothe mid-meltdown. But this view trivialises the breath's actual power. Breathing is one of the very few physiological processes that operates on both the automatic and the voluntary tracks. You can't will your heart to slow or your pupils to dilate. But your breath? That you can command. It is, quite literally, the nervous system's remote control.

Slow, measured breathing moves the body from sympathetic chaos—fight, flight, freeze—into parasympathetic recovery. This isn't spiritual conjecture; it's neurology. It's measurable. A deep exhale recalibrates the amygdala. A steady rhythm extends the perceived duration of time. With training, breath becomes a gateway to cognitive sovereignty—the space between provocation and reaction, the very terrain where wise decisions are made. In a culture that too often mistakes immediacy for authenticity, being able to pause is no small feat. It is, in fact, an act of radical autonomy.

But the breath is just the beginning. True resilience must also be constructed in thought—specifically, through cognitive reframing. Not the sticky-note optimism of internet affirmations, but a grounded discipline drawn from cognitive behavioural science. Reframing is the practice of catching distorted interpretations—those black-and-white narratives, imaginary mind readings, and doomsday projections—and interrogating them. It's not about slapping on a smile. It's about reclaiming precision in perception.

Because when setbacks strike, the brain doesn't simply assess—it stories. And more often than not, it tells poor stories with corrupted data. It fills silence with meaning. It turns neutral feedback into personal indictment. A failed pitch becomes an existential referendum. A delayed text becomes rejection. But resilience lives not in the ability to avoid feeling, but in the decision to question the logic of those feelings. The narrative you assign to an event can compound its damage or diffuse it altogether.

Enter the metaphor: emotional investing. Emotionally resilient people are not unlike long-horizon investors. They don't sell off at the first sign of red. They don't confuse volatility with collapse. When their internal markets dip—when doubt, fear, or shame spike—they don't liquidate their efforts or identity. They hold. They know that discomfort is part of the cycle, not evidence of failure. Reframing becomes their emotional dollar-cost averaging: steady recalibration through every season of the self.

This brings us to a tool far more powerful than it appears: the journal. Not a diary for unfiltered venting, but a structured ledger of patterns, recoveries, and reframed insights. The Resilience Journal makes the ephemeral concrete. It allows you to spot recurring internal narratives, measure your own mental bandwidth, and map the slow accumulation of psychological strength. In short: it gives you receipts. Not inspirational fluff, but your own data—proof of what you once feared and eventually outlived.

Writing externalises thought. It drags vague anxiety into specificity. It slows cognition just enough to make it observable. The sentence "everything is broken" becomes "I missed two deadlines and had a poor night's sleep." This distinction is not academic—it's everything. Specificity enables strategy. You can't plan your way out of chaos until you can name what chaos is.

But perhaps the most counterintuitive insight here is that resilience isn't built through grand transformations. It's built through micro-decisions. One breathing pattern before an interview. One cognitive reframe after a harsh critique. One honest line written down instead of shouted out. These are the reps. This is the work. Not dramatic. Not cinematic. Just relentless in its subtlety.

And that is the paradox of resilience—it is invisible when it's working. It doesn't trend. It doesn't come with badges. It's just there, holding you upright when conditions would buckle someone else. And yes, the resilient are often misread—perceived as naturally calm, lucky, or somehow less affected. But that's the illusion. In reality, they are trained. Not hardened. Not immune. Just practised.

This chapter is your invitation to join that training. To stop looking for inspiration after the crash, and start building insulation before it. Not through bravado. Through breath. Through clarity. Through dozens of quiet returns to centre when no one's watching. Because resilience, when you strip away the myth, is simply this: the ability to respond rather than react, again and again, until it becomes who you are.

Small Waits, Big Shifts

Uses micro-delays in everyday life to train macro-level patience

Patience is not a natural state. It is a trained response. And its true strength is not forged in life's defining moments, but in its smallest ones. While society often spotlights dramatic displays of willpower—finishing a marathon, launching a business, staying silent under provocation—what it overlooks are the *tiny waits* that accumulate silently, shaping our neurological defaults. *Micro-delays*—those fractions of a second or minutes we choose to endure discomfort without resolution—may appear insignificant, but they are the gymnasium in which macro-level patience is built.

In an attention-fractured culture obsessed with immediacy, the ability to delay action—*by even a few seconds*—has become a rare competitive advantage. And unlike talent, charisma, or capital, patience is entirely self-trained. No one is born with it. But everyone pays the price for its absence.

Consider this: the average person checks their phone **96 times per day**—roughly once every ten minutes. Not because the information is urgent, but because the *urge* is. That single act is a tiny surrender. A default to distraction. A conditioned reflex that erodes our capacity for delayed reward. Each time we indulge such urges without resistance, we compound the habit of impatience. Conversely, each time we insert a deliberate pause, we lay a new neural track—one where stimulus does not hijack behaviour.

This is the principle at the heart of *micro-waits*: **consciously introducing small delays into routine actions to expand emotional bandwidth**. Waiting ten extra seconds before opening a notification. Letting someone finish speaking fully before formulating a reply. Choosing the longer queue at the supermarket on purpose. These are not exercises in masochism—they are opportunities to *resist reflexive action*. And they matter more than they seem.

Why? Because the brain is plastic. It adapts not to what we *know* we should do, but to what we *repeatedly practice*. Every pause builds tolerance. Every withheld reaction becomes a vote for a more composed identity. The patience required to stick with a decade-long investment, sustain an unglamorous job, or parent with calm in chaos does not spring fully formed in the moment of need. It has been *pre-loaded into the system*, often without ceremony, in a thousand tiny waits.

The Stoics understood this deeply. Marcus Aurelius wrote not about grand public restraint, but the *daily disciplines* of the mind. "You have power over your mind—not outside events. Realise this, and you will find strength." What is that, if not the architecture of patience? And importantly, he didn't recommend passivity. He recommended control. The kind that can only be developed when one *notices urges*, *names them*, and *chooses not to follow*—at least not immediately.

Modern behavioural science aligns with this ancient insight. Delay discounting—a concept in psychology—refers to our tendency to devalue rewards the longer we have to wait for them. It is the cognitive mechanism behind impulsive decisions and short-termism. Yet research shows that people who develop high delay tolerance not only perform better academically and financially, but also report *greater life satisfaction*. Why? Because they experience their choices as *intentional*, not compulsive.

Micro-waits provide a laboratory for this training. Take, for example, the practice of *Intentional Inconvenience*: deliberately choosing a slower option to recondition your tolerance for delay. Opting for stairs instead of the lift. Handwashing dishes instead of using the dishwasher. Waiting for your thoughts to settle before replying to an inflammatory email. These acts may appear inefficient, even regressive, but they retrain the body and brain to *live without rushing*. And that shift has profound implications for long-term thinking.

In investing, entrepreneurship, and creative work, most breakthroughs arrive not through genius, but through the *willingness to persist through plateaus*. But persistence is not a heroic trait. It is simply the refusal to quit because reality didn't yield fast enough. And that refusal is built—not in crisis—but in the mundane. In waiting for your tea to steep rather than microwaving it. In pausing a beat before hitting "send." In walking past the impulse to interrupt. These are the rehearsal rooms for emotional endurance.

There is also a deeper philosophical question at play here: *what kind of life are we building if we cannot stand to wait?* If every idle moment is treated as a problem to be solved, every silence as something to fill, every delay as a personal affront—then what remains of sovereignty? The person who cannot wait is not free. They are *enslaved by time*. Conversely, the person who can *wait without torment* enjoys a kind of invisible power. They are not dragged by life's momentum; they are *anchored by intention*.

Importantly, micro-waits are not about deprivation. They are about *differentiating urgency from importance.* Just because something can be resolved immediately doesn't mean it should. The compulsion to always close loops, answer fast, move forward, is often a false proxy for effectiveness. In reality, the most patient systems are often the most robust. The oak outlasts the weed not because it grows faster, but because it grows deeper.

In practical terms, cultivating micro-delays can be embedded into daily rituals:

Wait 30 seconds after your phone buzzes before checking it.

Set a timer and sit in silence for one minute before beginning work.

When eating, pause for a breath between each bite.

Ask a question, then count to five before offering your perspective.

These are not spiritual practices. They are neurological strength training. They teach your system that *you are in charge of your impulses*, not the reverse. Over time, this translates into better decision-making in contexts that matter: holding a long-term investment during a volatile cycle; resisting the need to correct someone in conversation; standing firm when progress seems invisible.

The value of micro-waits is not in the delay itself, but in what they *reveal.* Each pause is a mirror. It shows you what you crave, what you fear, and where you default. But more than that, it gives you a choice: *to pause or to proceed; to consume or to consider; to repeat the pattern or redirect it.*

Small waits, practised deliberately, make patience a part of your nervous system—not just your philosophy. And that shift, though subtle, is radical. Because it rewrites the very script of modern life: *You must act fast, or you'll fall behind.* But here's the truth most won't admit: *those who train themselves to wait well rarely fall behind at all—they simply arrive where it matters most, with more clarity, more calm, and far less regret.*

Breathing Through the Breakdown

Integrates breathwork and somatic practices as resilience builders

When breakdown looms—whether in the form of burnout, anxiety, grief, or overwhelming stress—modern culture tends to prescribe intellectual solutions. Analyse the problem. Meditate. Journal. Reframe the thought. But in the heat of emotional dysregulation, words often fail. Thought is hijacked. Logic disappears. The body speaks before the mind can catch up. In such moments, no philosophical insight or motivational quote can anchor a person. What does? The breath.

Breathwork is not simply a wellness fad or spiritual accessory. It is the most immediate and controllable access point to the autonomic nervous system—the very system that governs our fight, flight, freeze, and fawn responses. Long before we think, we feel. And long before we feel, we breathe. Shallowly, rapidly, erratically when stressed. Slowly, deeply, rhythmically when safe. The implication is profound: if we can intentionally change the breath, we can change the body's perception of threat—and thus reclaim agency in moments that would otherwise feel hijacked.

The breath is the bridge between conscious will and unconscious physiology. And like any bridge, it can collapse under disuse or neglect. But it can also be reinforced. This is why elite athletes, trauma therapists, special forces operatives, and contemplative monks all prioritise breath training. Not for mysticism—but for resilience. Because resilience is not the absence of breakdown; it is the capacity to stay online when it hits—to remain anchored, aware, and responsive under pressure.

One of the most robust findings in somatic psychology is that unresolved stress and trauma do not only reside in thought—they embed in the body. They manifest as muscle tension, gut issues, clenched jaws, or shallow breathing patterns that become habitual. Somatic practices—like breathwork, grounding, and interoceptive awareness—retrain the nervous system to complete stress cycles. They help the body remember what safety feels like, not as a concept, but as a felt reality.

Consider a simple, evidence-based technique: **physiological sighing**. Two quick inhales through the nose, followed by a long, slow exhale through the mouth. This pattern, documented by Stanford neurobiologist Dr Andrew Huberman, mimics a natural reflex the body uses to restore calm. Just one or two rounds measurably reduces physiological arousal. It is available at any time, in any place, with no equipment. The ROI? An immediate shift in state—from reactive to responsive. Multiply that over hundreds of high-stress moments, and you are rewiring your resilience baseline.

Or take **box breathing**—four seconds in, four seconds hold, four seconds out, four seconds hold. This method, popularised by Navy SEALs and trauma therapists alike, balances sympathetic and parasympathetic nervous system activity. It cultivates what researcher Stephen Porges calls neuroception of safety—the body's unconscious evaluation of whether it is safe to relax. The goal here is not sedation. It's strategic self-regulation. The kind that allows you to think clearly while others panic.

Crucially, these tools must be trained before the breakdown. Just as a pilot does not learn to fly during a storm, resilience must be rehearsed in calm. A daily breath practice—five minutes in the morning, two minutes before sleep, a few rounds before a stressful meeting—is not a luxury. It is maintenance of the instrument through which you meet life. And it has a compounding effect. Over time, you recover faster. You escalate less. You begin to trust your body to carry you through emotional turbulence without collapse.

Yet breathwork is not a standalone fix. It must be integrated into a broader somatic approach that includes **body awareness**, **movement**, and **release**. Many people live entirely in their heads—narrating, analysing, rehearsing. But resilience lives in the body's memory. Practices like **tension and release exercises**, **tremor work**, or **self-massage** can discharge stored stress and recalibrate the nervous system's sensitivity to triggers. This is not softness. It is precision. A body that is informed, not overwhelmed, becomes a source of stability.

One overlooked method is **orienting**—a trauma-informed practice where you slowly turn your head and eyes to visually scan your environment, noticing what feels pleasant or neutral. This simple act tells the nervous system, "There is no threat here." It interrupts the internal narrative loop of anxiety with sensory information. It is especially useful when you feel "flooded" but cannot access complex cognitive tools.

Critically, these somatic interventions differ from avoidance. They do not suppress emotion. They create the physiological conditions in which emotions can be processed, rather than resisted. They allow grief to move through, anger to be metabolised, fear to dissolve—not by force, but by space. This is the opposite of numbness. It is feeling with capacity.

The long-term payoff of integrating breathwork and somatic practice is not just personal regulation. It is relational resilience. A regulated nervous system becomes a co-regulating force. You model calm. You hold presence. You de-escalate situations simply by not being pulled into their spiral. In workplaces, families, and social systems, these are not soft skills. They are infrastructural assets.

Historical wisdom echoes this truth. The Buddha taught anapanasati—mindfulness of breathing—as the foundation of equanimity. The Stoics trained themselves to pause before judgment, an act rooted in breath. Indigenous cultures used rhythmic movement and breath in ceremony to process collective emotion. Across epochs and geographies, the body has always known what the modern mind forgets: that resilience is not a thought—it is a felt state.

Of course, no technique is a panacea. Some breakdowns require medical, therapeutic, or structural intervention. But what this chapter insists is that we underestimate the foundational role of physiology in every emotional process. We try to out-think what we need to out-breathe. And in doing so, we ignore the most accessible, scalable tool for building endurance under pressure.

To integrate breathwork is not to reject thinking. It is to sequence it correctly. Breath first, then thought. Body first, then behaviour. Only when the nervous system is stable can the mind operate with clarity. This is the sequencing behind all durable performance—whether in leadership, parenting, creative work, or crisis response.

Ultimately, breathing through the breakdown is not about staying calm all the time. It is about learning how to come back—to centre, to clarity, to coherence. That is the essence of resilience. Not brute force. Not emotional stoicism. But somatic fluency: the ability to speak your body's language, to direct its energy, and to return it to balance, again and again, without drama.

In a world that moves fast, collapses often, and rewards reactivity, this is the quiet superpower: a nervous system trained to pause, breathe, and hold steady while the storm passes. And it begins not in crisis, but in practice.

Thought Reframing as Emotional Investing

Teaches cognitive behavioural tools to rewire emotional responses

The modern mind is inundated with data but starved of discipline. We track calories, steps, and spending, yet allow thoughts to roam unchecked—often in loops that deepen anxiety, resentment, or shame. Most people do not suffer from a lack of intelligence, but from a lack of *mental leverage.* They misallocate their emotional energy by reacting to thoughts as if they were facts, then wonder why inner peace remains elusive. In cognitive behavioural terms, this is an investment problem. The question is not "Do I feel this?" but *"What am I emotionally funding by thinking this?"*

Cognitive Behavioural Therapy (CBT), long studied for its clinical efficacy, rests on a deceptively simple premise: *what we think shapes what we feel, which in turn shapes how we act.* But reframing—changing the lens through which we interpret an event or belief—is not about denial or forced positivity. It's about *strategic cognition.* The mind can become either a compounding asset or a draining liability depending on how we train it to appraise situations.

Take, for example, a professional setback—a failed product launch, a missed promotion, a lukewarm review. The automatic thought might be: "I'm incompetent." The corresponding emotion is shame. The behavioural outcome? Withdrawal, avoidance, perhaps even sabotage of future efforts. Now reframe: "This was a useful feedback loop. I now know what doesn't work." The emotion becomes curiosity or resolve. The behaviour shifts to iteration, learning, and growth. Same facts. Different framing. Radically different return on emotional investment.

What distinguishes mature thinkers is not the absence of negative thoughts but the ability to *interrogate them swiftly and precisely.* This is where structured tools—borrowed from clinical psychology but increasingly used in high-performance coaching—come in.

One such tool is the **ABC model**:

A: Activating event

B: Beliefs about the event

C: Consequences—emotional and behavioural

For instance, let's say the activating event is being ignored in a meeting (A). The belief might be: "They don't respect me" (B), leading to frustration or self-doubt (C). But that belief is only one of many plausible interpretations. What if the real cause was distraction, not dismissal? By identifying and challenging that belief, we reclaim agency over the emotional consequence. *We cannot control the event, but we can optimise our interpretive equity.*

Another core CBT tool is **cognitive distancing**. This is not about suppressing thoughts but *de-fusing* from them—seeing them as mental events rather than identities. Instead of thinking, "I am a failure," one practices saying, "I'm having the thought that I'm a failure." It sounds minor. It is not. That small shift creates a wedge of meta-awareness—a pause between thought and belief. Over time, that pause becomes a choice. And choice is the beginning of freedom.

This practice parallels what behavioural economists observe in market psychology. When investors react to short-term volatility as if it were personal catastrophe, they sell in panic. When they reframe the same dip as a long-term buying opportunity, they remain calm—or act strategically. In both cases, the external conditions are constant. *Only the framing changes the outcome.* Emotional investing, then, is not just metaphor—it is mental portfolio management.

There is a growing body of evidence linking thought reframing to measurable physiological changes. A 2012 study by the University of California, Berkeley, found that reframing stress as a challenge rather than a threat reduced cortisol levels and improved performance under pressure. This is not mere psychology—it is *neurobiological rebalancing.* The story we tell ourselves about our situation literally rewires the brain's stress pathways over time.

Reframing also trains us in emotional granularity—the capacity to distinguish between subtly different feelings (e.g., frustration vs. disappointment, anxiety vs. anticipation). This is a crucial resilience skill. A person who says, "I feel bad," remains stuck in vagueness. But a person who says, "I feel discouraged because I interpret this silence as rejection," has already begun to regulate the emotion by specifying its roots. *Naming disarms blaming.*

However, there are conceptual risks to address. Thought reframing is not a call to ignore structural injustice, abuse, or real danger. Nor is it about gaslighting oneself into compliance. The mature use of CBT tools requires *discernment*—knowing when to adjust perspective and when to act externally. Not every problem is an inner narrative. But *every emotional reaction involves one.*

Ethically applied, thought reframing also builds *cognitive empathy.* The ability to understand that someone else's behaviour may reflect their internal lens, not a deliberate affront, prevents escalation and invites compassion. For example: a terse email might not signal hostility but distraction. A lack of praise might not signal disapproval but overwhelm. Reframing, then, is not only intrapersonal—it is relational intelligence.

The long arc of mental resilience hinges on repeated, skillful reframing. Over time, this practice accumulates. Patterns become habits. Habits become mindsets. And mindsets harden into dispositions that *either sabotage or sustain wellbeing.* This is why it's not enough to try reframing once or twice. Like financial investing, the value is in *long-term consistency*. The mind, like a portfolio, responds to compounding.

To that end, many experts advocate for structured mental training in the form of a **thought journal**. Not a passive diary, but an active record of distortions, reappraisals, and emotional outcomes. This form of metacognitive bookkeeping builds a feedback loop. It shows, over time, that the majority of distress comes not from events—but from unexamined assumptions about those events. Journaling, in this context, becomes an *audit of attention.*

Of course, reframing alone is insufficient in cases of clinical depression, complex trauma, or systemic oppression. In such contexts, cognitive tools must be paired with deeper therapeutic or structural work. But for the majority of everyday stressors—conflict, uncertainty, criticism—*the skill of reframing offers a high-leverage intervention.* It interrupts reactive cycles and opens a space for intentionality.

To summarise without summarising: thought reframing is not about silencing your inner critic. It's about becoming *a better fund manager of your inner economy.* It's about directing emotional capital toward beliefs that generate clarity, energy, and adaptive action—and away from those that erode stability or distort truth. It is slow work. But it is sovereign work.

Because once you understand that *your thoughts are not your identity, but your instruments*, you stop being a passenger to emotion and become an investor in resilience. And that kind of mental wealth pays dividends for life.

The Resilience Journal – Encourages readers to document their struggles, rebounds, and growth

We chronicle what we care about. Diaries document love and loss. Spreadsheets track investments. Medical charts record the body's vulnerabilities. Yet when it comes to one of the most crucial forms of long-term capital—our emotional endurance—most people leave no trail. They feel pain, navigate setbacks, occasionally recover, but rarely observe how. *Without recording resilience, we risk forgetting that we ever had it at all.*

This is where the practice of resilience journaling becomes not just reflective, but strategic. It is not about nostalgia, or self-indulgent introspection. It is a performance tool—a method for increasing emotional liquidity, cultivating narrative control, and identifying strength patterns that are invisible in real time. For intelligent professionals and long-term thinkers, the capacity to rebound is not a soft skill; it is a decisive edge. And like any edge, it sharpens with use.

Resilience is often mistaken as an innate trait: a static quality you either have or lack. In truth, it's a *process*—a behavioural loop of shock, assessment, adaptation, and re-engagement. But this loop is noisy and forgettable unless captured. The Resilience Journal converts the transient into the trackable. It gives structure to struggle. Not to romanticise hardship, but to metabolise it into insight.

To grasp its power, consider the cognitive science of retrieval practice. We know from decades of research in learning theory that writing things down—especially when prompted by tension, discomfort, or novelty—enhances recall, pattern recognition, and adaptive thinking. When people reflect on how they overcame previous breakdowns, their tolerance for ambiguity and pressure increases. That's not motivational fluff. That's neuroplasticity in action.

The stoic philosophers understood this centuries ago. Epictetus instructed students to write nightly summaries of where their intentions wavered or held. Marcus Aurelius's *Meditations* remains one of the most enduring case studies in written resilience—a battlefield general chronicling emotional discipline in the margins of imperial chaos. These weren't academic musings. They were self-correction mechanisms. The written word kept the inner compass calibrated.

Modern-day equivalents exist but often fall short. Gratitude journaling, for example, tends to flatten complexity. It encourages bypassing discomfort with affirmation. The Resilience Journal, by contrast, doesn't avoid friction—it frames it. It invites you to chart not only what hurt or failed, but *how you responded.* What resources did you reach for? What emotional narratives surfaced? What got tested—ego, identity, endurance? And perhaps most critically: What are you tempted to forget now that the crisis has passed?

Let's take a real-world example. Consider the recovery arc of a senior executive during the 2020 pandemic—a time when markets tanked, organisations froze, and uncertainty reigned. She began a nightly log, tracking not her wins or goals, but her stressors, responses, and decisions under fire. Within three months, she noticed a pattern: her decision quality improved when she journaled after conflict, not before bed. She shifted her routine, integrated breathing techniques post-entry, and refined her strategic clarity across teams. The journal didn't just record her leadership. It *shaped* it.

Another case involves a trauma therapist who uses a resilience journal during her own supervision process. Working with high-intensity clients, she found herself absorbing emotional residue—what psychologists term *vicarious trauma.* By using a structured prompt system in her journal (e.g., "What part of this session stayed with me?" or "What is unresolved in me?"), she improved both her boundary clarity and emotional recovery rate. Her journal wasn't reflective. It was *preventative care.*

The concept also has applications outside the helping professions. A quietly consistent investor—known for decades of compounding returns—uses a post-decision journaling technique to track emotional states before and after trades. Not the numbers, but the *narratives*: what headlines influenced his mood, what biases surfaced, what doubts he ignored or validated. Over time, this led to a profound realisation: most of his worst trades came not from analytical error, but from emotional impatience. His resilience journal became a volatility barometer—not for markets, but for his own mental state.

All three examples point to a critical insight: *tracking your responses to pressure creates a compounding advantage*. This is not just about remembering what happened, but detecting the micro-adjustments that build emotional capital. Much like financial journaling reveals cash leaks and investment patterns, a resilience journal uncovers the habits that quietly save—or sabotage—your future self.

Yet the real strength of a resilience journal lies not just in what it captures, but in how it teaches you to observe differently. In high-pressure contexts—whether professional, relational, or existential—most people default to one of two strategies: suppression or rumination. Suppression avoids the issue, rumination amplifies it. Journaling offers a third path: *integration*. It neither dismisses discomfort nor wallows in it. It dissects it. This act of structured self-observation interrupts the emotional feedback loop and creates enough distance to respond rather than react.

Cognitive behavioural therapy (CBT) offers a useful parallel. A foundational CBT tool is the thought record—a structured way of identifying distortions, separating emotion from evidence, and reframing narratives. The Resilience Journal builds on this logic, but personalises it. Instead of fitting your experience into a clinical form, it invites you to design a framework that reflects your real-world context. Over time, your entries reveal not just isolated moments of tension, but *patterns of recovery*—which thoughts regulate you, which derail; which environments nourish, which deplete.

For sceptics, especially those in high-stakes or highly rational professions, journaling can appear unscientific or inefficient. But this resistance often stems from a false dichotomy between emotional insight and strategic rigour. In reality, the two reinforce each other. A well-kept resilience journal is not emotional indulgence—it is executive function in narrative form. It tracks your behavioural data, organises your decision loops, and builds a personalised archive of stress-tested wisdom. The time spent journaling is not time away from performance—it is investment in *repeatable clarity*.

There is also a long-term benefit most people miss: *emotional continuity*. When life gets difficult—when crises overlap or setbacks compound—it's easy to lose faith in one's ability to rebound. That's where the journal becomes more than a tool. It becomes *evidence*. Evidence that you've been here before. That you've suffered before. That you've handled worse, or harder, or longer than what now feels impossible. This is not nostalgia. It's statistical reinforcement of your capacity to endure.

In this way, the resilience journal performs a quiet but radical function: it *externalises memory in service of inner strength*. We don't remember accurately under stress. We inflate failures and forget recoveries. The journal preserves fidelity. It brings past evidence to the present moment. It says, "You made it through *that*—you are not as fragile as you feel."

Some practitioners add a forward-facing element to their journals—what might be called preemptive resilience. This means recording *future stress simulations*: projecting potential stressors and pre-writing possible responses. For example, a founder anticipating an investor dispute might journal, "If X challenges my integrity, I will breathe twice, pause for ten seconds, and respond with data, not defensiveness." These entries don't guarantee control. But they *prepare the nervous system* by rehearsing regulation. This is psychological antifragility in action—turning the unknown into a domain you've already visited on paper.

For those wondering how to begin, there is no perfect format. Some use dated entries with consistent prompts ("What happened?" / "What did I feel?" / "What did I do?" / "What would I repeat or revise?"). Others prefer free-form narrative. Some use it daily, others weekly, still others only during volatility spikes. The method matters less than the *intention*: not to vent, but to study.

One powerful technique is what resilience researchers call *delayed decoding*. This involves writing the raw experience when it's fresh—but revisiting and annotating it days or weeks later. That annotation process reveals growth markers that were invisible during the heat of the moment. Over time, this cultivates metacognitive distance—one of the core pillars of mental resilience.

This practice also enhances self-trust. As entries accumulate, the journal becomes a mirror of integrity. It shows how often you told the truth under pressure. How often you stayed composed or recalibrated quickly. That record, built over months or years, becomes its own form of capital—a kind of *psychological net worth* that few people ever audit.

By capturing breakdowns and breakthroughs alike, the Resilience Journal reframes struggle as signal, not noise. It teaches the reader that setbacks are not anomalies to be erased but *case studies in capability*. The longer you maintain the practice, the more the journal evolves—from a place of solace to a system of strength.

And here lies the deeper insight: *growth is only as visible as your record of it.* Without the Resilience Journal, your progress may remain perceptual—felt but not proven. With it, your growth becomes measurable, reviewable, and—perhaps most powerfully—*reusable.*

This is not a sentimental hobby. It is strategic memory. It is the architecture of endurance. And for those committed to sustainable, long-term performance—financial, emotional, or otherwise—it may be the most underutilised tool of all.

Chapter 9
Resilience in Relationships

Human relationships—romantic, familial, collegial, or platonic—remain one of the most potent arenas for emotional volatility and psychological evolution. Yet, curiously, they are often the least rigorously examined. We dissect markets, habits, and health with surgical precision, but when it comes to how we relate to others, the conversation often dissolves into sentiment or cliché. This chapter resists that drift. It begins not by bemoaning the difficulty of relationships—that's already been conceded—but by offering something rarer: a case for relational resilience as a legitimate, measurable form of wealth. As consequential as your bank balance. As strategic as your investment plan.

To engage deeply with this idea is to consider a truth both simple and profound: our emotional operating system—complete with its triggers, blind spots, belief structures, and boundaries—doesn't just influence how we love and connect. It shapes how we live. Who we draw in. Who we keep out. Who we become in proximity to others. And, by extension, whether we flourish or fracture in the process.

This is not, to be clear, a chapter about how to "fix" your partner, manage difficult parents, or network more effectively. It is not relationship advice dressed up in new language. What we're exploring is relational infrastructure—the unseen framework that supports or sabotages connection. How we metabolise discomfort in close quarters. How we express need without collapsing into neediness. How we hold tension without issuing ultimatums, and repair ruptures without defaulting to either denial or domination. These are not "soft skills." They are adult competencies. And in their absence, even the most sincere love or friendship can become unsustainable.

Let's start with a proposition that might feel slightly disorienting at first: what if your relationship with intimacy mirrors your relationship with money? That isn't a metaphor, it's a diagnostic. People who compulsively hoard affection often do the same with savings—guarding what they fear will never be replenished. Those who overspend on emotion—who offer too much, too fast—frequently overextend themselves financially as well. The dynamics echo: risk appetite, emotional liquidity, crisis responses. Even status-seeking in love can parallel the pursuit of wealth for recognition rather than sovereignty. Both spheres demand discernment, boundaries, and delayed gratification—skills not often taught but always required.

Seen this way, emotional wealth becomes a system of deposits and leaks. Trust, clarity, and self-regulation accrue compound interest over time. But just as financial health can be eroded by chronic micro-spending, emotional dignity is often lost in a thousand small self-betrayals: the nods when we mean no, the silences we endure in lieu of truth, the appeasements that trade authenticity for approval. Relational resilience, then, is not simply the ability to endure. It's the ability to hold one's shape. To remain principled and present in the emotional furnace—not by armouring up, but by refusing to disown oneself in the name of keeping the peace.

This brings us to the gap—the ever-critical space—between reaction and repair. It is a slim moment, barely perceptible at times, but decisive. It is the pause between feeling triggered and acting on it. That pause is where relationship maturity either deepens or disintegrates. Stretching it takes practice. Using it takes courage. Because inside that breath is the choice to ask: Is this response coming from an old wound or a current reality? Am I speaking to my partner, or to a ghost of someone who once hurt me? Is this reaction serving resolution or simply discharging discomfort?

Make no mistake: this pause is not about suppression. It's not a call to freeze or defer feeling. It's a move toward sovereignty. A way of reclaiming authorship over your own emotional experience rather than letting it be dictated by external stimuli. Those who learn to pause—just long enough—are less likely to make emotionally expensive choices. They're less inclined to burn bridges they still need, or surrender dignity for the illusion of control. And the implications go beyond romance or conflict resolution. Regulating your emotional state is a foundational wealth-building move. Because impulse is costly. Reflection compounds.

We must also speak, unapologetically, about boundaries—not as brittle defences, but as elegant systems for protecting energy, values, and emotional liquidity. Too often, boundaries are misunderstood as emotional shutdowns or power plays. In reality, they are expressions of clarity. They define what we can responsibly sustain and what we cannot afford to underwrite with our time, attention, or nervous system. A healthy boundary says, "This is the cost of admission to my presence. This is the condition for my continued generosity." Not as a threat, but as a principle. Like a prudent investor managing exposure to high-volatility assets, the emotionally resilient person calibrates their availability in accordance with reality—not fantasy.

Boundaries are not designed to keep people out. They're built to keep integrity in. They don't kill intimacy—they purify it. They ensure that closeness is not earned through erosion, but through mutual coherence.

Much of what we'll examine here involves dismantling inherited scripts—those subconscious instructions we absorbed before we had the tools to challenge them. Scripts that taught us to conflate people-pleasing with kindness. That rewarded emotional contortionism and called it loyalty. That blurred the line between vulnerability and self-erasure. We'll ask better questions: Can I love someone deeply without becoming their emotional mule? Can I offer forgiveness without abandoning accountability? Can I stay in connection without losing my centre?

And no, resilience doesn't mean going it alone. True emotional sovereignty isn't a call to isolation—it's the gateway to genuine interdependence. A space where mutuality can thrive without manipulation. Where love is extended without ledger. Where walking away isn't a tantrum but a tender recognition of limits. This is what makes resilient relationships not just possible, but deeply rewarding. They don't hinge on perfection. They rely on presence. They survive friction not because the participants never err, but because they know how to course-correct without burning down the foundation.

Resilience in relationship isn't staying at any cost. It's staying aligned. It's knowing how to repair without self-abandonment and how to exit without turning history into blame. It's about choosing connection from strength, not desperation. Choosing to remain open even after disappointment, to set a boundary without a need to punish, to invest slowly and with discernment rather than sprint toward intensity just to feel alive.

This isn't about being emotionally unshakeable. It's about becoming emotionally fluent. And that fluency translates directly into every other domain of life. When we know how to stay centred in conversation, we're better negotiators. When we can absorb emotional ambiguity without collapse, we make more thoughtful decisions. When we no longer mistake intensity for intimacy, we stop investing in short-term highs and start cultivating long-term returns.

So, no, this is not relationship advice. This is a reckoning. A blueprint. A call to those who understand that relationships are not peripheral to wealth—they are the crucible in which our deepest values are tested, refined, and expressed. The world might urge you to optimise for chemistry, convenience, or performance. But inner wealth? It asks for something more rare: character, coherence, and the courage to stay open when staying open feels like risk.

Hard? Yes. But so is emotional bankruptcy.

Let's build with care.

The Patience to Listen – How Emotional Resilience Makes for Better Partners, Parents, and Friends

We often assume that listening is a passive act—the mere absence of talking. But true listening, the kind that forges trust, diffuses conflict, and affirms another's humanity, is among the most active, taxing, and *resilient* skills a person can develop. It requires more than silence. It requires the strength to withhold judgement, the discipline to remain present, and the humility to place understanding above control. In this sense, *listening is not something we do after we've mastered our emotions—it's how we master them.*

Emotional resilience—the ability to stay internally steady in the face of external volatility—is what makes sustained listening possible. Without it, we don't hear; we defend. We don't absorb; we rehearse our counterpoints. We don't witness another person; we scan for threat, disrespect, or inconvenience. It is only when we are not hijacked by our own emotional circuitry that we can afford to open space for someone else's truth, even when it's uncomfortable, unfamiliar, or inconvenient.

This article explores the high-return utility of patient listening in the architecture of strong relationships. We will examine why most people don't listen, what emotional regulation has to do with attentiveness, and how cultivating this underappreciated form of restraint can change the texture of intimacy across all domains—romantic, parental, professional, and social. Our goal is not to romanticise listening, but to treat it as a *strategic and ethical imperative* in the practice of resilient living.

Let's begin with a critical observation: *most listening is performance, not presence.* What passes for listening in modern discourse—whether in couples' therapy, boardrooms, or social media comments—is often a proxy for waiting. Waiting for the other to finish, waiting for one's chance to speak, waiting for a confirmation of one's biases. The root problem is not impatience; it is ego fragility. When a person lacks the emotional resilience to tolerate ambiguity, contradiction, or discomfort, they substitute interpretation for attention. They listen not to understand but to regain psychological control.

This inability to stay present during another person's expression—especially when the content feels like criticism, rejection, or an ideological threat—explains why so many conflicts escalate. *The emotionally untrained mind treats any tension as an attack.* Resilient listening, by contrast, operates on a different premise: that *not every difficult statement is a demand for agreement; some are invitations for understanding.* That distinction is what allows resilient people to stay open when others shut down.

The implications for relationships are profound. In romantic partnerships, for instance, miscommunication is not the main threat to connection—defensiveness is. Consider how many arguments begin with one partner expressing frustration, only to be met with counterarguments, historical grievances, or emotional withdrawal. What's often missing is a moment of attuned stillness: the capacity to hear the full content of someone else's pain without rushing to contextualise, correct, or collapse. This is not about being a doormat. It's about being a durable witness.

Resilient listening does not mean abandoning boundaries. It means having boundaries *so well-defined* that one does not need to react impulsively to discomfort. It means recognising that another person's emotional state is not a referendum on one's adequacy. The emotionally fragile partner panics at every sigh, interprets feedback as betrayal, and demands emotional precision from others as a condition of stability. The resilient partner *absorbs nuance without personalising everything*—not because they are indifferent, but because they are grounded.

In parenting, the stakes are even higher. Children are not yet skilled at regulating their inner worlds. When they cry, protest, act out, or shut down, they are communicating through raw, unrefined signals. The parent who lacks emotional resilience will interpret these behaviours as threats to their authority or evidence of failure. They will either clamp down with excessive control or collapse into emotional over-identification. Both responses short-circuit the child's development of self-trust.

By contrast, the emotionally grounded parent listens first—not because the child is always right, but because *being heard precedes learning.* When children feel seen and safe, they are more likely to internalise boundaries, adapt to correction, and cultivate their own resilience. But this requires the parent to tolerate emotional noise without rushing to fix it. *Listening in this context is not permissiveness—it is containment without coercion.*

In friendships, patient listening is a form of emotional capital. We often underestimate the extent to which people are starving for uninterrupted attention. In a culture that confuses performance for connection and speed for competence, simply *being the person who listens with full presence* is an irreplaceable gift. It is also an investment: the relationships that yield long-term emotional dividends are built not on novelty or convenience, but on the rare experience of being fully received.

But what allows someone to become a skilled listener in the first place? The answer is not found in communication techniques or active listening scripts. It is found in *emotional bandwidth.* Put simply: you cannot hear someone else clearly if you are busy surviving your own reactions. Resilient listening begins with nervous system regulation—whether through breathwork, mindfulness, or simply self-awareness. When the body is in a state of sympathetic arousal, everything sounds like danger. Every opinion becomes a battle. Every request becomes an imposition.

The listener must learn to become an *emotional regulator, not a re-enactor.* That is, rather than reflexively mirroring the emotional intensity of others, they hold space for it without absorbing it. This is not a stoic suppression of empathy. It is the creation of psychological safety. It tells the speaker: "You are allowed to feel, and I do not need to control, defend, or fix it to stay intact."

It is here that we encounter one of the deeper truths of emotional resilience: *the most powerful people are not those who dominate conversation, but those who do not need to.* They are the ones who can sit in silence without signalling withdrawal. Who can absorb another's distress without retaliating. Who can remain inwardly still while bearing witness to someone else's storm. This is not emotional weakness. This is what *emotional wealth* looks like.

Critically, this kind of listening does not imply agreement. It is possible to listen with full presence and still maintain disagreement, dissent, or divergent values. Resilience is what allows that differentiation to feel safe. Fragility demands consensus. Resilience makes room for multiplicity. In difficult conversations—about race, politics, identity, history, hurt—this skill is non-negotiable. *It is the precondition for collective coherence.*

The consequences of poor listening are not just interpersonal—they are systemic. Workplaces, communities, even entire societies fracture not because people disagree, but because people feel unheard. Policies collapse when leaders do not listen. Marriages dissolve when needs go unacknowledged. Children rebel not because they are defiant, but because they are misinterpreted. The repair begins not with better messaging, but with better receiving.

In sum, listening is not soft. It is structural. It is a method of engagement that requires clarity, stamina, and restraint. It is how we teach others they are safe. It is how we de-escalate emotional volatility. And it is how we hold the complexity of relationships without simplifying, avoiding, or overpowering them.

Listening is not the reward for resilience. *It is the training ground for it.*

This subchapter invites the reader to treat listening not as an afterthought or add-on, but as *an advanced form of emotional mastery.* We will examine the psychology behind reactivity, the neuroscience of attunement, and the practical ways we can cultivate the discipline to stay still long enough to let another person *exist fully in our presence.* That is the goal—not agreement, not appeasement, not even resolution. Just the radical, patient, generous act of letting someone else be seen.

Because the world doesn't change when we all talk louder. It changes when we learn to listen better.

Emotional Maturity in Love and Money – How Relationships Often Mirror Our Financial Attitudes

There is an unspoken ledger running through every close relationship—not a tally of deeds or affections, but a deeper psychological accounting system, tracking expectations, security, freedom, and control. When studied closely, the emotional patterns that shape how we love and the psychological patterns that shape how we handle money often turn out to be the same. *Emotional maturity and financial maturity are not just correlated; they are often cognitively and behaviourally indistinguishable.* The degree to which a person can tolerate uncertainty, delay gratification, manage anxiety, and invest in long-term outcomes shows up—almost identically—in both their bank statements and their intimate relationships.

This chapter explores the profound overlap between our emotional intelligence and financial behaviours—not as a metaphor, but as a functional mirror. We are not interested in cheap analogies ("money is love" or "emotions are currency"). We are interested in what the evidence, from psychology to behavioural economics, tells us about the ways *our internal emotional architecture predicts our capacity to partner, parent, earn, spend, and save wisely.*

At the centre of this exploration is the principle that *security is an inside job.* People who chase emotional security externally—through over-earning, controlling partners, or avoiding conflict—often replicate the same patterns in their romantic and financial lives. For example, the person who fears abandonment may hoard resources and affection alike, not out of malice, but because they equate closeness with volatility. The person who overspends impulsively often loves with a similar intensity—lavish, immediate, but lacking future-consciousness.

Take attachment theory as a starting point. Anxious attachment—characterised by emotional hypervigilance and fear of rejection—often manifests financially as under-saving, over-dependence, or financial enmeshment with others. Avoidant attachment—marked by discomfort with intimacy—frequently correlates with hyper-independence, over-saving, or controlling financial behaviours. Neither are financial disorders per se; they are *emotional strategies for managing fear*, repurposed in fiscal domains.

What this means is that asking someone about their relationship to money is not just a practical question—it's diagnostic. It tells us about their relationship to uncertainty, risk, and trust. It reveals whether they treat the future as a place to fear or to prepare for. And perhaps most importantly, it exposes whether they view resources (emotional or monetary) as tools for mutual enrichment or as instruments of control.

This is not abstract theory. In couples' therapy, financial conflict is among the top predictors of long-term dissatisfaction, not because money is inherently divisive, but because it is symbolically loaded. *Money decisions are rarely just about money.* They are about identity, control, self-worth, legacy, and power. A disagreement about a budget is often a disagreement about values. A dispute over spending may be a proxy war about autonomy or visibility. And decisions about joint accounts, debt, or saving are often veiled commentaries on trust and future commitment.

The emotionally mature partner understands that their financial stance is part of a broader relational ecosystem. They recognise that frugality can sometimes be a disguise for fear, that generosity can mask guilt, and that independence can be a defence against vulnerability. Rather than moralise these behaviours, they interrogate them. They ask: *What emotional script am I following? Where did I learn to associate love with sacrifice, or success with suffering?*

Consider the phenomenon of financial infidelity—a term used to describe the concealment of spending, debt, or financial choices from a partner. This is rarely about greed. More often, it is about shame. Shame around inadequacy, fear of judgement, or unmet needs. These are the same emotional undercurrents that drive secrecy and disconnection in romantic dynamics. *The betrayal is not the money; the betrayal is the breach of emotional transparency.*

Conversely, we also see how financial maturity reinforces relational health. The capacity to delay gratification—to invest in long-term goals, resist short-term temptations, and make uncomfortable but necessary choices—mirrors the emotional discipline needed to weather relational tension without emotional impulsivity. Saving is a form of patience. Budgeting is a form of boundary-setting. Negotiating shared financial goals is a form of communication. In this light, *money becomes a feedback loop for emotional development.*

Importantly, this discussion is not about how much money one has. Wealth does not confer maturity. Some of the most emotionally chaotic individuals possess great material affluence, while some of the most grounded, secure people live modestly. *The issue is not quantity, but orientation.* Does a person use money to avoid, control, impress, or escape? Or do they treat it as a neutral resource for intentional living?

A striking example can be found in the rising popularity of financial independence movements—those who choose to live below their means, invest early, and opt out of hyper-consumerist cultures. On the surface, these may look like financial strategies. But underneath, they often reflect *deep emotional maturity*: the willingness to live with less today for the sake of more freedom and flexibility tomorrow. The same principle applies to emotionally resilient partners, who can endure temporary discomfort in a relationship without resorting to blame or withdrawal.

There is also a gendered layer to this discourse. Women, historically underpaid and socially conditioned to associate worth with giving rather than keeping, often experience complex intersections between love and money. The expectation to nurture can manifest financially in undercharging, over-giving, or self-sacrificing behaviour. Men, conversely, are often socialised to derive self-worth from financial provision, which can create emotional suppression, overworking, or transactional attitudes in romantic settings. Both patterns reveal how *emotional immaturity, shaped by cultural programming, expresses itself through fiscal behaviours*.

The solution is not to demonise money or idealise emotionality. The goal is integration. Emotional maturity in love and money requires a dual capacity: to self-regulate in the face of tension, and to collaborate across difference. It means bringing awareness to the hidden scripts we inherited about worth, risk, and control. It means asking uncomfortable questions—about who we're trying to impress, what we're trying to compensate for, and whether we're using spending, saving, or sharing as stand-ins for intimacy.

Practically speaking, emotional maturity in this domain can look like:

– Talking about money without shame or aggression
– Making decisions collaboratively, not unilaterally
– Being honest about limitations without defensiveness
– Respecting the autonomy of each partner while still planning jointly

- Recognising that love does not require self-abandonment, nor does money guarantee emotional safety

These are not relationship hacks. They are *personal disciplines with systemic consequences.* Emotional maturity ripples outward: it creates more honest partnerships, more secure families, and more humane economic interactions. It allows couples to disagree without demeaning, to plan without coercing, and to see resources not as tests of loyalty but as shared stewardship.

Ultimately, love and money are both mirrors. They reflect back the stories we tell ourselves about value, control, and worthiness. If those stories remain unexamined, they play out unconsciously—through overspending, chronic resentment, or subtle emotional blackmail. But if we bring awareness to them, if we name and question the inherited scripts, we gain something priceless: the ability to love and live with clarity.

Because emotional maturity isn't what we bring once things are stable. It's what creates stability in the first place.

The Space Between React and Repair – The Unrecognised Power of the Pause

The difference between a conversation that escalates into rupture and one that deepens connection often comes down to just a few seconds—a breath not taken, a pause not held, a reflex not questioned. In the heat of relational tension, our biology demands reaction. It's fast, self-protective, and rooted in ancient neural pathways. Yet, in the context of modern relationships, this speed becomes a liability. *Maturity does not lie in suppressing our impulses, but in expanding the space between them and our actions.*

This article examines the strategic and emotional utility of the *pause*: that small but potent window between stimulus and response, where resilience, respect, and repair are made possible. Rather than viewing the pause as passive or avoidant, we frame it as a learned discipline—one that strengthens our capacity to self-regulate under pressure, communicate with clarity, and build trust even during moments of conflict.

Psychologists, neuroscientists, and behavioural theorists all converge on one truth: *the nervous system does not distinguish easily between emotional and physical threat.* When we feel criticised, ignored, or rejected, our body reacts as if it were endangered. This response, often labelled "amygdala hijack", shifts the brain's control centre from the reflective prefrontal cortex to the defensive limbic system. In this state, logic is impaired. Empathy is inaccessible. Language deteriorates into blame, silence, or escalation.

Yet the greatest irony of emotional maturity is that it is often most invisible when most important. The person who pauses before responding may look passive or disengaged. But internally, they are often performing the cognitive equivalent of heavy lifting: regulating heart rate, suppressing retaliatory urges, organising incoherent emotions into coherent speech. This is *not detachment—it is depth control.*

Real-world relationships offer countless examples. Consider a disagreement between spouses over a financial decision. One partner says, "You're always so irresponsible with money," triggering a spike in the other's cortisol levels. A typical reaction might be defensiveness—"At least I'm not stingy like you"—followed by a back-and-forth spiral that ends in mutual resentment. But a well-timed pause—perhaps a breath, a few seconds of silence, or even a simple, "Give me a moment to think about that"—interrupts the escalation cycle. *That pause is not retreat; it is preparation.* It creates space to choose response over reaction.

From a neuroscientific lens, this is a form of re-routing. Instead of allowing the limbic system to dictate the outcome, the pause recruits the prefrontal cortex—the seat of planning, empathy, and meaning-making. In this sense, *the pause is neurobiologically radical.* It reverses centuries of evolutionary programming that equates immediacy with survival. By pausing, we are not just being polite—we are resisting our most primal wiring.

This also explains why children and emotionally immature adults often struggle in conflict: they do not yet possess the inner scaffolding to delay expression. Their words arrive before their meaning is fully formed. Their tone precedes intention. They collapse the space between stimulus and response, because they haven't learned to inhabit it. Emotional resilience, then, is not just about bouncing back from adversity—it is about *sustaining internal composure during micro-adversities*, the everyday interpersonal frictions that demand our presence without triggering our defences.

In leadership, the same principles apply. A manager who reacts swiftly to criticism from a team member may assert authority in the short term but lose credibility and morale in the long run. The leader who pauses, listens, and reflects—who *chooses to interpret criticism as data, not disrespect*—models a form of psychological safety that no corporate policy can replicate. The best communicators are not necessarily the most articulate, but the most attuned to timing.

Culturally, the pause has been underestimated because of its invisibility. In a productivity-obsessed world, silence is often mistaken for stagnation. Yet silence between two people, if held with intentionality, can be a form of attunement. The pause is not the absence of communication—it is a higher-order form of it. It says: *I care enough about this interaction to slow it down. I choose not to treat this conversation as a threat.*

The concept of the pause is also integral to many contemplative traditions. In Buddhist psychology, the moment between impulse and action is where mindfulness lives. In Stoic thought, the discipline of assent—the idea that not every impression must lead to assent or action—is central to emotional freedom. Viktor Frankl, the Austrian psychiatrist and Holocaust survivor, put it succinctly: *"Between stimulus and response there is a space. In that space is our power to choose our response. In our response lies our growth and our freedom."*

The challenge, of course, is how to operationalise the pause. Telling someone to "just pause" in the middle of an argument is like telling someone to swim while they're drowning. It requires training—both physiological and psychological. Breathwork can help, particularly techniques that engage the vagus nerve and signal safety to the nervous system. Somatic awareness—tracking where tension sits in the body—can make us aware of our early warning signs. And journaling after conflict can create cognitive maps for recognising recurring triggers, so that future pauses become more accessible.

There's also an important ethical layer here. The pause is not just self-protective. It is *relationally generous.* It prevents us from saying things we can't take back. It gives others the dignity of being heard rather than interpreted. And perhaps most crucially, it gives us a chance to repair. Because no matter how self-aware we become, rupture is inevitable. We will misspeak. We will misread. The question is not whether conflict arises, but *how quickly and honestly we return from it.*

Repair is not a technique. It is an outcome made possible by the pause. The ability to say, "I overreacted," "I need to understand you better," or "Let me try again"—these are statements that *require ego deactivation.* And ego, when triggered, does not deactivate on its own. It needs time. Space. A deceleration of the nervous system. The pause is not just an interruption of reactivity—it is the foundation of reparation.

Consider how this shows up in parenting. A parent whose child defies them may feel disrespected and respond harshly, framing the behaviour as a moral failing. But a pause allows the parent to ask a better question: *What is my child feeling right now that they don't yet know how to express?* From this position, discipline can be firm without being punitive. Boundaries can be enforced without emotional withdrawal. *The pause, in this context, is what keeps correction connected to care.*

At a societal level, the inability to pause is evident in our cultural discourse. Political polarisation, online outrage cycles, and collective fragility all stem from the erosion of interpretive space. Nuance dies in the absence of delay. When everyone is reacting in real time, no one is reflecting. No repair is possible when the entire culture runs on limbic fuel. Relearning how to pause, then, is not just a private practice. It is a cultural corrective.

To be clear, the pause is not a blank cheque for avoidance. It is not silence as manipulation, nor disengagement disguised as maturity. The point is not to *withhold*, but to *withstand*—to hold space for discomfort without collapsing or retaliating. To remain in contact with the other, even while buying time for internal coherence.

In practical terms, this might look like saying:

– "I'm noticing I'm getting defensive—can we pause for a moment?"
– "This conversation matters. I want to get grounded before we continue."
– "I'm not ready to respond well right now, but I want to come back to this."

These are not evasions. They are signs of a person who respects the relationship enough to engage with clarity, not chaos.

The most resilient people are not those who never react—but those who have trained themselves to *interrupt the chain reaction.* They honour the space between feeling and speaking, between offence and response, between rupture and repair. And it is within this space that integrity, healing, and trust quietly accumulate.

Because the pause is not what happens when we stop responding. It's what allows us to respond from the part of ourselves most capable of love, leadership, and clarity.

Boundaries as Wealth Protection – Emotional Limits as Strategic Capital

Boundaries are often mischaracterised as lines drawn in fear, hostility, or retreat—defensive walls to keep others out. But this framing is both outdated and operationally inaccurate. In truth, boundaries are not walls; they are *filters.* They do not reject connection; they regulate it. And when set with clarity and conviction, they serve not only as emotional self-preservation but as *asset protection.* In this sense, emotional boundaries function as a form of *wealth insurance*—safeguarding the psychological capital we invest in work, love, and community.

This article redefines boundaries as an active resilience tool, essential not just for mental health, but for *long-term value preservation*—emotional, relational, and even financial. To mistake unlimited access for generosity is to overlook how emotional erosion begins: not with obvious trauma, but with subtle and repeated overextensions of the self. Over time, a lack of clear boundaries doesn't just deplete energy; it distorts identity, compromises judgment, and diminishes one's ability to discern where their obligations end and another's entitlement begins.

The central argument here is simple: Boundaries are not limitations on what you give; they are specifications of how you give without going bankrupt—emotionally, energetically, or existentially.

Emotional Economics: The Cost of Boundary Failure

Just as financial systems rely on credit limits, interest rates, and capital buffers, so too does emotional stability depend on parameters. Without clear boundaries, you accrue *emotional debt*—promises made under duress, obligations accepted from guilt, time allocated without alignment. These choices may win short-term approval but often result in *long-term depletion.* Emotional boundary failure is not always visible in loud breakdowns—it often manifests as subtle erosion: chronic fatigue, resentment, vague dissatisfaction, or the creeping loss of autonomy.

Many professionals experience this in workplace dynamics. Consider the employee who answers emails at midnight, never says "no" to an additional task, and avoids conflict under the guise of team spirit. On paper, this looks like commitment. But operationally, it's *an unsustainable drawdown on emotional liquidity.* Without enforced personal limits, their perceived value is tied not to competence but to availability—a fragile currency prone to exploitation and burnout.

In relationships, the parallel is just as stark. A partner who absorbs emotional volatility, who overfunctions to stabilise the other, or who continually sacrifices priorities for harmony may feel "supportive" in the short term. But over time, *resentment grows in the shadow of overgiving.* The relationship becomes a ledger where generosity is expected but seldom reciprocated.

Boundaries prevent this drift. They offer containment, not constraint. They clarify roles, responsibilities, and realistic capacities. And crucially, they allow trust to be built on *authentic consent* rather than silent self-erasure.

Boundaries and Emotional Asset Management

If time, attention, and emotional labour are finite resources—and they are—then the management of these assets demands intentionality. Boundaries serve this function. They *allocate emotional capital based on values, not pressure.* Just as an investor wouldn't put their entire portfolio into a volatile stock, a psychologically grounded individual does not give unrestricted access to volatile people or environments.

This is where the metaphor of *wealth insurance* becomes powerful. Insurance does not prevent risk; it mitigates exposure. It acknowledges that some loss is inevitable, but sets a cap on what's forfeited. Healthy boundaries do the same. They cannot shield you from every disappointment, breach, or conflict. But they ensure that your *core capital—dignity, self-trust, and inner stability—remains intact* even under strain.

Moreover, boundaries don't just preserve; they enhance value. By clarifying what is negotiable and what is not, they increase predictability in relationships—a key component of psychological safety. Counterintuitively, the more clearly you define your limits, the *more dependable you become.* People know what to expect from you, and you avoid the relational chaos that comes from inconsistent, reactive, or people-pleasing behaviour.

Psychological Safety is a Return on Integrity

One of the most underdiscussed returns on setting boundaries is the peace of self-respect. While the social risk of disappointing others is real, the *internal cost of betraying oneself is higher.* Every "yes" that violates your principles compounds over time into lowered self-trust and misalignment. And in this misalignment, you forfeit the very clarity needed to lead, connect, and create.

By contrast, when boundaries are established not in anger but in *calibrated conviction*, they increase self-coherence. You become harder to manipulate—not because you resist connection, but because your centre of gravity is internal. You respond rather than react. You clarify rather than comply. You speak with fewer words and greater weight.

This isn't abstract idealism—it's behavioural economics applied to selfhood. Emotional boundaries stabilise the yield on your time and effort. They reduce volatility in your relational landscape. And they protect your most important asset: the ability to invest in others without erasing yourself.

The Misconception of Boundaries as Rejection

A frequent cultural misunderstanding is to frame boundaries as forms of rejection. This is especially common among individuals raised in environments where needs were met inconsistently or where saying "no" was framed as betrayal. In such contexts, *boundaries feel like abandonment*—not just to others, but internally. Saying "no" triggers guilt not because it's wrong, but because it's unfamiliar.

To reframe boundaries as wealth protection, then, requires emotional re-education. It requires unlearning the false equivalence between availability and love, between compliance and care, between overextension and worth. It asks us to replace *martyrdom with stewardship*—not of others, but of ourselves.

This does not mean becoming rigid or unyielding. In fact, the most effective boundaries are *responsive, not reactive.* They evolve based on context and mutual respect. But what remains constant is the *underlying principle*: you cannot give sustainably unless you give from overflow—not obligation.

Implementing Strategic Boundaries

In practical terms, strategic boundary-setting might involve:

Protecting time blocks for uninterrupted focus without guilt or apology

Declining emotional labour requests that fall outside your consent or capacity

Communicating availability limits to colleagues or clients clearly and kindly

Defining what conversations, behaviours, or tones you will not engage with—privately or publicly

Choosing intentional disconnection (from digital communication, draining environments, or unresolved conflicts) to protect cognitive and emotional bandwidth

These are not grand gestures. They are *micro-defences with macro consequences.* They accumulate into a stronger, cleaner signal about who you are, what you value, and how you operate. They reduce friction, because your operating system becomes legible. And over time, they attract people and environments that align with that system—clients, partners, collaborators—while repelling those who seek to extract rather than exchange.

Closing Frame: Boundaries as Trust Infrastructure

To set a boundary is not to assume the worst of others; it is to honour the best in yourself. It is to act as a trustee of your own emotional wealth. Like any trustee, your duty is to *preserve and grow what has been entrusted to you.* Not hoard it. Not spend it recklessly. Not allow others to siphon it under the illusion of obligation.

Boundaries, properly understood, are not a rejection of intimacy—they are its precondition. Without them, relationships degrade into enmeshment or domination. With them, partnerships flourish in the soil of mutual respect.

In a world where visibility is currency and performative generosity often outpaces sustainable connection, boundaries offer something radical: a way to stay intact while still engaging fully. They let you show up, give generously, and remain whole.

Because protecting your peace is not self-indulgent. It's self-respecting. And in a noisy, extractive world, that self-respect is one of the few assets that appreciates over time.

Chapter 10
Raising Resilient Thinkers

It's no longer enough to raise clever children. Nor is it sufficient to cultivate politeness, academic accolades, or social charm. In a world saturated with stimulation and fast-tracked rewards—where volatility has become the backdrop of daily life—what truly distinguishes adults who thrive is not IQ or charisma, but cognitive resilience. That is, the capacity to sit with discomfort without fleeing into distraction. The ability to absorb disappointment without spiralling into despair. The willingness to hold paradox without retreating into tidy binaries. These qualities don't arrive as happy byproducts of intelligence—they're the hallmarks of a resilient mind. And like any form of mastery, they are developed, not inherited—deliberately, and often early.

This chapter sets out not to rehash parenting tropes, but to ask a question that cuts deeper than "How do I raise happy children?" Instead: "How do I help them think clearly, recover quickly, and endure ethically when the world is hard, the pace is slow, or outcomes feel unjust?" That inquiry is both philosophical and disarmingly practical. It nudges us to shift our gaze—from protection to preparation, from short-term calming to long-term capacity building.

Central to this is the idea of frustration tolerance. It's an unglamorous phrase, often neglected in modern parenting narratives, which tend to privilege emotional safety and validation—a worthy pursuit, no doubt, but sometimes taken to the extreme. In this well-meaning landscape, boredom is pathologised, failure softened to avoid the sting, and social slights quickly glossed over with distractions. But avoidance doesn't build resilience. If anything, it undermines it. Durable minds are not forged in padded rooms. They are shaped—gently, incrementally—through exposure to manageable discomfort, guided by presence and reflection. The

Cognitive resilience is not a given. It is cultivated—patiently, imperfectly, in countless small acts. This chapter won't offer quick fixes or silver bullets. What it offers instead is a durable framework—a lens and a set of tools that can reshape how we engage with those we are entrusted to guide. Whether you are raising children, mentoring the next generation, or leading teams, your influence extends beyond outcomes. It shapes the stories others will tell themselves when they encounter resistance. Will they collapse? Or recalibrate?

That difference, often, begins with you.

Let's begin the work of raising minds that don't just function—but endure. Not because it's easy. But because it matters more than ever.

The Inheritance of Emotional Wealth

It is tempting to measure legacy in numbers: the size of an estate, the contents of a portfolio, the presence or absence of financial security. But ask any psychologist, social worker, or adult reflecting on their upbringing, and a deeper truth becomes evident—*the most influential inheritance we receive is not monetary but emotional.* It is coded not in wills or trusts, but in tone of voice, patterns of response, and habits of self-regulation. Emotional wealth is not an abstraction. It is a transferable asset with real-world impact on how individuals think, relate, and recover.

This chapter challenges the cultural assumption that leaving financial stability is the ultimate parental succ[illegible]
resources do matter—they reduce st[illegible]
improve safety—they d[illegible]
chronic anx[illegible]
inher[illegible]

from conflict resolution skills to financial behaviour to mental health outcomes.

To understand this more clearly, we must first define what emotional wealth actually is. It is *not* about being cheerful or agreeable. It is the capacity to name emotions accurately, tolerate distress without collapse, and respond to difficulty with adaptive perspective. It includes empathy, boundaries, delayed gratification, emotional accountability, and the ability to self-soothe without destructiveness. These are capacities that allow individuals to *function effectively under pressure*, navigate relationships with maturity, and make decisions that align with long-term values.

Unlike material assets, emotional wealth cannot be transferred through paperwork. It must be modelled, mirrored, and reinforced in everyday interactions. A child who watches a parent apologise without defensiveness learns more about integrity than from any lecture. A teenager who sees an adult process grief without emotional shutdown is being taught how to metabolise pain. A young adult raised in a household where mistakes are met with calm inquiry rather than rage or shame carries forward a blueprint of psychological safety.

This modelling begins far earlier than most realise. Developmental neuroscience shows that children internalise emotional templates from caregivers well before they can articulate them. The patterns we demonstrate—whether we suppress, explode, avoid, repair—become part of a child's operating system. They learn whether emotions are safe to express, whether relationships can withstand conflict, and whether distress is a temporary state or a dangerous one. Th essons shape identity, coping, and even career paths.

lays out directly in financial
ancial stress was
ken

about value, spending, generosity, and limits may grow into a financially literate adult—not just in terms of budgeting, but in terms of *emotional neutrality toward wealth.* Emotional inheritance informs how we handle both scarcity and abundance.

Consider two hypothetical adults who each receive a significant financial inheritance at age 30. One was raised in an emotionally volatile environment where money was used to control or reward. They may view the inheritance as a source of tension, guilt, or identity inflation. The other was raised in an emotionally stable household where money was discussed with clarity and equanimity. They are more likely to integrate the inheritance into a thoughtful financial strategy rooted in purpose rather than ego or fear. Same assets, different outcomes. The difference lies in *emotional architecture*, not financial literacy alone.

In families of affluence, the absence of emotional modelling is particularly salient. It is not uncommon to find adult children of wealthy parents who struggle with basic emotional regulation despite elite education and material comfort. Generational wealth without generational resilience creates fragile success—externally stable, internally brittle. Emotional wealth acts as an internal stabiliser. It teaches that identity is not tethered to outcomes, that relationships matter more than performance, and that distress is manageable, not catastrophic.

The mechanisms by which emotional wealth is passed down are deceptively simple. They include:

– *Repair after rupture.* Not the absence of conflict, but the ability to recover from it with accountability and respect.

– *Emotional transparency with containment.* Naming feelings in real time, while staying anchored enough not to overwhelm others.

– *Boundaried warmth.* Demonstrating love without over-accommodation. Teaching that support includes limits, not just rescue.

– *Perspective in pain.* Modelling how to endure loss, failure, or disappointment with both realism and hope.

– *Delayed reactivity.* Showing that not every feeling requires immediate action, and that pause often precedes wisdom.

These behaviours do not require perfection—only consistency and humility. Adults who model these traits are not only building emotionally literate children; they are creating generational resilience that transcends bank balances.

Importantly, emotional wealth is not limited to parents. Mentors, teachers, coaches, managers—all play critical roles in shaping how emotional resilience is transmitted. In organisations, leaders who model calm under stress create cultures of safety that foster creativity and risk-taking. In schools, educators who validate frustration while encouraging effort help children convert struggle into stamina. Emotional inheritance is always in progress. It is shared across systems, not locked inside family units.

There is also a necessary reframing here for parents and caregivers who worry they haven't "done enough" financially. What matters more is *how they have shown up*, not what they have saved up. A child who inherits clarity, curiosity, and compassion is often far better positioned in life than one who inherits assets but lacks self-understanding. This is not an excuse for financial neglect—it is a recalibration of what truly supports thriving.

Moreover, emotional wealth is uniquely *anti-fragile.* It grows stronger with use. Whereas material inheritance can be depleted, emotional modelling can be passed down indefinitely, even retroactively. Adults who heal their own emotional patterns often rewire the narrative for their children, and even for siblings, partners, or employees. The repair of generational wounds is not symbolic; it is deeply practical.

To ignore emotional inheritance is to misread the full equation of legacy. We live in a culture that rewards display but often devalues depth. By turning attention to the quality of emotional modelling we provide, we not only raise better individuals—we build more resilient families, communities, and institutions. Emotional wealth, once properly recognised, becomes *the most stable currency of all.* It fuels the patience to invest, the capacity to care, the courage to fail, and the clarity to begin again.

And unlike any monetary gift, it cannot be taxed, stolen, or squandered overnight. It is held in the mind, the nervous system, and the memory. It shows up when a child is alone with disappointment and remembers to breathe. When a colleague owns a mistake without spiralling. When a parent passes on not just lessons, but lived examples of what strength under pressure truly looks like.

This is the inheritance worth prioritising. Not because it replaces financial provision, but because *it makes wealth livable, shareable, and sustainable.* Emotional wealth is what gives money meaning. Without it, we are rich and unsteady. With it, we may have less, but we carry more.

Teaching Frustration Tolerance

Modern parenting often prioritises immediate comfort over long-term capability. Yet, one of the most essential emotional tools we can equip children with is the ability to *tolerate frustration.* Not to eliminate it, avoid it, or soothe it away too quickly—but to face it, understand it, and move through it. Teaching frustration tolerance is not a luxury skill. It is foundational to raising emotionally resilient individuals who can navigate life's inevitable disappointments without crumbling or overreacting. It is also one of the least glamorised, most misunderstood facets of emotional development.

Frustration tolerance refers to the capacity to stay present and functional when goals are thwarted, when things don't go one's way, or when discomfort persists beyond what feels manageable. It is what enables a child to wait their turn, persist in problem-solving, accept "no" without emotional collapse, and experience disappointment without spiralling into shame or rage. Importantly, it is also the skill that underlies adult capacities like delay of gratification, emotional regulation under stress, and resilience in the face of failure or ambiguity.

This skill does not develop automatically. It is learned—and often painstakingly so—through repeated exposure to manageable levels of discomfort, paired with the consistent modelling of calm, regulated adult behaviour. The modern cultural impulse to shield children from all forms of frustration—through over-accommodation, instant gratification, or emotional micromanagement—ironically makes them *more fragile*, not more secure. By removing opportunities for practice, we remove the very conditions required for growth.

The cultivation of frustration tolerance begins in infancy but becomes especially salient in toddlerhood and early school-age years. The two-year-old who throws a tantrum when their toy is taken is not misbehaving; they are confronting a developmental edge. The role of the adult is not to eliminate the frustration, nor to punish the reaction, but to *hold the boundary and contain the distress*, showing the child through tone, posture, and presence that the discomfort is survivable. This experience, repeated hundreds of times across contexts, wires the nervous system to recognise that frustration is a signal—not a catastrophe.

One of the most effective but underused strategies in building this capacity is *naming and normalising the experience of frustration*. When an adult calmly says, "You're feeling really stuck because that didn't work the way you wanted," or "It's hard to be told to wait when you're excited," they are helping the child link their internal state with language, perspective, and containment. Over time, this builds emotional literacy—the precursor to regulation. The child learns not just what they feel, but *how to relate to that feeling with awareness instead of panic.*

Developmental psychologist Lev Vygotsky referred to the "zone of proximal development"—the sweet spot between what a child can do independently and what they can achieve with scaffolding. Frustration tolerance lives in that zone. It must be *challenged*, but not overwhelmed. This means adults must be willing to endure the temporary discomfort of witnessing their child's discomfort. In many families, this is the central bottleneck: the adult cannot tolerate the child's frustration, so they capitulate or distract. The child then learns that distress is both intolerable and effective—a message that undermines autonomy, confidence, and resilience.

It is crucial to distinguish between healthy frustration and emotional flooding. When a child becomes so dysregulated that they lose access to language, logic, or safety, they need co-regulation—not stoicism. The adult's task is to stay calm, physically present, and emotionally available, offering a regulated nervous system to anchor the child's experience. Over time, this co-regulation becomes internalised. The child begins to develop *self*-regulation—not by being told to "calm down," but by witnessing what calm looks and feels like in another.

This has clear applications in both parenting and education. In schools, students who are never challenged beyond their comfort zone often become avoidant or perfectionistic. Conversely, students who experience structured failure—followed by reflective feedback—become more intellectually courageous. They learn that mistakes are not indictments but invitations. That sense of psychological safety is not the absence of stress but the presence of support during stress.

Consider a student attempting a difficult maths problem. If the teacher rushes in to give the answer, the student loses the opportunity to sit in the gap between desire and success. If the teacher stands back entirely, the student may flounder. But if the teacher says, "This part looks tricky—take a minute to think. I'll come back," they are honouring the struggle while signalling belief in the student's capacity. *That moment of pausing—of not rescuing too soon—is the classroom equivalent of emotional scaffolding.*

Similarly, in families, frustration tolerance can be taught through everyday micro-experiences: delayed gratification, denied requests, waiting in queues, losing at games. The goal is not to make children suffer, but to help them *make meaning from moments of discomfort.* A child who can hear "not yet" and still feel seen is being prepared for a world that will often say "not now." This is one of the most powerful inoculations against entitlement, impulsivity, and chronic dissatisfaction.

Importantly, frustration tolerance has far-reaching implications for adult life. Adults who were never allowed to sit with disappointment often struggle with relationships, careers, and even health habits. They may react impulsively, avoid challenges, or seek immediate escape—through substances, technology, or blame—whenever things feel hard. On the other hand, adults who were supported through frustration learn to differentiate between temporary discomfort and structural injustice. They become more strategic, more patient, and more emotionally durable.

One under-recognised aspect of this skill is its relationship to *identity development.* When a child overcomes a frustrating task, they don't just gain a skill—they *change their self-concept.* They begin to see themselves as capable, competent, and trustworthy. This shift in identity—"I can handle hard things"—is one of the most durable psychological assets a person can possess. It protects against helplessness, victimhood, and learned avoidance.

Frustration tolerance also builds ethical maturity. It teaches that *just because we feel something intensely doesn't mean we should act on it immediately*. That truth, absorbed in childhood, becomes the foundation for impulse control, empathy, and moral reasoning. It allows space for consideration, perspective-taking, and thoughtful engagement with difference.

There are, of course, cultural tensions around this work. In some parenting paradigms, emotional expression is overly suppressed. In others, children are given unmoderated emotional power. Neither extreme serves development. The key is to *welcome emotion without enshrining it*. To say, in effect: "Your feelings are valid, and you still have choices." This balance—between validation and boundary—is the heart of emotional resilience.

Technology further complicates this terrain. The immediacy of digital feedback, entertainment, and gratification reduces opportunities for natural frustration. Parents and educators must now *design experiences that delay reward*, reintroduce boredom, and elevate effort. It is not about demonising technology, but about ensuring that *friction* remains part of development.

In practice, this might look like structured challenges, deliberate pauses before screen time, reflection after failure, and parental narration of their own frustrations ("I was really irritated when that happened, but I gave myself a few minutes before responding"). These practices transmit not just information, but *modelling*. And it is modelling—not instruction—that builds emotional muscle.

In sum, teaching frustration tolerance is not about hardening children. It is about expanding their emotional bandwidth. It is the slow, iterative work of preparing them for a life that will not bend to their every wish—but that will reward those who can stay calm, stay present, and stay engaged when things get tough. The adults who can do that themselves—and offer it without drama to the children in their care—are building more than behaviour. They are cultivating capacity. And that capacity is what ultimately determines how well a person can love, lead, work, and grow.

The Gift of Boredom

Few states of mind are as mischaracterised in modern culture as boredom. It is routinely dismissed as a nuisance, a void to be filled, or a problem to be solved. In an age defined by immediacy, novelty, and digital saturation, boredom has become almost taboo—something to be banished by a swipe, a scroll, or a stream of curated distraction. And yet, boredom is not a deficit. It is a developmental tool. Properly understood, *boredom is a psychological space rich with potential: a crucible for patience, creativity, self-inquiry, and problem-solving.*

To reclaim boredom as a gift requires not only a shift in perception but a reorientation of cultural priorities. In childhood and adulthood alike, the moments of boredom—those stretches of unstructured time where nothing demands attention—are not empty. They are fertile. They offer a context in which the mind, no longer occupied with consuming input, begins to *generate output.* Imagination awakens. Curiosity takes the reins. The inner world expands, no longer eclipsed by the noise of external stimuli.

The importance of boredom is particularly acute in childhood development. Decades of developmental psychology and educational theory have recognised that unstructured time fosters divergent thinking, resilience, and emotional self-regulation. When a child says, "I'm bored," they are expressing a state of unmet desire. The typical adult response—offering entertainment, redirection, or technology—is well-intentioned but counterproductive. It short-circuits the very discomfort that catalyses growth. The child never learns how to *sit with internal unrest long enough for creativity to emerge on the other side.*

There is a neurological basis for this. When the brain is not actively processing external input, it enters what neuroscientists call the *default mode network* (DMN). This system is associated with introspection, memory consolidation, and future planning. In essence, it is the mental workspace for self-reflection and idea incubation. The DMN is activated during boredom—provided the boredom is not instantly interrupted by stimulation. Research has shown that children and adults with frequent access to such states tend to develop stronger problem-solving skills and a deeper sense of self-awareness.

By contrast, hyper-stimulated environments—those that prioritise constant engagement and entertainment—train the brain to avoid stillness. This has consequences. A mind that has never learned to tolerate boredom becomes a mind that avoids discomfort of any kind. It seeks escape, not exploration. *The inability to endure boredom is not benign—it is a precursor to impulsivity, anxiety, and even addiction behaviours in later life.* When every lull is pathologised as a problem, the ability to cultivate inner resources atrophies.

The educational implications of this are profound. Classrooms that allow space for unstructured exploration, rather than cramming every minute with objectives, tend to produce students with greater intrinsic motivation and intellectual flexibility. The child who has spent time bored is more likely to generate original ideas, because they have been forced to look inward, to experiment, and to self-direct. The child who has never been bored may become an efficient test-taker but a passive learner—someone who waits to be told what to do rather than seeking out problems to solve.

This logic extends well into adulthood. Adults, too, need boredom—though they may label it differently. The entrepreneur facing a dry spell, the artist between commissions, the executive in a long meeting—these are all modern faces of boredom. And yet, it is often during these slow stretches that breakthroughs occur. *The strategic insight, the unexpected solution, the creative synthesis—these are frequently born not in the frenzy of doing but in the stillness of waiting.*

There is also an ethical and relational dimension to this. Boredom teaches patience—not the gritted-teeth variety, but the spacious patience that allows relationships to deepen and conversations to evolve. In friendships, in parenting, in long-term romantic partnerships, the ability to be with another person through stretches of mundanity is what anchors intimacy. *If we cannot tolerate boredom, we cannot build depth.* Everything becomes a performance, a dopamine hit, a highlight reel. Relationships flattened by novelty addiction become unsustainable under the weight of real emotional complexity.

Crucially, boredom also builds frustration tolerance. The child who learns to tolerate being bored is the child who can handle waiting, disappointment, and the temporary absence of stimulation. This is foundational for executive functioning—skills like delay of gratification, sustained attention, and impulse control. These are not just academic assets; they are life skills. Without them, adulthood becomes reactive, brittle, and chronically unfulfilled.

Parents, therefore, do children a disservice when they rush to entertain. A more constructive response to "I'm bored" might be: "Good. That means your brain is about to think of something new." Or: "Boredom is where ideas are born." These responses reposition boredom not as a void to be feared, but as a threshold to be crossed. They treat it with respect—and in doing so, they teach the child to do the same.

The reframing of boredom also invites cultural critique. In a capitalist logic that prizes productivity and optimisation, boredom is treated as waste. Every moment must be filled, monetised, or made useful. This framing ignores the paradoxical truth that *some of the most important human capacities—creativity, empathy, imagination—cannot be forced. They emerge when we stop trying to summon them.* Boredom is not unproductive; it is pre-productive. It is the soil in which future action germinates.

There are, of course, limits. Chronic understimulation or environmental deprivation is not the same as healthy boredom. A child in an impoverished or neglectful setting is not "growing through boredom"—they are surviving scarcity. The gift of boredom only emerges when there is a safe, enriched context in which to explore. It is not about abandoning children to solitude, but about *trusting them to find themselves within it.*

In practice, this means protecting unstructured time. It means resisting the impulse to overschedule, to programme every moment, to equate boredom with failure. It also means adults modelling their own relationship to stillness. A parent who reflexively picks up their phone at every lull cannot plausibly ask a child to sit with nothing. Children learn not only through instruction but through observation. They must *see adults doing nothing—and being fine with it*—to understand that stillness is not dangerous.

In the digital age, this is countercultural work. Algorithms are designed to eliminate boredom. Platforms compete to keep attention constantly occupied. But if attention is never allowed to rest, the mind never learns to meander. The result is a culture of reaction, not reflection. The task, then, is to *protect the slow spaces in which deep thinking can flourish.* This is not nostalgia—it is neuroscience.

The gift of boredom is that it restores a kind of cognitive sovereignty. It reminds us that our inner world can be as compelling as anything outside. It is not merely a buffer between meaningful experiences—it *is* the condition that makes meaning possible. It offers an invitation to reclaim the imagination, to make peace with our own minds, and to rediscover the slow power of undirected thought.

To teach children to value boredom is to teach them to trust themselves. To teach adults to re-embrace boredom is to remind them that reflection is not a luxury—it is a requirement. And to reframe boredom culturally is to assert that depth, not speed, is the true measure of intelligence.

Boredom, in the end, is not the absence of meaning. It is its prelude. And those who learn to sit through its awkward silence often emerge not with less to say, but with more worth hearing.

Modelling Calm in Chaos

The true test of leadership, parenting, or mentorship is not how one performs when circumstances are ideal—it is how one behaves in the midst of pressure, uncertainty, and conflict. In such moments, composure is not simply a private virtue. It is a *transmissible influence.* When a parent remains centred during a child's tantrum, when a manager retains clarity during organisational disruption, or when a teacher maintains warmth amid classroom escalation, those within their orbit do more than observe—they *mirror.* Human beings, particularly in groups or developmental relationships, attune not just to the words spoken, but to the nervous system of the person before them. *Regulation is contagious. So is dysregulation.*

At the heart of this phenomenon lies a neurological mechanism called co-regulation. It is the process by which one person's nervous system influences another's—subtly, often nonverbally. Infants rely on caregivers to help regulate their physiological arousal, calming through tone of voice, facial expression, and physical proximity. But this is not a phase we outgrow. Even as adults, we unconsciously borrow emotional cues from those around us. The leader who enters the room with grounded presence communicates safety. The parent who lowers their voice as tension rises invites de-escalation. *The one who holds the calm holds the influence.*

This is not simply a metaphor; it is a biological reality. The human nervous system is equipped with mirror neurons—specialised cells that activate not only when we perform an action, but when we observe it in others. These neurons are implicated in empathy, social learning, and emotional attunement. When a team sees their leader approach a crisis without panic, their mirror neurons register that stability as information. It is not rational persuasion; it is physiological synchrony. In this sense, *leadership is less about instruction and more about transmission.*

Children are particularly susceptible to this dynamic. They do not learn emotional regulation through lecture. They learn it by watching how adults behave under stress. A parent's response to spilled juice, a forgotten homework assignment, or a sibling conflict teaches more about resilience than any scripted life lesson. If the adult meets frustration with sarcasm, shouting, or shutdown, the child internalises those responses. If the adult instead breathes, pauses, and problem-solves, that template becomes a tool the child can one day access. *We cannot expect emotional maturity from children if we do not consistently model it ourselves.*

The stakes are equally high in professional settings. During crises—whether financial downturns, technical failures, or interpersonal ruptures—the team does not look to spreadsheets or policies for reassurance. They look to their leaders' faces, tone, and body language. Leaders who panic amplify fear. Leaders who deflect or deny create distrust. But leaders who acknowledge difficulty while remaining centred inspire trust and clarity. They signal that the system, while strained, is still functional. *This is not about suppressing emotion. It is about metabolising emotion in a way that preserves coherence.*

This distinction—between suppression and regulation—is essential. Suppression masks distress; regulation manages it. The former often leads to a simmering undercurrent of reactivity that erupts unpredictably. The latter requires self-awareness, presence, and the willingness to tolerate discomfort without immediately acting upon it. In practice, this means recognising one's physiological signs of stress—tightened jaw, shallow breathing, racing thoughts—and consciously intervening. Perhaps through grounding exercises, strategic pauses, or simply a few deep breaths. These micro-interventions are not signs of weakness. They are acts of *emotional professionalism*.

Moreover, this capacity to model calm becomes a stabilising asset in any environment. Consider the teacher in an overstimulated classroom who responds not by raising their voice but by speaking slower. Or the executive fielding aggressive questions during a public earnings call, who calmly repeats the facts without defensiveness. Or the parent navigating the chaos of a morning routine, choosing humour over exasperation. In each case, the individual offers not only leadership but *nervous system leadership*—anchoring the collective by regulating themselves.

Crucially, modelling calm does not mean being emotionless. It means *being emotionally honest without becoming emotionally uncontained.* It means acknowledging fear, frustration, or disappointment, but doing so from a place of integration rather than fragmentation. This authenticity builds relational credibility. Children, teams, and peers can sense when composure is performative. What earns trust is congruence—when the person's internal state and external behaviour are aligned, and when that alignment is oriented toward stability and repair.

The implications for resilience are profound. Systems—familial, organisational, educational—derive their resilience not just from policies or protocols, but from the emotional tone set by their leaders. When the people in charge model thoughtful responses over impulsive reactions, others learn that chaos is survivable, even instructive. They learn that stress is not an emergency in itself, but a signal to slow down, reassess, and respond deliberately. *In this way, regulation becomes cultural currency: a shared language of coping, communicating, and recalibrating under duress.*

There are, of course, limits to what regulation can resolve. Calmness cannot compensate for structural injustice, abusive dynamics, or chronic overload. But even in such contexts, the presence of a consistently regulated figure can be transformative. They become not a saviour, but a reference point—a reminder that groundedness is possible even when the environment is destabilising. Over time, this modelling helps others internalise those cues, developing what psychologists call *interoceptive awareness*—the capacity to sense and manage one's own internal states.

Modern neuroscience continues to affirm the role of co-regulation in developing emotional resilience. Studies in affective neuroscience and polyvagal theory show that the human autonomic nervous system is profoundly influenced by the tone of voice, rhythm of speech, facial expression, and perceived safety cues from others. *We regulate each other, whether we intend to or not.* That insight should humble us into greater responsibility—not just for what we say, but for how we show up, physiologically and relationally.

For parents and leaders alike, this reframes the idea of authority. Authority is not simply the ability to direct others. It is the ability to *stabilise a room.* To make others feel safer, clearer, more focused, even amid confusion. That authority is earned not through credentials, but through consistent, embodied behaviour. It is not something one claims—it is something one offers, through presence.

This principle has applications far beyond crisis moments. It also applies to the rhythms of daily life. The parent who navigates the school run with gentle humour. The manager who debriefs a failed project with compassion and curiosity. The team leader who pauses before answering an inflammatory email. These moments, while small, accumulate. They form the relational environment in which trust, innovation, and psychological safety either flourish or decay. *Calm is not a backdrop to productivity—it is a prerequisite for it.*

Importantly, modelling calm is not a solo act. It requires inner work: emotional literacy, somatic awareness, the discipline to interrupt reactivity. But it also requires external support. No one regulates well in isolation. Leaders and parents need their own networks of co-regulators—mentors, peers, therapists, friends—who help them return to centre when they drift. Modelling calm, therefore, is not about heroism. It is about humility. The willingness to self-regulate not for ego but for others. *To lead not by control, but by coherence.*

In the end, what we model in chaos becomes the emotional inheritance of those we influence. Our children do not remember our advice nearly as much as they remember our tone in moments of stress. Our teams do not retain every directive, but they do absorb the emotional temperature we set. If we want a generation of emotionally intelligent thinkers, collaborators, and problem-solvers, we must start not with instruction manuals, but with ourselves. *Not by asking others to calm down, but by demonstrating what calm looks like, feels like, and makes possible—even in the storm.*

Chapter 11
The Entrepreneur's Inner Game

Resilience is seldom tested as relentlessly as in the life of a founder. While the popular imagination paints entrepreneurs as iron-willed visionaries powered by caffeine and confidence, the inner landscape often tells a grittier tale—one of persistent uncertainty, long spells of invisibility, and the slow erosion of certainty. To build something from nothing is not just a matter of intellect, funding, or strategic finesse; it demands a fortified nervous system, one that can remain steady amidst contradiction and unresolved tension. In truth, the most formidable threat to a founder isn't always a market misfire or a failed funding round. More often, it's the subtle tyranny of emotional mismanagement: mistaking anxiety for urgency, seeking applause over alignment, and walking away—not because it's time, but because discomfort masquerades as a verdict. This chapter is a companion for navigating that inner terrain.

By design, startups embody a paradox few founders are adequately prepared for: the constant tug between speed and patience. "Move fast and break things," the mantra goes—iterate, pivot, hustle. Yet real businesses, the ones that last, unfold slowly. They require time to take root, stumble, recover, recalibrate. These two forces—urgency and patience—rarely sit easily together. One misjudged, and you're either sprinting toward burnout dressed up as ambition or lapsing into inertia cloaked as strategic restraint. Resolving this tension isn't about slogans or mindset hacks; it calls for nuance, the discernment to know when to press forward and when to hold still.

At the heart of that discernment lies emotional stamina—not stoicism, not repression, but the cultivated ability to metabolise discomfort without letting it cloud your judgment. A founder's advantage rarely stems from a clever growth hack or a beautifully crafted pitch deck. It often begins with their capacity to remain psychologically intact while moving through fog. Building something worthwhile without instant validation, without the dopamine hit of constant praise, requires a kind of internal economy that isn't governed by likes or investor buzz. You begin drawing momentum from your own coherence, not external confirmation. In that sense, the absence of applause becomes a crucible for clarity. The founder who can keep moving in the quiet is far harder to destabilise.

And make no mistake—this kind of emotional sovereignty is indispensable in a world where constant self-promotion is often mistaken for progress. We're conditioned to believe that visibility is synonymous with value. That if it isn't tweeted, it hasn't happened. And so, many founders build in public—not always from alignment, but from anxiety. Yet attention is not the same as traction. Exposure doesn't guarantee efficacy. Sometimes, the seasons of greatest growth are cloaked in silence. Those are the stretches where no one's watching and the only audience is your own integrity. There's a discipline to operating in the shadows—it forces you to get honest about what really drives you.

Still, conviction has its own traps. Not every hard season is a spiritual test to endure. Sometimes, quitting is exactly the right move. But there's a difference between making an informed exit and dressing up avoidance as strategic wisdom. Fear, when cleverly disguised as logic, becomes one of the most persuasive liars in the room. So how do you know when to hold, when to fold, when to pause? This chapter introduces a kind of diagnostic lens—a resilience filter, if you will—for interrogating the motives beneath your desire to walk away. Is this exit coming from clarity or exhaustion? From coherence, or from collapse? From your best judgment, or from the part of you that just wants the noise to stop?

These aren't philosophical musings. They're operational levers. Because startups rarely implode in a single stroke. More often, they fray quietly—through compromises made under duress, through decisions that betray timing, through the slow corrosion of conviction when urgency becomes a stand-in for ego. When a pause could have preserved alignment, but performative speed got the final word. In this context, resilience isn't about brute force—it's about quiet tenacity. A willingness to stay aligned amidst noise, to listen when the market whispers, and to know that what's loud isn't always what's lasting.

This chapter explores why emotional fluency—the ability to interpret and navigate one's own psychological weather—is not a soft asset but a strategic one. It's the differentiator between founders who pivot with clarity and those who panic into motion. Between those who use silence as a strategy and those who flee it out of fear. We'll look closely at the art of quitting—how to recognise when something is misaligned and worthy of departure, versus when you're simply inside a temporary storm that must be borne. In doing so, we reframe grit. It's not blind endurance. It's intelligent resilience: the ability to weather uncertainty without losing your sense of direction.

To build something meaningful in today's startup landscape is to invite interruption—of focus, of confidence, of self. And not just from the outside. Your own mind will often be the loudest heckler in the room. The real task, then, isn't simply to recruit better or iterate faster. It's to fortify the internal scaffolding—the psychological architecture that allows you to stand upright in the midst of ambiguity. That sort of structure isn't taught in accelerators or demo days. It's constructed slowly, privately. Through practices of stillness. Through deliberate pauses. Through the courage to wait, even when everything around you—and within you—is screaming for speed.

Strip away the myth, and entrepreneurship is as much an emotional craft as a commercial one. Not a sprint. Not a clean linear marathon. But a choreography of uncertainty: belief colliding with evidence, hope measured against data, vision carried across dry spells of doubt. The most successful founders aren't simply those with brilliant ideas—they are those who remain composed while waiting for the world to catch up. Who resist the urge to fill the void. Who understand that waiting, when intentional, is not stagnation but stewardship.

If the chapters preceding this one focused on resilience in the personal sphere—identity, relationships, emotional self-governance—this section brings those insights into the high-pressure theatre of creation. Because at stake is not merely the viability of an idea, but the wellbeing of the person tasked with shepherding it. And no funding round, no IPO, no acquisition is worth the erosion of the founder behind it.

In the pages ahead, we'll dive into frameworks, mental models, and stories from the trenches—tools to help you refine not just your venture, but your internal operating system. We'll explore how to navigate ambiguity without flinching, how to decouple your value from your metrics, and how to lead from inner stability rather than external compulsion. The goal isn't invincibility. It's emotional solvency: the ability to assess risk clearly, absorb setbacks wisely, and walk away clean when the time is right.

This is the inner game. And if we're honest, it may be the most undervalued asset in entrepreneurship today.

Why Founders Break First – Shows how entrepreneurship is more about enduring failure and slow traction than ideas

At the heart of every early-stage company lies a human system—emotions, perception, stamina. Despite the gloss of pitch decks and product-market fit graphs, entrepreneurship remains a test of psychological endurance disguised as an economic or technological exercise. The dominant narrative around startups is that failure stems from bad ideas, inadequate capital, or misread markets. But behind most collapsed ventures is not a fatally flawed concept—it is a founder who has run out of emotional runway. *Startups don't fail because ideas break; they fail because the people carrying them fracture first.*

This is not merely anecdotal. Across multiple founder interviews, postmortem analyses, and accelerator case studies, the pattern is unmistakable: burnout, co-founder conflict, chronic self-doubt, the crushing silence of slow traction—all of these precede financial insolvency. Ideas, no matter how brilliant, do not self-execute. They require sustained psychological oxygen—belief under pressure, clarity amidst ambiguity, and patience without applause. The early stages of building anything meaningful demand a tolerance for invisibility, contradiction, and prolonged uncertainty. And while many founders enter the arena ready to hustle, far fewer are prepared to *wait.* The greater the gap between expectation and reality, the heavier the emotional toll.

This tension is particularly acute in high-ambition ecosystems, where speed is glorified and scale is fetishised. Founders are implicitly taught to conflate motion with progress, fundraising with validation, and media visibility with product-market fit. But momentum built on anxiety is brittle. It can't sustain long sales cycles, product delays, or investor hesitations. It leads to reactionary decisions—premature pivots, bad hires, over-promising—because the real fear is not strategic failure, but personal irrelevance. *When the founder begins to mistake slow growth for personal inadequacy, the clock doesn't just start ticking for the company; it starts ticking for their mental clarity.*

Much of this emotional erosion occurs in silence. Founders are often isolated—not only by the demands of the role, but by the illusion that they must appear invulnerable to inspire confidence. Even in teams, they occupy a psychological altitude that few can reach, carrying a weight that is rarely visible to peers, employees, or investors. Underneath the curated optimism is often a private attrition: the anxiety of meeting payroll, the pressure of a high-burn runway, the frustration of broken tools or buggy rollouts. And unlike operational failures, which can be addressed through systems, this form of breakdown is internal, cumulative, and unspoken. *Founders don't burn out from doing too much; they burn out from holding too much alone.*

One of the most under-discussed reasons founders collapse early is the lack of traction—not failure, but the slow, silent void of no feedback. Not enough users, not enough revenue, not enough energy coming back into the system. In that vacuum, insecurity rushes in. Self-worth becomes tied to conversion metrics. Every rejection feels like an indictment of your vision or your value. Even when the idea is sound and the market promising, *the absence of visible progress feels like a referendum on the self.* And if the founder does not have the psychological tools to separate signal from self-image, their resilience corrodes.

This is compounded by the performative culture of entrepreneurship. Founders are often encouraged to build in public, to share roadmaps, wins, and learnings on social media. While transparency has its merits, it can quickly distort internal timelines. The public display of traction—however curated—creates an invisible pressure to match a pace that may not reflect reality. The result is a toxic comparison loop, where patience feels like failure, and quiet building feels like incompetence. *The startup ecosystem rewards visibility, but building something lasting often requires invisibility.*

Psychologists have long understood the cognitive and emotional toll of chronic uncertainty. Entrepreneurs live with near-constant ambiguity—about timelines, partnerships, markets, and even their own capacity. Without internal systems of grounding, this ambiguity morphs into anxiety, and then into erratic behaviour. Founders become less thoughtful, more reactive. They pivot not from insight, but from fear. They overcorrect. They chase novelty to escape stagnation. *But sustainable companies are not built on adrenaline; they're built on emotional sobriety.*

This brings us to a critical insight: *resilience is not the same as grit.* Grit implies pushing through. Resilience requires recalibrating. It is not heroic effort, but intelligent recovery. And founders who break often confuse the two—equating value with busyness, identity with output, and visibility with worth. When the feedback loop is exclusively external, the internal narrative gets outsourced. And in that outsourcing, the founder loses authorship of their own thinking. *They no longer know whether they're building because it's working, or just because they're afraid to stop.*

What, then, does emotional sustainability look like for entrepreneurs?

It begins with *honest self-tracking*: knowing your cognitive thresholds, recognising burnout signals early, and building routines that prioritise mental maintenance over performance optics. It also means *redefining progress*—valuing iteration over perfection, process over virality. Founders who learn to *read their own nervous systems as carefully as they read analytics dashboards* are better equipped to survive the slow middle. And the slow middle is where most companies either find their rhythm—or quietly expire.

There is also a systemic dimension to this. Incubators, accelerators, and boards often overlook the emotional infrastructure needed to support founders. A focus on KPIs without psychological scaffolding creates brittle companies—ones that may hit early numbers, but crumble under the weight of long-term demands. *Founder coaching, peer support systems, and trauma-informed advisory frameworks* are not optional luxuries—they are existential tools. Because it is entirely possible to have a viable idea, a decent team, and market access—and still implode. The data will show a failed company. But the cause? A founder who broke under the strain.

To be clear, this is not an indictment of entrepreneurial ambition. It is a recalibration. The problem is not that founders work hard; it is that they are rarely taught to *recover with precision.* Nor are they equipped to tolerate the most common experience in early-stage ventures: slow traction. Not public collapse. Just the steady erosion of certainty in the face of lukewarm response. *That is the crucible—and it is emotional, not strategic.*

In the end, this subchapter offers a reframing: ideas do matter, of course—but they are only as durable as the person carrying them. Product-market fit is irrelevant if the founder cannot stay mentally solvent long enough to iterate towards it. The work of endurance—of psychological pacing, expectation management, and emotional autonomy—is the real startup skill. Everything else is a toolset. This is the mindset.

And so, the founder's most important job is not simply to lead the company. It is to *outlast their own doubt, without letting it define their decisions.* That is where companies are built. Or quietly die.

The Startup Patience Paradox – Explores the tension between urgency and patience in startups

At the core of every entrepreneurial pursuit lies an inescapable tension: the simultaneous demand for speed and stamina. The startup world celebrates urgency—ship fast, scale now, pivot yesterday. But beneath that celebrated velocity sits an uncomfortable contradiction: the most impactful companies are not those that rush, but those that endure. This is the startup patience paradox. *To win in a market that rewards speed, founders must master the art of strategic slowness.* Not hesitation. Not complacency. But deliberate restraint—knowing when to pause, when to persevere, and when to prioritise depth over pace.

This paradox is not merely theoretical. It defines the psychological terrain every founder must navigate. In practice, building a startup demands sprinting within a marathon—racing against time for funding, market share, and validation, while simultaneously cultivating the slow, unglamorous patience required to build a viable product, culture, and business model. Urgency without patience leads to burnout, brittle strategy, and fragile foundations. Patience without urgency, on the other hand, results in irrelevance. The art lies in balancing these two temporal forces without allowing one to cannibalise the other.

Consider the widely mythologised startup stories—the overnight success narratives that dominate tech journalism and investor lore. They often erase years of obscurity, pivoting, and unsexy iteration. Stripe, Airbnb, Canva, even WhatsApp—each was built over years of trial, rejections, and underwhelming growth before gaining traction. What distinguished these companies was not just insight or timing, but *persistence under pressure without panic.* The real inflection points came not from velocity alone, but from an accumulated body of quiet, patient execution that eventually paid compound interest.

In early-stage startups, urgency tends to dominate. There are natural pressures: short runways, investor expectations, fast-moving competitors. The temptation is to over-index on visible activity—shipping features rapidly, announcing partnerships, hustling for users. But if the core product isn't solving a real problem or isn't technically stable, this rush becomes a form of theatre. *Urgency becomes noise.* And noise distracts from signal: actual user feedback, market signals, and internal clarity. Speed, in this sense, becomes a false proxy for momentum.

Ironically, too much urgency can inhibit the very thing it claims to accelerate—traction. Products get shipped before they're usable. Teams scale prematurely, diluting culture. Marketing spend outpaces product readiness. In trying to "move fast and break things," startups often break themselves. *Sustainable growth requires patience with processes, not just impatience with results.*

Yet, to suggest that patience alone is virtuous would be equally misguided. Many founders use patience as a mask for fear-based avoidance: they delay decisions, postpone launches, over-tinker, or wait endlessly for "perfect timing." This brand of patience is not strategic—it's passive. What distinguishes effective patience is intentionality: *choosing to delay action not out of fear, but out of prioritisation.*

A key to navigating this paradox lies in redefining what urgency and patience actually mean. Urgency should not imply recklessness—it should mean clarity. A precise focus on what matters most right now. Likewise, patience is not passivity—it is discipline. The discipline to *not chase every new opportunity*, to withstand the discomfort of obscurity, to resist the reflex to appease every investor's whim or mimic every competitor's move.

One real-world framework worth examining here is Amazon's emphasis on "long-term thinking." Jeff Bezos famously preferred metrics like customer lifetime value and infrastructure investments over short-term stock performance. Internally, Amazon moves quickly—on experiments, on hiring, on iteration. But strategically, it thinks in decades. This is *patient urgency* in practice: operational speed within a philosophically slow game.

Another example is Basecamp (now 37signals), which deliberately avoided venture capital and refused to scale by traditional Silicon Valley playbooks. Their success—measured not by valuation but by profitability, longevity, and user trust—was rooted in their insistence on building slowly and deliberately, even when the ecosystem rewarded the opposite. Their patience wasn't slowness; it was sovereignty.

For founders, then, the question becomes not "Should I move fast or be patient?" but rather *"Where should I move fast—and where must I move slow?"* Speed in customer discovery? Essential. Speed in hiring leadership? Dangerous. Speed in bug fixes? Non-negotiable. Speed in fundraising? Contextual. The ability to *discern temporal zones* within the business is the hallmark of a strategically mature founder.

Psychologically, the paradox also demands emotional bifurcation. Founders must be able to hold contradictory mindsets at once: relentless urgency in action, calm patience in outcome. This requires emotional regulation, not just cognitive clarity. When the default culture around you is hyper-reactivity—when every downturn feels existential and every news cycle is a referendum on your worth—it is easy to confuse visibility with progress and activity with effectiveness. *To stay patient in a room full of panicked actors is not laziness; it is leadership.*

One overlooked contributor to the patience deficit in startups is the funding model itself. Venture capital is structurally biased toward quick returns and exponential growth. Even though investors speak the language of resilience and long-term vision, their incentives often reward short-term inflection points: the next round, the next milestone. As a result, founders internalise a timeline that may not match the natural tempo of their product, market, or business model. This misalignment produces both strategic and emotional incoherence. *If your product is on a five-year maturity arc, but your investors expect scale in 18 months, you are being set up to fail—not due to capability, but due to incompatible clocks.*

The solution is not to reject urgency or delay accountability. It is to *own your timeline deliberately*. Founders must learn to manage not only their product roadmaps but also the narrative timelines imposed by others. This may involve reframing milestones to investors, educating the team on the long-game, or simply resisting the dopamine rush of false validation. Every company is a time-bound organism. The founders who thrive are those who control their tempo with intention.

Educationally, this has implications for how we train and mentor entrepreneurs. Current incubators and accelerators often focus on speed—pitch days, sprints, lean tests. Valuable tools, no doubt. But rarely do we see formal curricula on psychological pacing, expectation management, or timeline design. We optimise founders for fast starts, but not for *slow middles*. And it is the slow middle—those ambiguous months or years of moderate growth, delayed traction, and quiet iteration—that separate resilient builders from reactionary ones.

To build a company is to live inside contradiction. You must act today like it matters urgently, while understanding that the most important results may not arrive for years. You must ship now, but build for longevity. You must please investors, but honour your product truth. You must speak with confidence, but think with humility. And through it all, you must guard your psychological bandwidth, because burnout will kill your company long before market risk does.

In the end, the startup patience paradox is not a dilemma to solve, but a tension to navigate—daily, hour by hour. Every decision is a metronome. Too fast, and you lose precision. Too slow, and you lose relevance. The goal is not balance for its own sake, but *tempo with intention*. Knowing when to wait is just as powerful as knowing when to move.

For the founder willing to master this internal clock, the paradox becomes a power. Not a trap. And in a culture that prizes urgency above all, that is perhaps the rarest competitive advantage of all.

Delayed Praise, Deliberate Focus – Discusses building in obscurity and resisting validation

In an age where validation is instant and visibility is currency, the quiet discipline of building in obscurity has become not only rare—but radically valuable. For founders, creatives, and ambitious professionals alike, the current climate rewards those who *appear* successful before they *are* successful. Likes, shares, pitch decks, and public updates create a theatre of momentum that often overshadows the slower, harder, and far more essential work: refining ideas, making mistakes privately, and developing mastery without applause. *Delayed praise is not a punishment. It is protection.*

To resist early praise is to choose intentional obscurity. Not out of modesty or fear, but out of a commitment to substance over image. The paradox is striking: the more one seeks public affirmation in the early stages of a venture or craft, the more fragile the underlying work tends to become. This is not a theoretical argument. Empirical studies in behavioural psychology, notably in the domain of motivation science, have repeatedly shown that *early social validation can reduce long-term persistence.* When individuals receive praise for effort not yet solidified into skill or results, their internal motivation often diminishes.

This insight has been echoed in entrepreneurial circles, albeit less rigorously: stealth-mode founders tend to focus better. Artists who work outside the limelight tend to experiment more freely. Startups that launch quietly iterate faster. Why? Because without the pressure to be publicly perceived as competent, they are free to be *actually* competent. In the early phase of any meaningful pursuit, failure is not only inevitable—it is a necessary learning mechanism. External validation interrupts this process. It shifts the focus from problem-solving to image management.

Consider the psychological consequences. Public validation triggers dopamine surges that feel indistinguishable from genuine achievement. A product announcement that garners industry buzz. A thought leadership post that gets hundreds of shares. A fundraising round covered in the media. These moments feel like progress—but they are often *proxies* for progress. They reward perception, not proof. And over time, they condition individuals to optimise for impressions rather than impact. *Delayed praise breaks that loop.* It allows creators to be less reactive to outside noise and more attuned to internal standards.

This is not a critique of public recognition itself. Nor is it a romanticisation of hardship or invisibility. Rather, the argument is that *early validation should be approached with discernment*, particularly in domains where complexity demands focus. There is a meaningful difference between sharing work to receive feedback and sharing work to receive approval. The former is developmental. The latter is performative.

There is also a philosophical dimension to this. In *Meditations*, Marcus Aurelius cautions against becoming addicted to reputation, reminding himself: "It never ceases to amaze me: we all love ourselves more than other people, but care more about their opinion than our own." In business, this tendency is amplified by an ecosystem where social proof is a form of leverage. Fundraising, recruiting, partnerships—they often depend on perceived traction, not verified depth. Yet, the most durable companies—those that compound over decades—are built not on hype, but on obsessive clarity. Clarity that can only be cultivated in conditions of deliberate focus, often far from public view.

One compelling case study is the development of Dropbox. Long before its launch, founder Drew Houston spent months quietly refining a simple video that demonstrated the product's functionality. Rather than seeking validation from venture capitalists or Twitter, he focused on a narrow, solvable user problem: syncing files seamlessly. The restraint paid off. By the time Dropbox did go public, it had a real product solving a real problem—validated not by applause, but by adoption.

Similarly, Canva, now one of the most widely used design platforms in the world, spent years refining its backend technology before making noise. The team resisted the pull of premature press and chose instead to focus on infrastructure, interface fluidity, and intuitive onboarding. Their restraint in seeking praise allowed them to deliver a product that needed no exaggerated claims. *It simply worked better than anything else on the market.*

What these stories share is not just humility, but *strategic seclusion.* This form of deliberate focus is not passive. It is fiercely active. It means creating long before you market. Testing long before you scale. Practising long before you perform. And perhaps most crucially, *defining success in private terms before the world attempts to define it for you.*

There is also a resilience benefit embedded in delayed praise. Creators who build without expectation of applause develop a sturdier emotional architecture. Their sense of value becomes decoupled from market volatility or public reaction. This is especially vital in fields where early results are ambiguous, and feedback loops are long—research, product development, writing, education, design. *When attention is deferred, resilience is built.* Because the work must be sustained by something deeper than recognition: a sense of intrinsic purpose, curiosity, or commitment to mastery.

However, this is easier said than done. We live in an era optimised for exposure. Platforms are built to encourage frequent updates, optimise for engagement, and reward immediacy. Founders are told to "build in public." Creatives are nudged to "show their process." While there are contexts in which this transparency is powerful and even necessary, it must be wielded with discretion. *Visibility without focus is a liability.* It invites distraction, comparison, and premature judgement—all of which distort the creative and strategic process.

There is also a cultural impatience that makes delayed praise feel counterintuitive. In fast-paced industries, those who delay announcements risk being perceived as irrelevant. But this overlooks the asymmetric nature of value creation. The most transformative products, ideas, and breakthroughs are not born from speed—they are born from *sustained attention.* And sustained attention is fragile. It cannot coexist with constant external feedback. That's why some of the most generative periods in a creator or founder's life occur in what Cal Newport terms "deep work"—a state of unbroken concentration, shielded from the performative pressure of public platforms.

In practical terms, cultivating this mode of building requires structure. Time-blocking deep work hours. Reducing digital noise. Defining metrics of progress that are internal, not social. Protecting early-stage ideas from overexposure. Creating mechanisms for private feedback before public dissemination. These are not luxuries—they are strategic investments in cognitive clarity.

More fundamentally, this mindset requires a reframing of what praise is *for*. Praise is not oxygen. It is punctuation. It arrives after coherence has been built, not before. *Premature applause can interrupt the sentence.* The most valuable recognition is that which confirms something real, not merely anticipated.

For leaders building teams or companies, this principle has organisational consequences. Cultures that over-index on recognition can inadvertently produce performative behaviours. Teams optimise for what gets praised, not necessarily for what creates value. By contrast, cultures that reward deliberate focus—through thoughtful feedback, long-term goals, and protected thinking time—foster deeper contributions. *Delayed praise here is not neglect; it is respect for the process.*

Ultimately, to build with deliberate focus is to place long-term fidelity above short-term visibility. It is a form of temporal discipline. A commitment to let quality mature before calling for attention. The public may not see the hours, the trials, the drafts—but they will feel the depth when the work is finally revealed. And that is the point.

In a world of noise, obscurity is not a weakness. It is a workshop. And praise, when it finally arrives, should not come as oxygen—but as confirmation of what you already knew was real.

When to Quit—and When You're Just Scared – Provides a resilience filter to discern between wise exits and emotionally driven abandonments

Quitting is not failure. But knowing *when* to quit—and when you're merely fleeing discomfort—is a decision that demands more discernment than most people are trained to exercise. Endurance, while often romanticised, is not inherently virtuous. Nor is walking away an act of cowardice by default. The critical distinction lies in motive, clarity, and timing. Emotional resilience isn't just the capacity to persist; it is the ability to pause, evaluate, and act from alignment rather than panic. *There is a vast difference between letting go of a pursuit that no longer serves your values and abandoning one that merely feels difficult in the moment.*

Modern work culture doesn't make this easy. On one hand, entrepreneurial mythology glorifies grit: "Never give up." "Push through the pain." "Success is just around the corner." On the other, mental health discourse rightly emphasises the cost of burnout, misaligned goals, and toxic tenacity. Between these poles, the real question—the human question—is how to recognise the internal cues that signal either wise departure or reactive withdrawal. To answer this, we must interrogate the psychological architecture beneath the act of quitting.

Fear masquerades as logic. Especially under pressure. When traction is slow, when feedback is sparse, when isolation grows heavy, the mind constructs what cognitive behavioural theorists call *cognitive distortions*—internal narratives that overstate risk and understate capability. "This will never work." "I'm not cut out for this." "Everyone else is ahead." These thoughts often emerge not from reality but from emotional depletion. If decisions are made in this state—without reflection, without anchoring—they tend to result in regret, not relief.

Contrast this with strategic withdrawal. Quitting with discernment is an act of strength. It reflects a capacity to *measure opportunity cost*, to honour emerging data, to acknowledge shifts in personal priorities or market conditions. This is what the philosopher and management thinker Peter Drucker referred to as "planned abandonment": the proactive ending of initiatives that no longer produce value, thereby freeing up attention for higher-leverage pursuits. The difference is not the act of stopping—it is *why* and *how* it is done.

A practical resilience filter must therefore include both internal and external diagnostics. Internally, one must ask: *Am I emotionally regulated enough to make this decision?* If the answer is no—if you're in the grip of exhaustion, shame, or panic—then any impulse to quit is likely distorted. This is not the moment for a final decision. It's the moment for rest, reflection, and recalibration. In contrast, if the desire to exit emerges *after* careful thought, grounded analysis, and open dialogue, then it warrants real consideration.

Externally, the diagnostic includes factors like feedback loops, market traction, alignment with personal values, and available alternatives. Is the project failing because of temporary headwinds—or because its assumptions no longer hold? Has the core idea been invalidated by data, or simply under-tested? Have you exhausted creative pivots or prematurely defined the effort as doomed? *Strategic quitting occurs when further investment is unlikely to yield proportionate returns—not just when progress feels hard.*

One of the most damaging myths in entrepreneurship is the "sunk cost fallacy." Founders, artists, and professionals alike often persist *not* because a project is still viable, but because they've invested so much already. Time. Money. Identity. The logic becomes circular: "I've put too much into this to stop now." But economic reasoning—and emotional wisdom—suggest the opposite. Resources already spent are gone. What matters is what remains:

energy, time, and attention. *Protecting these is not weakness; it is stewardship.*

However, discerning between fear and insight requires self-awareness. One of the most effective tools for this is journaling—not in a performative, gratitude-log sense, but as a form of mental debugging. Writing out the thought process behind your impulse to quit clarifies whether it's reactive or reflective. Patterns emerge. False beliefs are surfaced. Emotions are named. In many cases, the simple act of documenting your inner logic creates just enough distance from it to reveal whether it's trustworthy.

Another tool is structured feedback. Talk to those who have context and distance. Not generic cheerleaders, and not doom-mongers, but those who can hold tension: "This is hard *and* you're capable," or "This may not be worth pursuing further *and* that doesn't mean you've failed." Wise mentors do not give answers. They offer frameworks. One such framework comes from decision science: *pre-mortems*. Imagine quitting and fast-forward six months. What happened next? Relief, regret, redirection? Now imagine sticking with it. What happened next? Despair, or unexpected traction? The emotional clarity often lies in *projecting forward and observing imagined consequences.*

Importantly, fear-based quitting often mimics wisdom in its urgency. It feels *certain.* That certainty is a red flag. Fear narrows focus, compresses time, and demands resolution—usually by escape. Wisdom, by contrast, is quieter. It creates space. It accepts ambiguity. It suggests a decision but doesn't shout it. If your desire to quit is accompanied by frantic energy, that's not intuition—it's probably panic. *Wait until you can hear yourself think again.*

Consider the case of Basecamp (formerly 37signals), a software company that chose to deliberately limit its product suite, reduce its customer base, and reorient its entire culture around sustainability. To some, this looked like retreat. To the founders, it was a sober reassessment. They quit the path of hyper-growth not because they were scared, but because they no longer wanted to play that game. That is the hallmark of wise quitting: the decision is not about what you *can't* do, but what you *won't* do anymore—because the cost is no longer acceptable.

Now contrast that with the story of Elizabeth Holmes and Theranos. What began as a bold vision to revolutionise healthcare became an exercise in denial and deception. Refusing to quit became pathological. The warning signs were there. The product wasn't viable. Internal dissent was high. Ethical lines were crossed. But instead of strategic withdrawal, the company doubled down—trading truth for image, and resilience for bravado. This is the other side of the coin: staying the course not from courage, but from illusion.

The through-line across all such examples is this: *Resilience is not stubbornness*. It is the ongoing capacity to align with reality as it changes. That includes the reality of your limits. The reality of your values. The reality of the market. To persist when something is hard but meaningful is noble. To persist when something is broken but familiar is inertia. The only way to tell the difference is to listen—not just to the noise in your head, but to the deeper signals that emerge when you stop trying to force certainty.

There is no perfect algorithm for when to quit. But there are reliable questions. What pain am I trying to avoid? What fear is driving my urgency? What would I decide if I wasn't tired or afraid? What evidence am I ignoring? Who benefits if I keep going—and who pays the price? If I had to rebuild from scratch today, would I rebuild this?

Quitting well is a skill. It requires humility, presence, and a willingness to disappoint others. But it also creates room—for renewal, for redirection, for wiser bets. And perhaps most importantly, it ensures that the energy of your life is invested not in avoiding fear, but in pursuing something worth enduring for.

Not everything hard is worth pushing through. Not everything painful is a signal to stop. The challenge is learning to know the difference. The prize is a life built on choices you can stand behind—not because they were easy, but because they were *true.*

Chapter 12
Redefining Success for the Long Game

If the last ten years have shown us anything, it's this: our dominant definitions of success—speed, scale, visibility—are not only fragile, they're often psychologically corrosive. Burnout is no longer an anomaly. Disillusionment? Practically woven into the fabric of so-called high performance. And chronic dissatisfaction—well, that has become the silent tax paid by those playing the game too fast, too loud, and too publicly. Somewhere along the way, success was stripped of its depth and reduced to a sprint: how quickly can you rise, how far can you be seen? What fell away, almost unnoticed, was the quiet suggestion that "enough" might not be failure, but wisdom. That mastery takes time. And that enduring achievement isn't the result of relentless velocity, but rather of steady, deliberate alignment—often invisible to onlookers, sometimes even to ourselves.

This chapter doesn't propose productivity tweaks or motivational fuel. It's a reorientation. A reframing of the entire pursuit. What if success isn't a trophy but a tempo? What if the true metric isn't what we accumulate, but what we can consistently sustain without self-erasure? The invitation here is not to lower your standards, but to raise the level of discernment with which they're chosen. In a world that applauds the theatre of overwork and rewards the optics of constant motion, it's no small act to ask oneself: "What, exactly, am I building—and do I want to live inside it?"

We begin, somewhat defiantly, with *The Joy of Enough.* Not the Instagrammable version, but the rigorous kind—the type that asks you to interrogate your relationship with sufficiency. In an economic system that thrives on deficit—not just of goods and time, but of self-worth—contentment becomes almost subversive. It refuses to equate value with accumulation. And perhaps more critically, it allows us to question the cult of hustle for what it often is: a culturally sanctioned form of avoidance. Because let's be honest—some of our busyness is little more than a strategy for evading stillness, silence, and the self. But here's the hard truth: there is no compound return on self-abandonment. Enough is not the end of ambition—it's the beginning of intelligent, self-authored action.

From there, we expand into *Playing the Infinite Game.* Originally introduced by James Carse and later retooled by Simon Sinek for modern business parlance, this framework provides an alternative to the linear, winner-takes-all mindset so prevalent in startup and corporate cultures. Finite games are obsessed with rules, rankings, and endpoints. Infinite games ask only this: can you keep evolving? The mistake, of course, is treating careers, relationships, or even identities as though they were finite games. This segment unpacks that delusion—and challenges the grip of streaks, exit strategies, and "first-mover advantage" as markers of meaning. The real art of the long game is in resisting the urge to measure prematurely. The resilient mind builds capacity, not just track records. Infinite players aren't trying to win—they're trying to become.

And then we arrive at a less glamorous, more demanding proposition: *Becoming the Calm in the Storm.* Leadership, at its essence, has little to do with grandiosity and everything to do with nervous system regulation. It's the capacity to transmit steadiness—not because everything is under control, but because you are. In unstable environments—be they teams, households, or entire nations—the calmest person in the room becomes the de facto anchor. This isn't sentimentality. It's an advanced discipline that sits squarely at the intersection of emotional clarity, narrative coherence, and ethical conviction. The chapter draws from leaders who did not rise through noise, but through depth. Founders who steered their companies through chaos not with charisma, but with consistency. Parents who taught resilience not through lectures, but through the quiet repetition of their own regulated presence. The true currency of influence is no longer charisma—it's coherence.

The thread connecting all of this? A different kind of success. One that can sit with ambiguity, that can resist the seduction of spectacle, and that can remain tethered to principle even as the marketplace trades in volatility. We are drowning in metrics and starving for meaning. In such a climate, progress is not measured by reach or revenue alone, but by the quality of our internal traction—how well we hold to what matters when everything around us pulls for compromise.

This isn't a handbook for optimisation. It's something closer to a philosophical audit. You won't find tricks here. You'll find provocations. And they might land uncomfortably: What if thriving doesn't require being seen? What if pausing is more strategic than pushing? What if the richest lives are lived quietly—and in plain defiance of the metrics we've come to idolise? These aren't indulgent questions. They're structural ones. Because no strategy, however clever, can compensate for a life misaligned with itself.

To redefine success for the long game is not to abandon ambition. It's to rewire it. To shift its engine from external applause to internal coherence. The long game doesn't mean slow. It means considered. It doesn't mean timid. It means selective. And it's not about waiting for the right moment—it's about building the kind of foundation that doesn't collapse when the winds change.

What follows is less a roadmap than a compass. It's for those exhausted by the chase and curious about design. For those prepared to swap urgency for leverage, and spectacle for substance. For those beginning to suspect that endurance, not intensity, is the rarest skill of all. And for anyone brave enough to hold their breath—when the rest of the world starts gasping.

Beyond Metrics: What Really Lasts

There is a curious irony at the heart of modern success: the more measurable our lives become, the easier it is to lose sight of what actually matters. Leaders, founders, creatives, even parents—many wake up every day in pursuit of numbers: revenue goals, follower counts, engagement rates, test scores, productivity apps, and progress dashboards. These metrics offer clarity, a sense of control, even validation. But too often, they become not tools, but tyrants. *When numbers become the primary lens through which we evaluate worth, effort, or legacy, we risk impoverishing the very life they were meant to enrich.*

It is not that metrics are inherently misleading. Quite the contrary: measurement has been one of humanity's great innovations. From astronomy to engineering, data has helped us understand the world, spot patterns, refine systems. But when applied to human growth, relational trust, or long-term meaning, its utility has sharp limits. *You cannot spreadsheet the depth of a friendship, nor chart the compounding value of integrity.* Yet these are the very qualities that define resilient lives—and lasting impact.

In business culture especially, the fixation on metrics is both cultural and psychological. Venture capitalists scan monthly recurring revenue like cardiologists examining vital signs. Executives obsess over key performance indicators, believing they reflect not just performance, but worthiness. Startups chase hockey-stick growth because "traction" often determines survival. In academia, impact factors can decide careers; in art, virality now trumps mastery. All of these metrics serve a function, but none tell the full story. They rarely capture the slow accretion of trust, the cost of burnout, or the quiet wisdom of knowing when *not* to scale.

To understand what truly lasts, we need a different evaluative lens—one that honours resilience, relational depth, and the moral arc of our decisions. Emotional wealth, in this context, is not an abstraction; it is the accumulated strength of character, values, and perspective that sustain us when the metrics falter or fade. This subchapter is not a rejection of metrics, but a critical interrogation of their dominance. It asks: What are we counting, and why? What do we ignore because it is hard to quantify? What values are being reinforced by the very things we measure?

Consider the case of an entrepreneur who scales a company to a $50 million valuation in three years, only to lose their health, marriage, and inner clarity in the process. By standard definitions, they have succeeded. But by what standard have they *lived*? Conversely, consider a teacher who quietly shapes hundreds of lives over decades with no accolades, no followers, and no scalable brand. The effects of her work may not be seen in real time, but will echo across generations. Her success cannot be distilled into charts, yet it is deeply *durable*. This isn't sentimentality—it is a sober recognition that *impact is not always visible on a quarterly report.*

This issue becomes even more acute when viewed through the lens of time. *Metrics tend to favour the short-term.* They reward urgency, visibility, and immediate returns. But the most meaningful forms of success—character formation, legacy, ethical leadership, the raising of thoughtful children—unfold slowly. They often require years of patience before they produce visible fruit. In this way, overreliance on short-term metrics can systematically devalue long-term virtues.

Even in our personal lives, metrics shape perception in insidious ways. How many books you read in a year can become more important than what those books changed in you. Fitness apps reward streaks but not inner discipline. Social platforms encourage us to perform rather than connect. Over time, this habitual externalisation of worth leads to an internal emptiness. We become data-rich, meaning-poor. *We know how to optimise, but not how to endure. We track performance, but not purpose.*

Philosopher Byung-Chul Han, in his critique of contemporary culture, argues that society has shifted from a disciplinary model to a performance-based one—where individuals are no longer suppressed by external rules but driven to *self-exploit* through incessant productivity. In this landscape, metrics are not merely tools—they are ideologies. They tell us what to value. And they do so silently, pervasively, and often unexamined. *To live wisely in a metric-driven world is to interrogate the silent scripts we've inherited.*

There is also a psychological toll. Research in behavioural economics and positive psychology consistently shows that extrinsic motivation—when overemphasised—erodes intrinsic interest. A child praised solely for grades may lose the love of learning. A founder driven solely by valuation may lose sight of original purpose. *When our inner compass is calibrated to what earns applause, we lose our capacity to navigate quietly but rightly.* Emotional resilience, in contrast, requires a tolerance for ambiguity, an anchoring in values, and the discipline to remain steady even when no one is watching.

What would it mean, then, to shift our success criteria from the externally quantified to the internally cultivated? To assess our lives not by public visibility, but by private coherence? One model lies in what author David Brooks calls the distinction between *résumé virtues* and *eulogy virtues*. The former are achievements we list—roles held, goals met, titles earned. The latter are the deeper qualities that others remember us by: humility, integrity, kindness, courage. While society is built to reward résumé virtues, our legacy is built on the eulogy kind. And it's the latter that outlasts every performance metric we chase.

Reframing success in this way is not just philosophically elegant—it has practical implications. Leaders who anchor in values are more likely to build cultures that endure. Parents who model depth over achievement raise children with emotional stamina. Founders who resist the lure of inflated metrics are freer to focus on solving real problems with patient strategy. And individuals who prioritise inner clarity over external approval are better equipped to weather disappointment, recalibrate when needed, and derive meaning even from setbacks.

None of this requires abandoning excellence. In fact, it demands a more rigorous kind. It is far easier to optimise for what is visible than to live in alignment with what is true. It's easier to chase likes than to foster character. But the latter, though slower and less glamorous, proves more durable. Emotional wealth, in this sense, is the ability to operate from a centre that does not rise and fall with the metrics. It is the capacity to act with integrity even when no one is measuring.

There are, of course, tensions here. One cannot simply ignore metrics in a world that trades on them. Results matter. Accountability matters. Data has a role. But a mature relationship with metrics means using them without *being used* by them. It means treating data as signals, not verdicts. It means knowing when to value qualitative insight over quantitative output. And most importantly, it means defining success on terms that remain valid even when the numbers aren't flattering.

This kind of resilience has historical precedent. Many of the thinkers, artists, and visionaries we now revere were overlooked or misunderstood in their own time. Vincent van Gogh sold only one painting in his lifetime. Emily Dickinson's genius was barely known beyond a small circle. Socrates was sentenced to death by a jury of his peers. By the metrics of their era, they failed. But their work endured because it was not crafted for applause—it was born of conviction. *Success measured by metrics may peak quickly; success measured by depth often unfolds posthumously.*

And even in our lifetimes, we've all seen examples of this quieter strength. The mentor who shaped careers with no demand for credit. The friend who showed up at the lowest moment without broadcasting it. The colleague who consistently chose the right thing over the easy thing. Their influence cannot be graphed, but it is unmistakable. They do not just succeed—they *matter*. And in a world obsessed with what's trending, mattering is the more radical act.

To cultivate this stance requires reorienting how we ask questions. Instead of "How many people saw it?", we might ask "Did it move the people who needed it most?" Instead of "What's the ROI?", we might consider "What's the moral cost—or gain?" Instead of "How fast did it scale?", we can ask "Did it deepen what it touched?" These are not soft questions. They are hard, ethical ones. They demand reflection, discernment, and the courage to step off the conveyor belt of conventional validation.

In the end, every metric is a proxy. But proxies, by definition, are substitutes—helpful approximations, not truths. What lasts are not the numbers, but the lives shaped, the values embodied, the integrity sustained when compromise would have been easier. And if we're serious about building systems, relationships, and legacies that endure, then we must continually resist the pressure to let metrics define meaning.

This subchapter, then, is not a critique of metrics—it is a recalibration of attention. It challenges the reader to move from visibility to vision, from performance to presence, from reaction to reflection. It asks not "What did you build?", but "What did it stand for—and who did it serve?" And perhaps most critically, it offers a quiet, radical invitation: *Build lives that make sense in the absence of applause.*

Because what really lasts is not what we measured, but what we made space for when the world wasn't watching.

The Joy of Enough – Explores Contentment as a Radical Wealth Goal

It is a curious contradiction of modern ambition that while we accumulate more than any generation before us—more information, more convenience, more opportunity—we are simultaneously less convinced that we have enough. In economic terms, this is often explained by hedonic adaptation: the tendency to quickly return to a baseline level of satisfaction despite significant gains. But beneath this well-known psychological phenomenon lies a deeper cultural issue. We have internalised the belief that *enough* is a moving target, and in doing so, we have turned contentment into a form of subversion. To want less, to choose sufficiency over maximisation, is now a countercultural act. Yet this is precisely where enduring wealth—emotional, mental, relational—resides.

To understand the radicalism of contentment, we must begin by disentangling it from complacency. Contentment is not the absence of drive. It is the disciplined ability to define and honour thresholds. It asks: how much is enough to live with integrity, to build with care, to give without depletion? And perhaps more importantly: who gets to decide what enough looks like? In a world saturated with status symbols and gamified metrics, the default answer is everyone *but* the individual. Market culture thrives on dissatisfaction. It profits from comparison. But genuine wealth—the kind that does not corrode with time or collapse with market shifts—starts where comparison ends. *Contentment is the only metric that cannot be externally hacked.*

The practice of enough is not theoretical. It shows up in the choices we make with time, money, energy, and attention. Consider the entrepreneur who builds a profitable business but declines to scale endlessly, choosing creative autonomy over exponential growth. Or the professional who walks away from a higher-paying role because it would compromise health or family life. Or the household that stops chasing square footage once their home meets the needs of connection and rest. These decisions are not always legible to a productivity-obsessed society. But they are often the truest indicators of internal alignment. *Knowing what to pursue is strategy; knowing when to stop is wisdom.*

Economists have long wrestled with the diminishing returns of income and utility. The Easterlin Paradox, named after the economist Richard Easterlin, observes that while income is positively correlated with happiness within countries at a point in time, over time, rising incomes do not reliably produce rising happiness. Beyond a certain threshold—enough to meet basic needs and afford a measure of security—more money yields marginal gains in well-being. The problem is not in having more, but in never knowing when more ceases to be meaningful. As Daniel Kahneman famously quipped, "Money doesn't buy you happiness, but lack of money certainly buys you misery." Enough, then, is not an anti-growth argument—it is a plea for growth with *discernment.*

Modern psychology adds further nuance. The field of positive psychology identifies autonomy, competence, and relatedness as core psychological needs. Contentment—far from being passive—activates all three. It demands the autonomy to reject societal pressures, the competence to meet one's needs effectively, and the relational awareness to value connection over consumption. In this light, choosing enough is not an abdication of ambition, but a redirection of it. It prioritises depth over breadth, essence over excess.

Philosophical traditions across cultures have long echoed this sentiment. The Stoics warned against the tyranny of desire and emphasised virtue as the true measure of a good life. In Eastern philosophy, the Taoist concept of *wu wei* (non-striving) encourages flowing with the natural rhythms of life rather than constant exertion. The Buddhist idea of *santosha* translates directly as contentment and is considered a foundational practice. Even in modern secular ethics, thinkers like Alain de Botton and Wendell Berry have argued that meaning is not found in accumulation, but in coherence—between values and actions, between limits and longings.

What makes contentment radical today is that it requires opt-outs. It demands that we resist not just external pressures, but internalised narratives of lack. It requires us to notice the subtle language of scarcity embedded in corporate marketing, digital media, and even professional norms. Productivity apps don't ask, "Did you work meaningfully today?" They ask, "How many tasks did you complete?" Social platforms don't reward quiet contribution—they reward visible, optimised self-branding. Contentment, then, becomes a form of quiet resistance: the ability to say, "I am already living well," even if the world can't quantify it.

This does not mean rejecting ambition. It means interrogating it. *Ambition guided by enoughness* asks: will this next goal bring me closer to integrity, or merely status? Will scaling up create more impact—or dilute my presence? Is this next investment aligned with a life I actually want to inhabit, or one I've been told to admire? These are not soft questions. They are architectural. They determine the shape of our lives.

There are economic consequences, too. Households, organisations, and even nations that embrace the joy of enough often display higher resilience. They are less debt-driven. They are better positioned to navigate downturns because their structures are not optimised for perpetual growth. Minimalist businesses—those that keep operations lean, customer focus sharp, and decision-making values-based—tend to survive longer even if they grow slower. They are less exposed to volatility because they are not hostage to overextension.

At the interpersonal level, contentment is contagious. Leaders who model sufficiency signal to their teams that rest is not a reward for exhaustion—it is a condition for clear thinking. Parents who live within their means teach children that self-worth is not tethered to material display. Partners who express gratitude rather than dissatisfaction contribute to relationships that are generous, not transactional. In this sense, *enough is not just a private philosophy—it is a relational ethic.*

Of course, the pursuit of contentment is fraught with tension. It is not a single decision, but a series of micro-disciplines. It requires continual reflection: has my sense of enough changed? Am I expanding because it is needed, or because I am restless? Am I building in alignment with my values, or out of fear of falling behind? These questions are hard to ask in a world that equates stasis with failure. But they are essential if we are to move from a life of constant reaction to one of considered design.

To teach the joy of enough is to offer a counterweight to our culture's dominant scripts. It is to remind ourselves—and others—that sustainability is not just ecological, but emotional. That growth is not always proof of wisdom. That *enough* is not mediocrity—it is mastery over the endless loop of dissatisfaction. And perhaps most profoundly, that when we truly know what is enough for us, we stop being manipulated by what is enough for everyone else.

In this light, contentment becomes not the end of ambition, but the beginning of freedom. It frees us from performing lives we do not want. It frees our time for pursuits that nourish. It allows us to measure success not by how far we outrun others, but by how well we align with our own deepest truths. And in a time defined by noise, speed, and constant escalation, that alignment is not just rare. It is revolutionary.

Enough is not less. It is clarity. It is the decision to stop chasing—and start living.

Playing the Infinite Game – Frames Life and Success as Long, Evolving Journeys—Not Zero-Sum Games

In a world that rewards speed, scale, and immediacy, the idea of *playing the long game* is often reduced to a tired cliché—something to trot out when success is delayed or setbacks accumulate. Yet when framed correctly, it is neither an excuse nor a romantic notion. It is a strategic worldview that challenges the most entrenched assumptions about progress, value, and meaning. The concept of the "infinite game," as articulated by philosopher James P. Carse and later popularised in business strategy by Simon Sinek, posits a clear distinction between two types of pursuits: finite games, with fixed rules and clear winners; and infinite games, whose purpose is not to win, but to continue playing. This distinction is not merely philosophical—it has practical consequences for how we lead, build, relate, and endure.

Modern life is dominated by finite metrics. Quarterly earnings. Exam scores. Follower counts. Award seasons. Promotions. These are bounded contests, often governed by arbitrary timelines and shallow success markers. They create a high-pressure environment in which short-term tactics are mistaken for long-term vision, and optics are prioritised over substance. This mode of thinking breeds fragility. It encourages individuals and institutions alike to optimise for visibility, not viability. When success is framed as a zero-sum game—where one person's win is another's loss—collaboration atrophies, innovation is sacrificed for expediency, and resilience gives way to burnout. *Playing the infinite game reframes the question from "How do I win?" to "What am I building that lasts?"*

The infinite game demands a reorientation of goals. It does not disregard metrics, but subordinates them to a deeper mission. A business playing the infinite game is not merely chasing revenue but seeking relevance and longevity. A teacher committed to the infinite game is not simply maximising test scores but cultivating lifelong learners. A parent is not raising a child to perform, but to flourish independently. This shift in orientation—from performance to sustainability—is subtle but revolutionary. It requires patience, humility, and a capacity for delayed gratification that defies most institutional incentives.

History is rich with examples of individuals and organisations that embraced this logic. Consider the early years of Patagonia, a company that consistently prioritised environmental stewardship over short-term profits. Its now-famous decision to run an ad discouraging customers from buying its jackets was not a stunt—it was a signal that the company was playing an infinite game. Likewise, the open-source movement in software is built on the principle that collective progress often outpaces proprietary advantage. Contributors are not playing to win market share in the traditional sense. They are advancing a broader ecosystem—one in which value is distributed, not extracted. *The infinite game privileges contribution over conquest.*

From a psychological perspective, playing the infinite game fosters traits associated with long-term wellbeing: grit, adaptability, perspective, and internal locus of control. Carol Dweck's research on growth mindset intersects here—those who see their abilities as improvable over time tend to persist in the face of failure. They are not derailed by temporary setbacks because they are invested in an evolving arc, not a single performance. Similarly, Angela Duckworth's work on grit highlights sustained interest and effort as key predictors of achievement. But such persistence only makes sense if one's definition of success is allowed to evolve—if the game itself is infinite.

There is also a strong ethical dimension. The infinite game holds us accountable not just for outcomes, but for the systems we sustain. A leader playing the infinite game does not maximise shareholder value at the expense of employee wellbeing or environmental health. A public servant playing the infinite game considers the next generation, not just the next election cycle. These are not acts of self-sacrifice—they are strategic acts of stewardship. They recognise that reputational capital, trust, and legacy are slow-return assets, but ultimately more durable than any quarterly gain.

The practical tension, of course, lies in navigating a world built to reward finite achievements. Infinite players must survive in finite systems—funding rounds, hiring seasons, media cycles. This does not mean abandoning measurable targets. It means contextualising them. An infinite player might chase growth not because growth is the goal, but because it funds deeper experimentation. They may accept public recognition not as validation, but as leverage to expand impact. They will track performance—but as a diagnostic, not an identity. *Infinite thinking is not about rejecting performance culture—it's about reclaiming its purpose.*

One of the most overlooked benefits of this worldview is the psychological freedom it offers. When you stop measuring your worth by rankings, deadlines, or comparative milestones, you reclaim authorship of your own narrative. You can make unconventional choices without fearing reputational damage. You can prioritise depth over speed, craft over trend, people over optics. This is not about retreating into idealism—it is about building the kind of stamina that complexity requires. In today's climate of volatility, the most valuable trait is not intensity but endurance. And endurance is only sustainable when fuelled by intrinsic clarity, not external validation.

Philosophically, the infinite game aligns with many enduring traditions. In Stoicism, the wise life is not one that seeks victory, but one that seeks coherence with values. In Buddhism, the concept of *right effort* suggests that progress must be consistent with ethical intention. In African philosophy, the idea of *ubuntu* reminds us that personal flourishing is inseparable from communal thriving. These frameworks share a common insight: the game of life is not won through dominance, but through continuity, contribution, and integrity.

Crucially, infinite players are not passive. They compete, but selectively. They care about performance, but in the right time horizon. They are ambitious, but their ambition is tethered to substance, not spectacle. They take risks—but ones calibrated for the long arc, not immediate optics. They may walk away from accolades if those accolades distort the deeper game. They may endure obscurity, loss, even ridicule—because they understand that *the most important work is often invisible until it isn't.*

To play the infinite game is to choose legacy over ego. It is to ask not "How do I win?" but "What kind of player am I becoming?" And in that reframe lies the most enduring form of success. A person playing an infinite game does not panic at detours. They expect reinvention. They welcome complexity. They do not see a failed venture as a personal failure, but as data for refinement. They do not tie their worth to a single product, job title, or accolade. Instead, they cultivate a portfolio of experiments—each one aligned with an evolving mission.

In practical terms, this looks like founders who resist hyper-scaling and instead invest in culture and sustainability. It looks like educators who forgo performative teaching for transformative learning. It looks like artists who turn down viral trends in favour of meaningful craft. It looks like professionals who take strategic sabbaticals to renew their sense of purpose. These are not signs of stagnation. They are signals of clarity.

To live well, lead well, and build well in the 21st century, we must recover the discipline of infinite thinking. We must learn to navigate finite structures without becoming hostage to them. We must elevate endurance as a metric, resilience as a design principle, and contribution as a strategy. Because the ultimate test of any life, organisation, or idea is not whether it wins—but whether it keeps evolving.

The infinite game doesn't reward those who finish first. It rewards those who keep showing up with integrity, curiosity, and a willingness to change.

Becoming the Calm in the Storm – True Leadership is Measured by the Stability We Offer in Chaos

When systems fray, when certainty dissolves, and when the tempo of crisis eclipses the tempo of thought, the quality of leadership is no longer judged by charisma, credentials, or vision decks—it is measured in emotional voltage. Who stays grounded when others flail? Who absorbs complexity without transmitting panic? Who—regardless of role or title—becomes the anchor others instinctively trust? In every domain, from boardrooms to classrooms, operating theatres to family kitchens, leadership's truest metric is not what it creates under perfect conditions, but what it stabilises under pressure. *To become the calm in the storm is not a personality trait. It is a strategic, practiced skillset.*

This chapter concludes with a principle that is at once simple and seismic: in moments of instability, *people do not look for the loudest voice or the cleverest fix; they look for the most regulated nervous system in the room.* Neuroscience and organisational psychology converge on this truth. Emotions are contagious, and leaders—whether formal or emergent—act as the primary carriers. According to research from the HeartMath Institute and Harvard Medical School, emotionally coherent individuals can entrain those around them; in contrast, those caught in internal chaos unwittingly export that chaos, often magnifying the volatility they seek to resolve. In high-stakes situations, *emotional regulation is not just a wellness buzzword—it becomes operational infrastructure.*

Consider emergency medicine. A lead trauma surgeon, under extreme conditions, must not only decide and act swiftly but also model calm to their team. The difference between a coordinated effort and a cascade of avoidable errors often rests not on knowledge, but composure. Similarly, in aviation, captains are trained not merely for technical competence, but for maintaining psychological equilibrium under mechanical failure. And in the corporate sphere, the CEOs who steer organisations through downturns, litigation, or sudden reputational crises are almost always those who display a calm congruent with confidence—not false optimism or repression, but a deep, embodied sense of agency amidst uncertainty. *True calm is not the absence of stress. It is the presence of clarity under stress.*

But how is such calm developed? The answer lies not in temperament, but in training. Emotional self-regulation is a composite of meta-cognition, nervous system awareness, and meaning-making. It requires us to first recognise our internal state—am I escalated, frozen, reactive?—and then shift our state before speaking, deciding, or reacting. This is not intuitive under pressure, which is why high-functioning teams—from elite military units to crisis negotiators—train for it repeatedly. They rehearse chaos to habituate composure. For leaders in more civilian domains, this may look like practising mindfulness not as a luxury, but as a discipline; building recovery into routines; normalising feedback loops that address escalation early; and constructing environments where emotional contagion is recognised, named, and managed.

An often-misunderstood element of this practice is *boundaried empathy.* Leaders who offer calm do not do so by absorbing everyone's stress like a sponge. Instead, they create psychological safety by demonstrating emotional boundaries. They listen actively, validate emotions without amplifying them, and—crucially—do not confuse leadership with saviourism. Being the calm in the storm means standing *with* people in their difficulty, not *rescuing* them from it. In parenting, for example, this might mean saying, "I see that this is hard and I'm here with you," rather than panicking or rushing to fix the discomfort. In management, it may mean hearing someone's fear about a project and acknowledging the uncertainty, while also orienting the team back to what *can* be controlled. Calm, then, is not about surface stillness—it is about calibrated co-regulation.

There is also a philosophical dimension. Leadership under duress exposes what one truly believes about human nature, risk, and control. Those who react with brittle overconfidence or performative calm often reveal a deeper insecurity—a need to be seen as unshakable rather than to *be* genuinely grounded. True calm is humble. It admits what it does not know. It resists the fantasy of perfect control. It refuses false certainty in favour of principled clarity. When chaos hits, the question is not "Do I have the answer?" but "Can I hold the space until the right questions emerge?" That holding—intellectual, emotional, ethical—is the scaffolding on which good decisions are built.

Leadership theorist Ronald Heifetz draws a critical distinction between technical problems and adaptive challenges. The former have known solutions; the latter require redefinition, experimentation, and cultural work. Calm leadership excels at the latter. It holds competing perspectives without collapse. It allows for complexity without paralysis. It decouples speed from haste and urgency from panic. It fosters environments where people can speak truthfully, experiment responsibly, and metabolise discomfort without falling apart. *In short, calm is what enables adaptation—not by freezing action, but by pacing it.*

From a systems perspective, calm is anti-fragile. It does not merely restore baseline; it strengthens collective coherence over time. Consider the difference between leaders who create dependency through micromanaged crisis response versus those who build distributed calm—cultures where stability is a shared practice, not a top-down directive. The latter model is more scalable, more sustainable, and—crucially—more empowering. When team members, children, or communities are trained to self-regulate and co-regulate, they become less reactive, more creative, and more resilient. The leader becomes less a hero and more a hub.

Importantly, calm is not synonymous with slowness. It is fully compatible with urgency when needed. But it redefines urgency as *purposeful velocity*, not frenetic activity. It invites action that is informed, intentional, and in integrity with long-term goals. Calm leaders move fast *because* they are clear—not in spite of clarity. They filter signals from noise. They spot leverage points. They know when to pause and when to push. And when they do push, others follow not out of fear, but trust.

This ethos of calm extends beyond professional spheres. It is relational capital. Children model their emotional response systems on those of their caregivers. Teams model psychological norms based on leader conduct. Communities fragment or cohere based on the behaviours of those they look to in times of disorientation. The most transformative leaders do not generate movement through dominance; they generate momentum through presence. *And presence, in the midst of chaos, is what rehumanises the moment.*

To cultivate such presence is not a matter of personality but of decision. It is a choice to train—mentally, emotionally, physiologically—for the storms that will inevitably come. It is a decision to anchor one's leadership not in charisma but in credibility. And it is an ongoing commitment to examine how our reactions either stabilise or destabilise those around us. As the final insight in this chapter, it reinforces a radical but enduring truth: *the most effective leaders are not those who promise certainty, but those who model stability in the face of uncertainty.*

In closing—though not to conclude, for calm is not an endpoint but a way of being—this is the invitation: audit the spaces you influence, whether large or intimate. Ask not only, "What am I achieving?" but also, "What emotional climate am I cultivating?" Are people bracing around you, or breathing more deeply? Are they reacting, or reflecting? Are you broadcasting urgency without clarity, or modelling steadiness without sedation? These are the real metrics. And in a culture saturated with volatility, the one who learns to offer regulated presence, even when outcomes are unknown, becomes not just a better leader—but a necessary one.

Conclusion
The Final Dividend

Every serious pursuit must, at some point, confront a deeper reckoning: What actually lasts? Not what dazzled in the short term, nor what ticked boxes or earned applause—but what withstands time, tension, and truth. And perhaps more importantly—why. This final chapter doesn't tie things up with a neat ribbon, nor offer the warm glow of congratulatory closure. Instead, it extends an intellectual challenge: to revisit what's been laid out thus far, not through the lens of urgency or aesthetics, but through a more demanding frame—What is the real return on a life lived with attention and integrity?

If previous chapters charted the mechanics—resilience, strategy, relational clarity—this one steps back from the canvas. It asks you to look not at the strokes, but at the whole composition. The wider arc. The texture of the thing you're making with your time and energy. And if we're honest, the most meaningful dividends aren't public. They're not on your LinkedIn profile. They can't be tallied in followers or multiplied in revenue streams. The actual yield is far quieter: the tone of your inner voice, the sturdiness of your nervous system when the stakes rise, the emotional imprint you leave in rooms long after you've exited. That's the real legacy.

It's tempting, of course, to reduce the dividend to metrics—a bank balance, a title, a well-crafted obituary. But those are only proxies. Polished veneers that rarely speak to substance. The actual yield comes from choices made under pressure, principles upheld in private, and boundaries held without drama or announcement. The work beneath the work. And its reward? A kind of inner sovereignty. The capacity to trust your own calibration. To be clear without being brittle. To remain rooted in the face of ambiguity, when the easier path would be noise or conformity.

This final section, then, is neither recap nor epilogue. It's a reframing. A synthesis that challenges you to ask not simply what you've done, but what it has prepared you for. What are you actually building through the daily rituals of your parenting, your leadership, your creativity, your silence? What imprint are you leaving—not just in outcomes, but in the emotional atmospheres others must now inhabit because of you? These are not indulgent reflections. They're operational ones. Because in a culture where values are auctioned off for attention and principles are constantly up for renegotiation, the rarest form of leverage is clarity—and the ability to hold to it without theatrics.

You'll notice, perhaps, a familiar thread running through this chapter: a return to the long game—not as a posture, but as a governing logic. The short game is seductive. It rewards spectacle, reaction, and immediacy. But it rarely builds anything that holds. The long game is harder to measure. It rewards resilience, pacing, and quiet conviction. It's rarely the loudest that outlast; it's those most unwilling to compromise the architecture of their values. And in this frame, survival isn't the triumph. It's presence—unrushed amid urgency, grounded amid complexity, generous even under constraint—that signals mastery.

Across the book, emotional wealth has surfaced as a quiet refrain. Here, we press into it more deliberately. What are you compounding? Truly. Have your relationships grown deeper, or have they become more performative? Has your attention sharpened toward what matters, or has it been swallowed by digital static? Are your decisions rooted in coherence—or fatigue? These may sound abstract. They're not. They're operational diagnostics, camouflaged as philosophical questions. Because philosophy only becomes real at the point of pressure—and what you actually practise when challenged reveals far more than what you claim when comfortable.

And then there's regret. That stubborn, inevitable shadow. The question is not whether you have any—you do, and so does everyone. The more illuminating question is: what do you *do* with it? The emotionally impoverished either deny or deflect regret, flattening complexity in a bid to preserve self-image. The emotionally wealthy metabolise it. They study it. They refine themselves through it. It becomes feedback, not failure. Another form of compounding. Wisdom, after all, is not the absence of error—it's the refusal to waste it.

Leadership, too, distils in this final reckoning. The titles fade. The big wins blur. People rarely remember every policy or strategy. But they do remember how you made them feel—especially when things got hard. Did you offer clarity, or add confusion? Did you hold the centre, or demand others carry it for you? Were you the one who brought coherence to a room spinning in complexity, or did you become one more source of noise? Leadership leaves a residue. Not because you were infallible, but because you were anchored—especially when it counted.

There's a subtle but profound thread here about ambition—not abandoning it, but purifying it. Distilling it to something cleaner, less externally prescribed. What do you want, truly—once the metrics are stripped away? Does your ambition nourish you, or deplete you? Is it regenerative, or extractive? Do you crave attention, or impact? These aren't semantic distinctions. They're existential ones. You can chase everything the world celebrates and still have built nothing inside yourself that will hold under weight.

And finally—perhaps most challengingly—this chapter insists on legacy not as myth or monument, but as modelling. If emotional wealth is the dividend, emotional modelling is the transmission. You pass it down whether you mean to or not. Through presence or absence, through tone or reaction, through what you tolerate and what you honour. Do you teach the people around you—your children, your teams, your students—how to sit with complexity?

How to make space between trigger and response? How to endure without armouring? These are the scripts we hand off, intentionally or otherwise. They outlive the résumés. They shape cultures, not just careers.

So no, this isn't a celebratory ending. It's a provocation to begin—differently. With more intention. With fewer borrowed frameworks and more earned convictions. With a bias toward depth, not display. To think in decades, not quarters. To cultivate emotional clarity with the same seriousness as strategic skill. To measure your strength not by what you control, but by what you can hold without needing to grasp. And to understand—truly—that the ultimate measure is not how far you've risen, but how little of yourself you had to lose along the way.

That, finally, is the dividend that endures: you—undiminished, unperformative, and anchored in something no crisis, trend, or critic can take from you. The rest? That's just background noise.

Returns Aren't Always Measured in Dollars

There is a paradox at the heart of our modern world: while the tools of acceleration—technology, communication, finance—have never been more powerful, the inner qualities that allow one to withstand velocity have never been more scarce. We live in an era where immediacy is worshipped and impatience is subsidised. Attention spans have collapsed. Decision cycles are compressed. Results are demanded yesterday. Amid this hyper-optimised machinery of noise and urgency, it is easy to confuse speed with progress, visibility with impact, and growth with success. But the future does not belong to those who can move fastest. It belongs to those who can hold their ground with clarity, composure, and conviction while others flinch, chase, or burn out.

The patient are not waiting. They are winning slowly.

Patience—properly understood—is not passive. It is not the absence of action, nor the indulgence of delay. Rather, patience is the rare and rigorous discipline of choosing depth over display, substance over signal, and timing over tempo. It is the self-command to resist the seductions of premature reward in order to build something enduring. And this restraint—strategic, self-imposed, and often invisible—is what separates those who create long-term value from those who merely perform urgency.

This chapter asks the reader to examine their definition of return: What are you optimising for? What are you measuring that truly matters? In a culture that quantifies worth in likes, revenue, followers, and quarterly reports, it is a radical act to value peace of mind, strategic obscurity, or a good night's sleep. To invest in trust, not just transactions. To prioritise coherence over exposure. To build your resilience in silence and let compounding—emotional, intellectual, relational—do the speaking.

Consider this: a founder who keeps their head clear while their competitors burn capital on vanity metrics; a teacher who mentors over decades without chasing prestige; a parent who models stability through tough times instead of dramatics. None of these roles make headlines. Yet all of them generate *intergenerational dividends* that outlast the visible wins.

This is not romantic idealism. It is a strategic reframe. In fields as diverse as behavioural economics, evolutionary psychology, and complex systems theory, there is growing recognition that endurance—not dominance—is the ultimate advantage. The systems that last are those that adapt intelligently, absorb shocks, and recover with grace. In biological ecosystems, fragility often masquerades as strength—until it breaks. In human systems, the same holds true. An entrepreneur, investor, or leader who internalises this principle stops chasing short-term applause and starts cultivating antifragility: the ability to gain from disorder, not just survive it.

This subchapter advances the thesis that *measuring progress purely in financial, numerical, or externally validated terms is intellectually and practically insufficient.* The metrics that truly govern long-term advantage—emotional stability, moral clarity, interpersonal trust, cognitive range—are neither flashy nor easily monetised. But they shape the arc of sustainable leadership far more than dashboards and data spikes.

We will explore how *grace under pressure* is not a soft skill but a core differentiator. How *restraint,* in high-stakes environments, signals not weakness but control. And how *poise*—that quality of calm assertiveness in complexity—creates a gravitational field of trust, particularly in environments saturated with volatility.

Throughout, you will be asked to rethink assumptions: about what success looks like, when progress is real, and why enduring composure may become the most important currency in the years ahead.

If the last era rewarded noise, scale, and speed, the next will reward discernment, stillness, and sustainability. Those building slowly are not behind. They are outlasting.

In traditional economic thinking, value is assessed through transactions, profits, and quantifiable outcomes. But these instruments fail to capture the invisible returns that compound quietly in human systems—within teams, families, institutions, and inner lives. Consider a founder who, during a downturn, holds steady instead of panicking. Revenue might contract temporarily. Investors may grow restless. But beneath the surface, her capacity to manage pressure without broadcasting fear fosters an organisational culture of psychological safety. This does not show up in the balance sheet—but it will determine whether her company survives the next shock.

Not all value is visible. Not all returns arrive on schedule.

The greatest investors understand this instinctively. Warren Buffett's discipline, for instance, is not merely in selecting undervalued assets, but in withstanding boredom, public doubt, and irrational exuberance over decades. His success has as much to do with emotional mastery as it does with spreadsheets. Similarly, in leadership, it is often the quiet decisions—the ones made without fanfare—that define character: choosing not to escalate a conflict, not to reply with anger, not to indulge every demand for attention. In these moments, restraint becomes an asset, not a liability.

This orientation—towards long arcs and subtle returns—is a cultural anomaly. But it is precisely what positions individuals and institutions for enduring relevance. We are living through an age defined by overstimulation and under-reflection. The velocity of information has outpaced our psychological capacity to metabolise it. In such a context, those who develop the inner infrastructure to *stay calm, stay focused, and stay out of the fray* have a competitive edge.

The historian Yuval Noah Harari noted that one of humanity's most profound evolutionary advantages was not brute force or even intelligence, but our ability to cooperate flexibly at scale. Trust is the substrate of this cooperation. And trust, unlike performance metrics, is slow to build, easy to destroy, and impossible to hack. That makes it the ultimate long-term return.

But here's the dilemma: our professional culture often penalises slowness. We equate urgency with seriousness, speed with competence, and noise with relevance. This creates a misalignment between what is rewarded in the short term and what matters in the long run. Leaders are pushed to appear decisive even when discernment is needed. Creators feel pressure to publish constantly, even if quality degrades. Investors abandon solid strategies for the thrill of immediate gain. In every field, the risk is the same: *sacrificing longevity for visibility.*

To resist this pressure requires not only psychological resolve but a redefinition of wealth itself. If wealth is not just financial surplus but also emotional bandwidth, temporal sovereignty, and strategic control, then patience becomes a form of compounding. The more you resist false urgency, the more optionality you preserve. The more you conserve energy, the more precisely you can deploy it when stakes are real.

Restraint is not the opposite of ambition. It is its refinement.

Consider the architect who turns down an opportunity to build quickly in order to design with integrity. The teacher who nurtures a struggling student away from the spotlight. The civil servant who protects a policy decision from media distortion by saying less, not more. These acts of invisible fidelity to excellence rarely make headlines. But they create trust, coherence, and long-term effectiveness. In time, they *yield influence that is earned, not granted.*

Philosophically, this position echoes ideas from Stoicism, Buddhism, and systems theory. From Marcus Aurelius to Lao Tzu, enduring thinkers have argued that maturity lies in mastering response over reaction, pacing over pushing, and intention over impulse. In systems language, a well-regulated system is not the fastest one but the most adaptive—the one that preserves coherence in the face of change. That requires patience, which is a function of clarity and context, not passivity.

So how do we practise this in a world designed to interrupt, provoke, and extract? The answer lies in developing internal infrastructure: reflective routines, clarity of principle, intentional design of pace. It means knowing what you're building for—*and what you're not.* It means resisting the temptation to perform progress and instead, *engineering for durability.*

And perhaps most importantly, it means understanding that the real dividend is not applause, scale, or fame—but the quiet confidence that you are operating on your own terms, with your own rhythm, towards outcomes that matter beyond the metrics.

About the Author

Leandro Vos is a behavioural strategist and emotional resilience educator whose work bridges the gap between timeless wisdom and modern performance. With a background in psychology, Eastern philosophy, and behavioural economics, he has spent over a decade studying how patience, emotional regulation, and strategic restraint shape real-world outcomes in wealth, leadership, and personal growth. His global approach blends Stoicism, neuroscience, and human stories into deeply impactful teachings. Leandro speaks not just to the mind—but to the emotional core of those seeking clarity, composure, and long-term fulfillment in a world driven by noise and speed.

www.ingramcontent.com/pod-product-compliance
Lightning Source LLC
Chambersburg PA
CBHW031338230926
51848CB00002B/294